New Expanded Second Edition

MONEY
FOR
FILM&VIDEO
ARTISTS

New Expanded Second Edition

MONEY
FOR
FILM&VIDEO
ARTISTS

Researched by DOUGLAS OXENHORN

aca BOOKS
American Council for the Arts
New York, New York

Copublished with Allworth Press

Published by American Council for the Arts
One East 53rd Street, New York, NY 10022.

Director of Publishing: Robert Porter
Assistant Director of Publishing: Julia Dubner

Book and Cover Design by Celine Brandes, *Photo Plus Art*

Library of Congress Cataloging-in-Publication Data
Money for Film and Video Artists / researched by Douglas Oxenhorn.
        p.   cm.
      ISBN: 1-879903-09-1
        1. Motion pictures—Scholarships, fellowships, etc.—United States—Directories. 2. Video art—Scholarships, fellowships, etc.—United States—Directories.
      I. Oxenhorn, Douglas 1962-   . II. American Council for the Arts.
      PN1998.A1M56   1993
      791.43'079'73—dc20   93-38044
                                                        CIP

CONTENTS

ACKNOWLEDGMENTS

This publication would not have been possible without the hard work and support of many people. Thanks to David Bosca, Director of Information Services at the American Council for the Arts, and Robert Porter, Director of Policy, Planning and Publishing for overseeing the scope and clarifying the purpose of this book, and for their dedication to it. Warmest thanks to John von Bergen for his extraordinary assistance and to Julia Dubner, Assistant Director of Publishing, for her kind patience and skilled production work despite an incredibly hectic schedule. Finally, thanks to the many individuals who took the time to respond to my phone calls and faxes. Without their help this book would not exist.

—D.O.

HOW TO USE THE GUIDE

In this single volume, we have assembled a unique resource compendium of the myriad programs of support and assistance for professional, individual artists in the U.S. and Canada.

In assembling these 221 organization profiles (including 33 completely new entries) we have learned that support for artists comes in a wide variety of forms and from diverse sources. We have uncovered programs that offer free or low-cost access to production and post-production equipment and facilities. Other programs offer several million dollars in fellowships, operate slide registries or conduct how-to workshops; some operate on an international scale, while others provide service on a community-wide basis. We've tried to collect information from the largest government agencies to the smaller nonprofit groups. You may be surprised at how many places can provide help.

This book is intended to simplify your search for the various kinds of assistance that you need to advance your career. We have arranged the profiles alphabetically by organization name. Each entry includes the organization's name, address, phone number and contact person. In addition, where available, we have included the fax number and, for deaf and hearing impaired artists, the TDD number, or Telephone Device for the Deaf. We have marked two entries with the symbol † to alert the reader that we have been unable to verify the accuracy of the information since the last edition. Following the contact information, each entry is divided into three sections for quick reference.

The "Profile of Financial Support to Artists" is intended to give you an idea of the size and scope of the program. It includes the total amount of funding and value of in-kind support that the organization gives to individual artists, the total number of applications for funding that the organization receives from individual artists, the number of individuals that receive funding, and the dollar range of grants to individuals. At a glance, you will be able to determine how many opportunities exist and how many people compete for them.

The "Direct Support Programs" section details fellowships, project support, professional development grants, emergency assistance, and residency programs that serve individual film and video artists. Equipment access grants, public art and arts-in-education programs may also be included here, depending on the scope of the program, the standardization of the application and selection process, and the availability of direct funds for individual artists. This section also outlines each program's eligibility requirements, scope, and application/selection process.

Pay particular attention to what, if any, restrictions there may be on an artist's eligibility to apply for a program. Most programs have some restriction on citizenship, residency, age, art forms, or other special requirements that limit who is eligible to be considered for an award. For example, if under Residency, an entry says "North Dakota," that means only those artists who live in the state of North Dakota are eligible to apply. In this case, if an artist from Illinois ignores the guidelines and sends in an application anyway, it will not be considered. On the other hand, if a category says "Open," it means there are no restrictions at all in this area. For example, if the entry says "Residency: Open," then the program considers applications from artists no matter where they may reside. *No miracles come from ignoring eligibility requirements, only ill will and unnecessary work for both the staff of the funding organization and the artist.*

In the description of the application/selection process, you will find information on deadlines; the organization's preferred method for making an initial contact; the application procedure, including required support materials; the selection process; the notification process; and reporting requirements. The deadlines supplied here are subject to change, and you should always contact the organization to confirm dates. If a listing indicates SASE, it means that you should supply a self-addressed envelope with the proper postage on it. This request is sometimes made for those requesting guidelines and applications. More frequently, it is requested of artists who want to have slides or other supporting materials returned after their application has been reviewed.

The "Equipment Access" section describes low-cost or free access to production and/or post-production equipment for film and video in various formats. Discounted rates are usually reserved for producers working on noncommercial work, and further restrictions may apply. Restrictions are explained under the comments heading. Media centers frequently upgrade equipment, so a phone call to check on any additions may be worthwhile. Producers interested in equipment access programs may also want to contact their local cable television companies. Many carry public-access channels that offer equipment usage and/or broadcast time for independent producers.

The "Technical Assistance Programs and Services" section encompasses a wide range of activities that benefit artists. These include workshops, seminars, resource libraries, arts-in-education programs, fiscal sponsorship, screening opportunities, slide registries, public art programs, festivals, and marketing, legal, accounting and grantwriting assistance.

Many organizations confine their programs to artists living in certain areas or to specific types of support. Not all programs are for everyone. To help you find the programs for which you are eligible and which best match your needs and interests, we have provided four indexes. The Alphabetical Index of Organizations lets you quickly locate the organizations you are most interested in researching. The Index of Organizations by Geographic Area lists the organizations according to the area served: listings include individual states, the U.S., Canada, and international organizations. For practical reasons, most media centers are listed according to the state in which they are located, but many do not require residency in that state for equipment access programs. The Index of Organizations by Medium and Format allows you to determine which media centers have production or post-production equipment compatible with the film or video format you are using. Producers seeking equipment access should also consult the equipment access heading in the Index of Organizations by Types of Support: some organizations provide discounted rates at a variety of off-site facilities. The Index of Organizations by Type of Support lists organizations according to the services they provide:

■ ART IN PUBLIC PLACES/COMMISSIONS. Organizations that sponsor or administer art in public places programs and other commissions.

■ ARTISTS' COMMUNITIES. Organizations that provide a working retreat for artists. Some request that residents pay a fee but offer stipends or full or partial fee waivers to artists in financial need. Though film and video equipment and facilities are generally limited, communities can provide media artists with an opportunity to pursue pre-production activities, such as scripting.

■ ARTS IN EDUCATION/COMMUNITY RESIDENCIES. Organizations that sponsor, administer, or select artists for school/community residency and visiting artist programs.

■ DISTRIBUTION/MARKETING/PUBLIC RELATIONS. Organizations that offer information on or assistance with distribution, marketing, or publicity, including several national nonprofit distribution centers in the U.S. and Canada.

■ EMERGENCY ASSISTANCE. Organizations that provide financial support for artists facing work-related or personal emergencies.

■ EQUIPMENT ACCESS. Organizations that offer low-cost or free access to on-site and off-site production or post-production equipment and facilities.

■ FELLOWSHIPS/AWARDS. Organizations that offer financial support to artists based on past accomplishments or on potential for future success. These grants generally carry few or no restrictions on how the money is spent.

■ FESTIVALS. Organizations that sponsor or supply information on festivals.

■ FINANCE. Organizations that provide information on or assistance with taxes, recordkeeping, accounting, or financial management.

■ FISCAL SPONSORSHIP. Organizations that act as nonprofit fiscal agents for independent producers seeking funding from other sources.

■ HEALTH. Organizations that offer group health plans for artists or information on healthcare options or art hazards.

■ INTERNATIONAL OPPORTUNITIES/EXCHANGE PROGRAMS. Organizations that sponsor residencies or independent work or study abroad.

■ INTERNSHIPS. Organizations that offer internships.

■ JOB OPPORTUNITIES/CAREER DEVELOPMENT. Organizations that maintain job banks, publicize employment opportunities, or conduct career development workshops.

■ LEGAL ASSISTANCE AND ADVICE. Organizations that provide information or referrals on legal matters.

■ PROFESSIONAL DEVELOPMENT/TECHNICAL ASSISTANCE GRANTS. Organizations that provide financial support for general professional development activities such as travel to conferences or seminars, consultation fees, and promotional efforts. Sometimes these grants may be used for the production or exhibition of work deemed critical to an artist's career.

■ PROJECT SUPPORT. Organizations that offer grants for the development, production, or completion of a specific project.

■ REGISTRIES. Organizations that maintain registries or directories of individual artists. Slide registries are often used to select artists for commissions.

■ SCREENINGS/EXHIBITIONS. Organizations that sponsor screenings, broadcasts, or exhibitions of independent works on a regular basis.

■ STUDY GRANTS. Organizations that offer grants for independent study, workshop attendance, or study at an institution. Artists interested in study grants should also consult the Professional Development/Technical Assistance Grants heading.

■ TRAVEL GRANTS. Organizations that offer grants for travel, often for project development or professional development purposes. Artists interested in travel grants should also consult the Professional Development/Technical Assistance Grants heading.

One last thing. You can help us and other artists by sharing what you have learned on your own. If you know of programs that aren't listed here, please complete and return the card inserted in this book so that we can include them in the next edition.

THE GUIDE

ACADEMY OF MOTION PICTURE ARTS AND SCIENCES/ACADEMY FOUNDATION

8949 Wilshire Boulevard
Beverly Hills, CA 90211
310-247-3059
CONTACT: GREG BEAL, PROGRAM COORDINATOR

PROFILE OF FINANCIAL SUPPORT TO ARTISTS

Total Funding/Value of In-Kind Support: $125,000 for FY 1992-93
(figures reflect Nicholl Fellowships only)
Competition for Funding: Total applications, 3,855; total individuals
funded/provided with in-kind support, 5
Grant Range: $25,000

DIRECT SUPPORT PROGRAMS

➤ **NICHOLL FELLOWSHIPS IN SCREENWRITING**

Purpose: To foster the development of the art of screenwriting
Eligibility:
    Special Requirements: Previous recipients ineligible; professional
    screenwriters for theatrical films or applicants who have sold
    screen or television rights to any original story, treatment, screen-
    play, or teleplay are ineligible
    Art Forms: Screenwriting for feature-length films
Type of Support: $20,000; recipients expected to complete a screen-
play during fellowship year
Scope of Program: 5 awards in 1992-93

Please read carefully!
Do not contact any listed organization unless you fulfill all eligibility requirements.

Application/Selection Process:
  Deadline: May 1, annually
  Preferred Initial Contact: Write for application/guidelines; include SASE
  Application Procedure: Submit application form, feature screenplay, $25 fee
  Selection Process: Organization staff, jury of individuals from outside of organization, committee of Academy members
  Notification Process: Letter 3-5 months after deadline
  Formal Report of Grant Required: Yes

➤ **STUDENT ACADEMY AWARDS**

Purpose: To recognize the importance of student filmmaking to the future of the motion picture industry and to acknowledge the talent and achievements of student filmmakers

Eligibility:
  Citizenship: n/a
  Residency: Open
  Special Requirements: Awards given to completed films only; open to all students enrolled in a full-time, accredited university or college; film must have been made in a teacher/student relationship
  Art Forms: Film

Type of Support: $2,000, $1,500 and $1,000 awards in each of four categories: dramatic, experimental, documentary, animation; prior to receiving awards, recipients are flown to Los Angeles for a week of workshops, seminars and a banquet

Scope of Program: 12 awards annually

Application/Selection Process:
  Deadline: April 1, annually
  Preferred Initial Contact: Send legal-size SASE after January 1 to receive entry form
  Application Procedure: Submit entry form and a print of completed film to Regional Coordinator (coordinators listed by region on entry form)
  Selection Process: Films are judged on a regional level by a jury; winning films from each region are then judged by members of the Academy of Motion Picture Arts and Sciences for final awards
  Notification Process: Regional winners are notified by their regional coordinators; national winners are notified by the Awards Administrator by the first week of June
  Formal Report of Grant Required: No

ACTS INSTITUTE, INC.

P.O. Box 10153
Kansas City, MO 64111
816-753-3553
CONTACT: CHARLOTTE PLOTSKY, ADMINISTRATOR

PROFILE OF FINANCIAL SUPPORT TO ARTISTS
Total Funding/Value of In-Kind Support: n/a
Competition for Funding: n/a
Grant Range: n/a

DIRECT SUPPORT PROGRAM
➤ **CASH GRANT PROGRAM FOR COLONY RESIDENCIES**

Purpose: To serve as a last resort for artists who have been accepted at an artists'/writers' colony and need financial assistance that the colony is unable to provide

Eligibility:
　Citizenship: n/a
　Residency: Open
　Age: 18 or older
　Special Requirements: Artist must have been accepted at an artists' colony and been unable to procure financial support from the National Endowment for the Arts, from his or her state arts council, or any other source
　Art Forms: All disciplines

Type of Support: $200-$800 towards cost of residency

Scope of Program: $2,100 awarded to 5 artists between 12/90 and 12/92; program wil be re-evaluated at end of 1993

Application/Selection Process:
　Deadline: December 1 (summer residencies), June 1 (winter residencies)
　Preferred Initial Contact: Write for application/guidelines; must enclose SASE or materials will not be sent
　Application Procedure: Submit application form, $10 processing fee, samples of work, project budget, acceptance letter from colony, rejections for financial aid from the National Endowment for the Arts and state arts council, artist's statement, references
　Selection Process: Panel of artists
　Notification Process: Letter within 60 days
　Formal Report of Grant Required: Yes

Please read carefully!
Do not contact any listed organization unless you fulfill all eligibility requirements.

ALABAMA STATE COUNCIL ON THE ARTS (ASCA)

One Dexter Avenue
Montgomery, AL 36130
205-242-4076
FAX: 205-240-3269
CONTACT: RANDY SHOULTS, COMMUNITY DEVELOPMENT PROGRAM MANAGER

PROFILE OF FINANCIAL SUPPORT TO ARTISTS

Total Funding/Value of In-Kind Support: $69,000 for FY 1993 (figures for Fellowship, Folk Life and Technical Assistance grants only)
Competition for Funding: Total applications, 90; total individuals funded/provided with in-kind support, 30
Grant Range: $500-$5,000 in FY 1993

DIRECT SUPPORT PROGRAMS

➤ **FELLOWSHIPS**

Purpose: To encourage professional development of individual Alabama artists
Eligibility:
    Citizenship: U.S.
    Residency: Alabama, 2 years prior to application
    Special Requirements: Previous grantees ineligible for 4 years; no funding for academic study in pursuit of a college degree
    Art Forms: Disciplines rotate on a 2 year cycle: Crafts, design, dance, theater in odd-numbered years; visual arts, media arts/photography, literature, music in even-numbered years
Type of Support: $5,000 or $10,000
Scope of Program: 16 awards in FY 1993
Application/Selection Process:
    Deadline: May 1, annually (applications must be received by that date, not just postmarked)
    Preferred Initial Contact: Call or write for application/guidelines
    Application Procedure: Submit application form (original and 2 copies), samples of work, SASE for materials to be returned
    Selection Process: Professional advisory panel, ASCA council and staff
    Notification Process: 4-5 months after deadline
    Formal Report of Grant Required: Yes

➤ **TECHNICAL ASSISTANCE GRANTS**

Purpose: To provide funds for artists in need of assistance in marketing their work, establishing a portfolio, learning tax laws and accounting basics, grantseeking, or perfecting a particular artistic technique

Eligibility:

Citizenship: U.S. or permanent resident

Residency: Alabama, 2 years prior to application

Special Requirements: Artists may submit only 1 technical assistance application per grant period; no funding for academic study in pursuit of a college degree

Art Forms: All disciplines

Type of Support: Up to $1,000 for attending workshops or seminars, studying under another artist, or other educational opportunities except for pursuit of a college degree

Scope of Program: Limited funds

Application/Selection Process:

Deadline: While funds last (fiscal year begins October)

Preferred Initial Contact: Call or write for application/guidelines

Application Procedure: Submit application form (original and 2 copies), samples of work, budget for proposed use of funds, additional explanation of why the grant would be of benefit and how it would be used, SASE for materials to be returned

Selection Process: Professional advisory panel, ASCA council and staff

Notification Process: 4-5 months after receipt of application

Formal Report of Grant Required: Yes

➤ **ARTIST RESIDENCIES**

CONTACT: BARBARA GEORGE, ARTS IN EDUCATION PROGRAM MANAGER

Purpose: To allow artists to share their knowledge with students, teachers and the community

Eligibility:

Residency: open

Special Requirements: Artist must have ability to work well in educational settings

Art Forms: Visual arts, crafts, media (photography, film, video, audio), design arts, folk arts, dance, literature, music, theater

Type of Support: 2-week to 10-month residencies; fees vary depending on length of residency; acceptance in the program is not a guarantee of work, but means inclusion in a list of artists provided to sponsoring schools and community organizations

Scope of Program: 15 in FY 1993

Application/Selection Process:

Deadline: February 1, annually (application must be received by that date, not just postmarked)

Preferred Initial Contact: Write or call for application/guidelines

Please read carefully!
Do not contact any listed organization unless you fulfill all eligibility requirements.

Application Procedure: Submit application form (original and 2 copies), samples of work, a brief discussion of how the residency would be conducted, SASE for materials to be returned
Selection Process: Panel review
Notification Process: n/a

TECHNICAL ASSISTANCE PROGRAMS AND SERVICES

Programs of Special Interest: The council reviews in-state and out-of-state artists for school and community residencies (contact Barbara George, Arts in Education Program Manager); maintains the Alabama Artists Bank and Slide Registry; and subsidizes, through the Presenter Program, the booking of performances and exhibitions.

ALASKA STATE COUNCIL ON THE ARTS (ASCA)

411 West 4th Avenue
Suite 1E
Anchorage, AK 99501-2343
907-279-1558
TDD: 800-770-8973 (Statewide Relay Service)
FAX: 907-279-4330
CONTACT: G. JEAN PALMER, GRANTS OFFICER

PROFILE OF FINANCIAL SUPPORT TO ARTISTS

Total Funding/Value of In-Kind Support: $54,145 for FY 1992
Competition for Funding: Total applications, 138; total individuals funded/provided with in-kind support, 40
Grant Range: Up to $5,000

DIRECT SUPPORT PROGRAMS

➤ **INDIVIDUAL ARTIST FELLOWSHIP GRANTS**
Purpose: To assist experienced, professional artists in the creation of original works of art and in the development of their careers
Eligibility:
Residency: Alaska
Special Requirements: No full-time students; previous grantees ineligible for 3 years, preference given to artists who have never received an ASCA fellowship; collaborative projects ineligible
Art Forms: Visual arts, crafts, photography, traditional Native art eligible in odd-numbered years; music composition, choreography, media arts, literature eligible in even-numbered years
Type of Support: $5,000

Please read carefully!
Do not contact any listed organization unless you fulfill all eligibility requirements.

Scope of Program: 5 awards in FY 1992

Application/Selection Process:
　Deadline: October 1, annually
　Preferred Initial Contact: Call or write for application/guidelines
　Application Procedure: Submit application form, samples of work
　Selection Process: Peer panel of artists, board of directors
　Notification Process: By letter in late November
　Formal Report of Grant Required: Yes

➤ **ARTIST TRAVEL GRANTS**

Purpose: To enable individual artists to attend events that will enhance their artistic skills or professional standing

Eligibility:
　Residency: Alaska
　Special Requirements: Originating artists only; no full-time students; previous grantees ineligible for 1 year, preference given to artists who have never received a Travel Grant
　Art Forms: Visual arts, photography, media arts, literary arts, musical composition, choreography, and other arts involving the creation of new works

Type of Support: Maximum $600 to cover up to two-thirds of travel costs to attend workshops, conferences, or seminars, or to undertake projects; travel may be in-state, national or international

Scope of Program: 22 grants, totalling $10,145, awarded in FY 1992

Application/Selection Process:
　Deadline: 30 days before departure; awards made on first-come, first-served basis (fiscal year begins in July)
　Preferred Initial Contact: Call or write for application/guidelines
　Application Procedure: Submit application form, resumé, samples of work
　Selection Process: Decision by executive director
　Notification Process: Letter within 2 weeks of application's receipt
　Formal Report of Grant Required: Yes

TECHNICAL ASSISTANCE PROGRAMS AND SERVICES

Programs of Special Interest: Staff assistance is available for guidance on arts planning, artist promotion, project development, and grant application development.

Please read carefully!
Do not contact any listed organization unless you fulfill all eligibility requirements.

ALBERTA COMMUNITY DEVELOPMENT—ARTS AND CULTURAL INDUSTRIES BRANCH

10158-103 Street, 3rdFloor
Edmonton, Alberta
Canada T5J 0X6
403-427-6315
FAX: 403-427-9122
CONTACT: BILL STEWART, CULTURAL INDUSTRIES OFFICER

PROFILE OF FINANCIAL SUPPORT TO ARTISTS

Total Funding/Value of In-Kind Support: $127,000 for FY 1993-94

Competition for Funding: Total applications, n/a; total individuals funded/provided with in-kind support, 50

Grant Range: Up to $10,000

DIRECT SUPPORT PROGRAMS

➤ **FILM/VIDEO PRODUCTION GRANT PROGRAM**

Purpose: Production grants provide financial support for independent filmmakers and videomakers for short films and videos

Eligibility:
    Citizenship: Canada (landed immigrants also eligible)
    Residency: Alberta
    Art Forms: Film, video

Type of Support: Production grants, up to $10,000 to assist, not entirely underwrite, the cost of a project

Scope of Program: 12 grants, totalling $80,000, in FY 1992-93

Application/Selection Process:
    Deadline: May 15 and November 1, annually
    Preferred Initial Contact: Call or write for information
    Application Procedure: Submit application form, letters of reference, samples of work (if available)
    Selection Process: Jury, board of directors
    Notification Process: Letter
    Formal Report of Grant Required: Yes

➤ **THE QUEBEC-ALBERTA TELEVISION PRIZE/
THE ALBERTA-QUEBEC CINEMA PRIZE**

Purpose: To award individuals for excellence in innovation in Canadian television and cinema

Eligibility:
    Citizenship: Canada (landed immigrants also eligible)
    Residency: Canada

Please read carefully!
Do not contact any listed organization unless you fulfill all eligibility requirements.

Special Requirements: Awards given to directors only
Art Forms: Film, video
Type of Support: $2,500 award
Scope of Program: 2 television prizes, 2 cinema prizes annually
Application/Selection Process:
Deadline: April or May, annually; contact for exact date
Preferred Initial Contact: Call or write for information
Selection Process: Jury
Notification Process: Phone call to recipients; Television Prize announcements made in Summer, Cinema Prize announcements made in Fall
Formal Report of Grant Required: No

TECHNICAL ASSISTANCE PROGRAMS AND SERVICES
Programs of Special Interest: Alberta Culture and Multiculturalism offers consultations and a variety of workshop and seminar programs relating to professional development. The National Screen Institute-Canada provides training and development programs for filmmakers (contact the National Screen Institute-Canada, 10022-103 Street, Suite 300, Edmonton, Alberta, Canada T5J 0X2; 403-421-4084).

ALLIED ARTS FOUNDATION

105 South Main, Room 201
Seattle, WA 98104
206-624-0432
FAX: 206-624-2606
CONTACT: EXECUTIVE DIRECTOR

PROFILE OF FINANCIAL SUPPORT TO ARTISTS
Total Funding/Value of In-Kind Support: n/a
Competition for Funding: Total applications, 73; total individuals funded/provided with in-kind support, 5
Grant Range: Grant amounts vary according to available funds

DIRECT SUPPORT PROGRAM
➤ **ALLIED ARTS FOUNDATION GRANTS**
Purpose: To provide seed grants for emerging artists/organizations in the Puget Sound region
Eligibility:
Residency: Must serve or live in Puget Sound region

Please read carefully!
Do not contact any listed organization unless you fulfill all eligibility requirements.

Age: Open
Special Requirements: Professionals only; individuals eligible for only 1 award per year
Art Forms: All disciplines
Type of Support: $200-$500 grants in 1992
Scope of Program: Varies according to available funds; $3,000-$4,000 annually
Application/Selection Process:
    Deadline: Fall and spring, annually; contact for exact dates
    Preferred Initial Contact: Write or call for information
    Application Procedure: Submit application form
    Selection Process: Beneficiary Committee
    Notification Process: By letter, 1 week after deadline
    Formal Report of Grant Required: No

TECHNICAL ASSISTANCE PROGRAMS AND SERVICES

Programs of Special Interest: Allied Arts Foundation also acts as a fiscal sponsor. An affiliated organization, Allied Arts of Seattle, serves as an arts advocate, publishes a directory of regional arts organizations, and provides seminars and workshops on a variety of topics.

THE AMERICAN FILM INSTITUTE (AFI)

2021 North Western Avenue
P.O. Box 27999
Los Angeles, CA 90027
213-856-7600

PROFILE OF FINANCIAL SUPPORT TO ARTISTS

Total Funding/Value of In-Kind Support: n/a
Competition for Funding: n/a
Grant Range: Up to $20,000

DIRECT SUPPORT PROGRAMS

➤ **INDEPENDENT FILM AND VIDEOMAKER PROGRAM**
Phone: 213-856-7787

Purpose: To encourage and support the continued development of the moving image as an art form through funding productions that emphasize creative use of the media
Eligibility:
    Citizenship: U.S. (permanent residents also eligible)
    Residency: Open

Please read carefully!
Do not contact any listed organization unless you fulfill all eligibility requirements.

Special Requirements: Professional, experienced artists only; no students; noncommercial projects only
Art Forms: Film, video
Type of Support: Up to $20,000
Scope of Program: 10-12 grants awarded annually
Application/Selection Process:
Deadline: September 15, annually
Preferred Initial Contact: Call or write for application/guidelines
Application Procedure: Application requires submission of previously completed film or video art, an application form, script or treatment, resumé, project budget
Selection Process: Individuals from outside of organization, peer panel of artists
Notification Process: Phone call to recipients, letter to nonrecipients; announcements made by end of July, annually
Formal Report of Grant Required: Yes

➤ **DIRECTING WORKSHOP FOR WOMEN**

CONTACT: LINDA VITALE, PRODUCTION TRAINING DIVISION
Phone: 213-856-7622

Purpose: To offer mid-career professional women in the media arts their first opportunities to direct a dramatic project
Eligibility:
Citizenship: U.S. (permanent residents also eligible)
Residency: Open
Age: 18 or older
Special Requirements: Women only; must have considerable professional experience in television, film, video, or the dramatic arts but not yet had the opportunity to direct dramatic films or television; must reside and work in the U.S. or its territories during grant period
Art Forms: Film, video; participants will work with video.
Type of Support: $5,000 grant to direct 30-minute narrative videotape; 2 weeks of seminars and hands-on training before start of individual production; access to production equipment and editing facilities
Scope of Program: 12 grants, totalling $60,000, over last 18- to 24-month cycle
Application/Selection Process:
Deadline: Varies annually; contact for exact date
Preferred Initial Contact: Write for application/guidelines
Application Procedure: Submit application form, $50 fee, references, resumé
Selection Process: Organization staff, peer panel of artists, individuals outside of organization and board of trustees

Please read carefully!
Do not contact any listed organization unless you fulfill all eligibility requirements.

Notification Process: Letter or phone call, approximately 3 months after application deadline
Formal Report of Grant Required: No

➤ **TELEVISION WRITERS SUMMER WORKSHOP**

CONTACT: LINDA VITALE, PRODUCTION TRAINING DIVISION
Phone: 213-856-7622

Purpose: To provide a learning environment for promising new talents to hone their scriptwriting skills and to apply what they have learned by developing a script

Eligibility:
  Citizenship: U.S. (permanent residents also eligible)
  Residency: Open
  Age: 18 or older
  Special Requirements: Preference to new writers with media or theater backgrounds who have no major commercial television writing credits
  Art Forms: Scriptwriting for television

Type of Support: Workshop ($450 fee; scholarships with $1,000 living stipend available)

Scope of Program: 3 scholarships per year

Application/Selection Process:
  Deadline: Late winter/early spring, annually; contact for exact date
  Preferred Initial Contact: Call or write for application/guidelines
  Application Procedure: Submit application form, $35 fee, samples of work, references, resumé
  Selection Process: Organization staff, peer panel of artists, individuals from outside of organization and board of trustees
  Notification Process: Phone call or letter, approximately 2 months after application deadline
  Formal Report of Grant Required: No

TECHNICAL ASSISTANCE PROGRAMS AND SERVICES

Programs of Special Interest: AFI also administers Visions of U.S.: Home Video Competition, sponsored by Sony Corporation, which awards state-of-the-art video equipment to winners in five categories: fiction, nonfiction, experimental, music video, and applicants 17 years of age and under. Deadline in June, annually; contact for specific date. For more information, contact Lee Briggs, Visions of U.S., P.O. Box 200, Hollywood, CA 90078; 213-856-7743.

Please read carefully!
Do not contact any listed organization unless you fulfill all eligibility requirements.

THE AMERICAN-SCANDINAVIAN FOUNDATION

725 Park Avenue
New York, NY 10021
212-879-9779
CONTACT: KIEKO MATTESON, FELLOWSHIP PROGRAM ADMINISTRATOR

PROFILE OF FINANCIAL SUPPORT TO ARTISTS
Total Funding/Value of In-Kind Support: $195,000 for FY 1993-94
Competition for Funding: n/a
Grant Range: $2,500-$15,000

DIRECT SUPPORT PROGRAMS
➤ **AWARDS FOR STUDY IN SCANDINAVIA**

Purpose: To encourage advanced study and research in Scandinavia

Eligibility:
>   **Citizenship:** U.S. (permanent residents also eligible)
>   **Special Requirements:** Must have completed undergraduate education; language competence (as necessary), the special merit of pursuing the project in Scandinavia, and evidence of confirmed invitation or affiliation are important factors; conference attendance and study at English-language institutions are ineligible for support
>   **Art Forms:** All disciplines and scholarly fields

Type of Support: $2,000 grants for short visit to Scandinavia; $10,000 fellowships for a full academic year of research or study

Scope of Program: $193,500 available for 1993-94

Application/Selection Process:
>   **Deadline:** November 1, annually
>   **Preferred Initial Contact:** Call or write for application/guidelines
>   **Application Procedure:** Submit application form, $10 fee, samples of work, resumé, project description
>   **Selection Process:** Committee
>   **Notification Process:** Letter by mid-March
>   **Formal Report of Grant Required:** Yes

Please read carefully!
Do not contact any listed organization unless you fulfill all eligibility requirements.

APPALSHOP, INC.

306 Madison Street
Whitesburg, KY 41858
606-633-0108
FAX: 606-633-1009
CONTACT: MIMI PICKERING, COORDINATOR, SOUTHEAST MEDIA FELLOWSHIP PROGRAM

PROFILE OF FINANCIAL SUPPORT TO ARTISTS
Total Funding/Value of In-Kind Support: $53,900 for FY 1993
(figures reflect Southeast Media Fellowship Program only)
Competition for Funding: Total applications, 198; total individuals
funded/provided with in-kind support, 19
Grant Range: $500-$8,000

DIRECT SUPPORT PROGRAMS
➤ **SOUTHEAST MEDIA FELLOWSHIP PROGRAM (SEMFP)**
Purpose: To assist independent media artists in the Southeast by pro-
viding grants for the production of personally conceived works in
film and video
Eligibility:
 Citizenship: U.S.
 Residency: Alabama, Florida, Georgia, Kentucky, Louisiana, Missis-
 sippi, North Carolina, South Carolina, Tennessee, Virginia, 1 year
 Special Requirements: No full-time students; artist must have
 overall control of content and primary creative responsibility for
 project; no commercial or instructional projects
 Art Forms: Film, video
Type of Support: Up to $8,000 for residents of Kentucky, Louisiana,
Mississippi, North Carolina, South Carolina, Tennessee; up to
$5,000 for residents of Alabama, Florida, Georgia, Virginia; Equip-
ment Access Grants from South Carolina Arts Commission Media
Arts Center available for Betacam video production, 16mm film production, Beta SP video editing, 16mm film editing, S-VHS video pro-
duction, post-production, computer graphics system, audio/
electronic music studio; grantees must pay for shipping production
equipment to and from their location
Scope of Program: 15 cash grants, totalling $53,900, in 1993; 4
equipment access grants in 1993
Application/Selection Process:
 Deadline: February, annually; contact for exact date
 Preferred Initial Contact: Call or write for application/guidelines

Please read carefully!
Do not contact any listed organization unless you fulfill all eligibility requirements.

Application Procedure: Submit application form, $4 for return shipping, samples of work, resumé, project budget, support material (optional)

Selection Process: Independent panel of artists and arts professionals

Notification Process: Letter 4 months after deadline

Formal Report of Grant Required: Yes

EQUIPMENT ACCESS

Film: Production and post-production for 16mm

Video: Production and post-production for 3/4" and VHS

Comments: Rates for facilities, equipment, and crews range from no charge to commercial rates, depending on the nature of the project. A recording studio is also available.

TECHNICAL ASSISTANCE PROGRAMS AND SERVICES

Programs of Special Interest: Appalshop exhibits and broadcasts independent films and videos, and provides fundraising and distribution assistance.

ARIZONA CENTER FOR THE MEDIA ARTS

P.O. Box 40638
Tucson, AZ 85717
602-628-1737

TECHNICAL ASSISTANCE PROGRAMS AND SERVICES

Programs of Special Interest: The center offers workshops on funding and new equipment; consultation services regarding funding, distribution, and festivals; and a screening facility.

ARIZONA COMMISSION ON THE ARTS

417 West Roosevelt Street
Phoenix, AZ 85003
602-255-5882
TDD: 800-367-8939 (Arizona Relay Service)
FAX: 602-256-0282
CONTACT: KRISTA ELRICK, VISUAL ARTS DIRECTOR

PROFILE OF FINANCIAL SUPPORT TO ARTISTS

Total Funding/Value of In-Kind Support: $115,000 for FY 1993

Please read carefully!
Do not contact any listed organization unless you fulfill all eligibility requirements.

Competition for Funding: Total applications, 375; total individuals funded/provided with in-kind support, 73

Grant Range: $300-$7,500

DIRECT SUPPORT PROGRAMS

➤ **VISUAL ARTS FELLOWSHIPS**

Purpose: To allow individual artists to set aside time to work, to purchase supplies and materials, to achieve specific artistic career goals, and to further their professional development

Eligibility:
    Residency: Arizona
    Age: 18 or older
    Special Requirements: No students enrolled for more than 3 credit hours at a college or university
    Art Forms: Visual arts; eligible media rotate on 3-year cycle among 3-dimensional (apply in 1993), 2-dimensional (1994), and film/video/photography (1995)

Type of Support: $5,000-$7,500

Scope of Program: Varies; budget divided among disciplines in proportion to number of applicants

Application/Selection Process:
    Deadline: September, annually; contact for exact date
    Preferred Initial Contact: Call or write for application/guidelines
    Application Procedure: Submit application form, samples of work, technical description of work, resumé, reviews of work (optional), exhibition catalogs (optional), miscellaneous documentation (optional)
    Selection Process: Panel of out-of-state arts professionals
    Notification Process: April

➤ **ARTIST PROJECTS**

Purpose: To support artist projects that allow the artist increased time to research and develop ideas or new works, that stretch the artist's work or seek to advance the artform, that bear relevance to the artist's community, or that involve interdisciplinary collaborations with other artists or non-artists

Eligibility:
    Residency: Arizona
    Age: 18 or older
    Special Requirements: No students enrolled in more than 3 credit hours at a college or university; previous grantees not eligible
    Art Forms: All disciplines, innovative work encouraged

Type of Support: Up to $5,000 for project-related costs

Scope of Program: $20,000 allotted for 1993-94

Please read carefully!
Do not contact any listed organization unless you fulfill all eligibility requirements.

Application/Selection Process:
    Deadline: September annually, contact for exact date
    Preferred Initial Contact: Call or write for application/guidelines
    Application Procedure: Submit application forms, biographies of artists involved, samples of work
    Selection Process: Panel of out-of-state artists
    Notification Process: April
    Formal Report of Grant Required: Yes

➤ **PROFESSIONAL DEVELOPMENT GRANTS**

Purpose: To provide Arizona artists and organizations representing artists assistance in attending out-of-state conferences that will contribute to their professional growth

Eligibility:
    Residence: Arizona
    Special Requirements: Artists usually limited to one Professional Development Grant per year; assistance usually not provided for artist to attend same conference for 2 successive years
    Art Forms: All disciplines

Type of Support: Up to $750

Scope of Program: $35,000 budget for 1993

Application/Selection Process:
    Deadline: 6 weeks before conference
    Application Procedure: Submit materials describing conference (if available) and letter of request outlining conference date and location, how attendance would be beneficial, total costs involved, amount and source of other financial assistance

TECHNICAL ASSISTANCE PROGRAMS AND SERVICES

Programs of Special Interest: Individuals may apply for inclusion on the selective Artists Roster, which provides information to community sponsors interested in the Artists in Residence—Schools; Artists in Residence—Communities; Bicultural Arts; and Traveling Exhibitions programs. The commission's Arts Services Program and Arts Resource Center furnish artists with information about business-related issues.

ARKANSAS ARTS COUNCIL (AAC)

1500 Tower Building
323 Center Street
Little Rock, AR 72201
501-324-9150/9766
TDD: 501-324-9811
FAX: 501-324-9154
CONTACT: SALLY A. WILLIAMS, ARTIST PROGRAMS COORDINATOR

TECHNICAL ASSISTANCE PROGRAMS AND SERVICES
Programs of Special Interest: Film and video artists may apply for inclusion in the AAC's Artists-in-Education roster. The AAC assists artists who cannot afford legal services through referrals to the University of Arkansas at Little Rock Law School Legal Clinic. The Arts Council Library offers a wide selection of reference materials.

ARTIST TRUST

1402 Third Avenue, #415
Seattle, WA 98101
206-467-8734
FAX: 206-467-9633
CONTACT: PROGRAM COORDINATOR

PROFILE OF FINANCIAL SUPPORT TO ARTISTS
Total Funding/Value of In-Kind Support: $81,000 for FY 1992
Competition for Funding: Total applications, 1,300; total individuals funded/provided with in-kind support, 56
Grant Range: $100-$5,000

DIRECT SUPPORT PROGRAMS
➤ ARTIST TRUST FELLOWSHIPS
Purpose: To allow individual artists time to create
Eligibility:
    Citizenship: U.S. (resident aliens eligible)
    Residency: Washington State, 1 year
    Special Requirements: Washington State registered voter (except resident aliens); no students; practicing professionals only; originating artists only

Please read carefully!
Do not contact any listed organization unless you fulfill all eligibility requirements.

Art Forms: Dance (choreography), design, theater, visual arts, crafts, literature, media (including screenwriting, film production, video, audio art), music composition

Type of Support: $5,000; recipient must participate in and report on a "Meet the Artist" activity outside of his or her community

Scope of Program: 17 awards (2 each in dance, design, theater, crafts, literature, media, music composition; 3 in visual arts)

Application/Selection Process:
    Deadline: Multiple deadlines depending on discipline; contact for details
    Preferred Initial Contact: Call or write for application/guidelines
    Application Procedure: Submit application form, samples of work, resumé, copy of voter's registration card (except resident aliens), proof of residency (copy of driver's license or tax return)
    Selection Process: Peer panel of artists, board of directors
    Notification Process: Letter 8-12 weeks after deadline
    Formal Report of Grant Required: Yes

➤ **GAP (GRANTS FOR ARTIST PROJECTS)**

Purpose: To allow artists to pursue their own creative development through projects such as development, completion, or presentation of a new work; publication; travel for artistic research or to present or complete work; workshops for professional development

Eligibility:
    Residency: Washington State
    Special Requirements: No students; must be Washington registered voter
    Art Forms: All disciplines

Type of Support: $100-$1,000 for specific project

Scope of Program: 46 grants in FY 1992

Application/Selection Process:
    Deadlines: 2 per year, usually in spring and fall; contact for exact dates
    Preferred Initial Contact: Call or write for application/guidelines
    Application Procedure: Submit application form, samples of work, resumé, project budget
    Selection Process: Committee of artists and arts professionals
    Notification Process: Letter 8-12 weeks after deadline
    Formal Report of Grant Required: Yes

TECHNICAL ASSISTANCE PROGRAMS AND SERVICES

Programs of Special Interest: Artist Trust maintains an information clearinghouse of programs and services of interest to Washington State artists. A booklet on healthcare options (published in 1989) is available. A quarterly journal for Washington State artists is also

Please read carefully!
Do not contact any listed organization unless you fulfill all eligibility requirements.

available. The journal contains lists of grants, commissions and other opportunities for artists; information on health, legal and tax questions; and articles. Artist Trust has conducted educational campaigns about freedom of expression, censorship, and public art.

ARTISTS SPACE

38 Greene Street
New York, NY 10012
212-226-3970
CONTACT: GARY NICKARD, PROGRAMS COORDINATOR

TECHNICAL ASSISTANCE PROGRAMS AND SERVICES
Programs of Special Interest: The Artists File is a computerized slide file which contains the work of over 4,000 artists and which is free to participating artists and researchers. Artists from all disciplines and from around the country are presented at Artists Space.

ARTISTS' TELEVISION ACCESS (ATA)

992 Valencia Street
San Francisco, CA 94110
415-824-3890
CONTACT: KRIS ATKINS, PROGRAMMING DIRECTOR

EQUIPMENT ACCESS
Video: Production and post-production for VHS, S-VHS
Comments: Equipment access is available at subsidized rates to artists, community organizations, and people on limited incomes.

TECHNICAL ASSISTANCE PROGRAMS AND SERVICES
Programs of Special Interest: ATA programs "Other Cinema," a weekly Saturday night film/video screening, and produces "Artists' Television," a weekly half-hour public access art and documentary film/video cablecast. Guest curators program a weekly Friday night screening/performance series. Artists are not charged exhibition entry fees and are paid honoraria whenever possible. ATA coordinates an intern program for the community, including local colleges and universities, and offers low-cost video production and post-production workshops.

Please read carefully!
Do not contact any listed organization unless you fulfill all eligibility requirements.

ARTPARK

P.O. Box 371
Lewiston, NY 14092
716-745-3377 (Oct-Mar)/716-754-9001 (Apr-Sep)
CONTACT: JOAN MCDONOUGH, PARK PROGRAMS DIRECTOR

PROFILE OF FINANCIAL SUPPORT TO ARTISTS

Total Funding/Value of In-Kind Support: $377,000 for FY 1990

Competition for Funding: Total applications, 600; total individuals funded/provided with in-kind support, 100

Grant Range: n/a

DIRECT SUPPORT PROGRAMS

➤ **ARTPARK RESIDENCIES**

Purpose: To offer artists opportunities to experiment, collaborate, and develop their work

Eligibility:
    Citizenship: U.S. (workshop visa holders also eligible)
    Special Requirements: Practicing professional artists only; no students
    Art Forms: Visual arts (including film and video), crafts, performing arts

Type of Support: 1- to 6-week residencies including $450 weekly fee, $200 weekly living allowance, and allowances for travel and materials; residents work as project, craft, workshop, or performing artists

Scope of Program: 100-150 residencies per year

Application/Selection Process:
    Preferred Initial Contact: Call or write for guidelines
    Application Procedure: Submit $20 fee, resumé, samples of work (project, craft, and performing artists), description of proposed work or workshop (craft, workshop, and performing artists); project artist finalists make 1-day, expenses-paid site visit, then present project proposals
    Selection Process: ArtPark staff (craft, workshop, and performing artists); guest curator and ArtPark staff (project artists)
    Notification Process: Letter
    Formal Report of Grant Required: Yes

THE ARTS AND HUMANITIES COUNCIL OF TULSA (AHCT)

2210 South Main Street
Tulsa, OK 74114
918-584-3333
FAX: 918-582-2787
CONTACT: GEORGIA WILLIAMS, DIRECTOR OF EDUCATION PROGRAMS

PROFILE OF FINANCIAL SUPPORT TO ARTISTS

Total Funding/Value of In-Kind Support: $200,000 (includes Artists-in-Schools program) in 1992
Competition for Funding: n/a
Grant Range: $1,000

DIRECT SUPPORT PROGRAMS

➤ **JINGLE FELDMAN GRANT FOR INDIVIDUAL ARTISTS/SCHOLARS**

Purpose: To allow artists, writers, and scholars to create new works, complete works in progress, or pursue new avenues of artistic expression and scholarly endeavor
Eligibility:
  Residency: Tulsa area resident, 1 year
  Art Forms: Visual art (includes crafts, photography, film/video, performance art), writing, performing and humanities
Type of Support: $1,000 awards
Scope of Program: 4 awards for a total of $4,000 annually
Application/Selection Process:
  Deadline: April 1, annually
  Preferred Initial Contact: Call or write for prospectus
  Application Procedure: Submit application form, support material
  Selection Process: Independent juror (peer artist or scholar) with proven excellence in the field
  Notification Process: Letter to all applicants, phone call to recipients
  Formal Report of Grant Required: Yes

TECHNICAL ASSISTANCE PROGRAMS AND SERVICES

Programs of Special Interest: Career advancement opportunities are offered such as: resumé and portfolio counseling, referral for regional/national exhibits, master classes, grantwriting assistance, statewide and regional networking with Oklahoma Visual Arts Coalition, Individual Artists of Oklahoma, Tulsa Artists' Coalition, Na-

Please read carefully!
Do not contact any listed organization unless you fulfill all eligibility requirements.

tional Association of Artists' Organizations. Income opportunities for teaching artists in all disciplines are available through the council's Arts-in-Education programs: Artists-in-the-Schools, Harwelden Institute for Arts in Education, Community Arts School Tulsa (CAST), Tulsa Summer Arts.

ARTS AND SCIENCE COUNCIL OF CHARLOTTE/ MECKLENBURG, INC. (ASC)

214 North Church Street
Suite 100
Charlotte, NC 28203
704-372-9667
CONTACT: HELLENA H. TIDWELL, VICE PRESIDENT, RESOURCE MANAGEMENT

PROFILE OF FINANCIAL SUPPORT TO ARTISTS

Total Funding/Value of In-Kind Support: $18,500 for FY 1992-93

Competition for Funding: Total applications, 80; total individuals funded/provided with in-kind support, 24

Grant Range: $200-$1,200

DIRECT SUPPORT PROGRAMS

➤ **REGIONAL EMERGING ARTISTS GRANT PROGRAM**

Purpose: To enable individuals to advance their development as professional artists

Eligibility:
Residency: 1 year residency in Cabarrus, Gaston, Iredell, Lincoln, Union and/or Mecklenburg Counties
Age: 18 or older
Special Requirements: No students; previous grantees ineligible
Art Forms: Dramatic arts, literary arts (includes screenwriting/ playwriting), music, dance, visual arts (includes media arts, photography), multi-disciplinary, interdisciplinary

Type of Support: $200-$1,200 to support project that furthers artist's career

Scope of Program: $18,500 awarded annually

Application/Selection Process:
Deadline: Late summer/early fall, annually; contact for exact date
Preferred Initial Contact: Call or write for application/guidelines

Please read carefully!
Do not contact any listed organization unless you fulfill all eligibility requirements.

Application Procedure: Submit application form, resumé, samples of work, letters of recommendation
Selection Process: Panel of artists representing the six participating counties, ASC board and staff
Notification Process: Letter 2-3 months after application
Formal Report of Grant Required: Yes

TECHNICAL ASSISTANCE PROGRAMS AND SERVICES

Programs of Special Interest: ASC staff offer grantwriting assistance for ASC's Emerging Artist Program, North Carolina Arts Council grant programs, and other select local grant programs that the artist has researched; call at least 1 week in advance for appointment. The Cultural Education Research Handbook lists artists who are qualified to teach or perform in local schools; artists who live within a 200-mile radius of Charlotte/Mecklenburg are eligible for inclusion.

THE ARTS ASSEMBLY OF JACKSONVILLE, INC.

128 East Forsyth Street
3rd Floor
Jacksonville, FL 32202
904-358-3600
FAX: 904-353-5100
CONTACT: GRANTS AND SERVICES MANAGER

PROFILE OF FINANCIAL SUPPORT TO ARTISTS

Total Funding/Value of In-Kind Support: $50,000 for FY 1991-92
Competition for Funding: Total applications, 44; total individuals funded/provided with in-kind support, 14
Grant Range: Up to $5,000

DIRECT SUPPORT PROGRAMS
➤ ART VENTURES FUND
CAREER OPPORTUNITY GRANTS FOR ARTISTS
Purpose: To assist artists in attaining the "next level" of their professional development by funding expenses such as materials, advanced study with a mentor, contracting professional services for a project, travel, equipment rental or purchase, living expenses during pursuit of a specific project
Eligibility:
   Citizenship: U.S.
   Residency: First Coast area of Florida (Duval, St. Johns, Baker, Clay, Nassau counties), 1 year

Please read carefully!
Do not contact any listed organization unless you fulfill all eligibility requirements.

Age: 18 or older
Special Requirements: No students
Art Forms: Visual arts, literary arts, film/video, music, performing arts

Type of Support: Up to $5,000

Scope of Program: 14 awards in FY 1991-92

Application/Selection Process:
Deadline: Fall, annually; contact for specific date
Preferred Initial Contact: Call or make appointment to seek technical assistance
Application Procedure: Submit application form, samples of work, 2 letters of recommendation, resumé, project budget; evaluation panel may schedule on-site visits to applicants
Selection Process: Panel of artists and foundation staff member, Art Ventures Fund Advisory Committee
Notification Process: Letter
Formal Report of Grant Required: Yes

➤ **FLORIDA TIMES-UNION**
ARTS EDUCATION MATCHING GRANT PROGRAM
Purpose: To provide matching funds for schools, PTAs, arts organizations, and artists who wish to provide Duval County school students with basic arts education experiences as a supplement to basic curriculum

Eligibility:
Citizenship: U.S.
Residency: Duval County
Special Requirements: School principal must agree to present project; must have 1:1 matching funds
Art Forms: All disciplines

Type of Support: Up to $500 matching grant

Scope of Program: 27 grants in 1992

Application/Selection Process:
Deadline: Summer, annually; contact for specific date
Preferred Initial Contact: Call or write for information
Application Procedure: Attend workshops, meetings for program development
Selection Process: Peer panel review
Notification Process: Letter
Formal Report of Funding Required: Yes

TECHNICAL ASSISTANCE PROGRAMS AND SERVICES
Programs of Special Interest: The Arts Assembly of Jacksonville administers an Artist in Residence program for Duval County schools and distributes to First Coast schools a resource guide publicizing

Please read carefully!
Do not contact any listed organization unless you fulfill all eligibility requirements.

arts education programs available from individual artists. The organization showcases 1,500 artists in the annual multi-disciplinary Arts Mania festival, which includes special programming by and for the disabled. An annual arts education conference also provides a showcase opportunity for artists.

ARTS COUNCIL FOR CHAUTAUQUA COUNTY

116 East 3rd Street
Jamestown, NY 14701
716-664-2465
CONTACT: PHILIP MORRIS, EXECUTIVE DIRECTOR

PROFILE OF FINANCIAL SUPPORT TO ARTISTS
Total Funding/Value of In-Kind Support: $4,000 for FY 1993
Competition for Funding: Total applications, 7; total individuals funded/provided with in-kind support, 3
Grant Range: $500-$1,000

DIRECT SUPPORT PROGRAMS
➤ FUND FOR THE ARTS PROJECTS POOL FELLOWSHIPS/
DECENTRALIZATION GRANTS
CONTACT: DAVID MUNNELL, ARTS PROJECT POOL; SU EWING, DECENTRALIZATION GRANTS COORDINATOR
Purpose: Fellowships, awarded solely on the basis of creative excellence, assist the career development of Chautauqua County artists; decentralization grants expand and upgrade the arts and cultural programming in Chautauqua and Cattaraugus counties
Eligibility:
  Residency: Chautauqua County, 1 year (Cattaraugus County residents also eligible for decentralization grants)
  Age: 18 or older
  Special Requirements: Decentralization grant applicants must be sponsored by nonprofit organization; previous grantees ineligible for 1 year
  Art Forms: All disciplines
Type of Support: $1,000 fellowships, up to $3,000 decentralization grants
Scope of Program: 3 fellowships, 0 decentralization grants to individuals in FY 1993
Application/Selection Process:
  Deadline: October 17, annually

Please read carefully!
Do not contact any listed organization unless you fulfill all eligibility requirements.

Preferred Initial Contact: Call or write for application/guidelines
Application Procedure: Submit application form, samples of work, references, resumé, project budget, proof of residency
Selection Process: Individuals outside of organization
Notification Process: Letter after panel recommendations approved by board
Formal Report of Grant Required: Yes

TECHNICAL ASSISTANCE PROGRAMS AND SERVICES
Programs of Special Interest: The council offers a Group Health Program for working artists and their families and a reference library and workshops that address artists' needs. The council refers artists to local organizations to hold workshops and lectures/demonstrations.

ARTS COUNCIL OF HILLSBOROUGH COUNTY

1000 North Ashley, Suite 316
Tampa, FL 33602
813-229-6547
FAX: 813-229-6547
CONTACT: SUSAN EDWARDS, DIRECTOR, PROGRAM SERVICES

PROFILE OF FINANCIAL SUPPORT TO ARTISTS
Total Funding/Value of In-Kind Support: $29,000 for FY 1991-92

Competition for Funding: Total applications, 79; total individuals funded/provided with in-kind support, 23

Grant Range: Up to $1,500

DIRECT SUPPORT PROGRAMS
➤ **EMERGING ARTIST GRANTS**
Purpose: To assist promising local artists and arts groups in advancing their careers
Eligibility:
  Residency: Hillsborough County residents only
  Special Requirements: Previous grantees ineligible for 2 years
  Art Forms: All disciplines
Type of Support: Up to $1,500 for a specific project
Scope of Program: 23 awards in FY 1991-92
Application/Selection Process:
  Deadline: Two deadlines (spring and fall), annually; contact for exact dates

Please read carefully!
Do not contact any listed organization unless you fulfill all eligibility requirements.

Preferred Initial Contact: Call or write for application/guidelines
Application Procedure: Submit application form, samples of work, resumé, project budget, supporting materials (e.g., reviews, catalogs)
Selection Process: Panel of artists and arts professionals, board of directors
Notification Process: Letter 5 weeks after deadline
Formal Report of Grant Required: Yes

TECHNICAL ASSISTANCE PROGRAMS AND SERVICES

Programs of Special Interest: The council sponsors workshops for artists in areas such as basic business matters, marketing, public relations, fundraising, grantwriting, and taxes. The council also offers tax and insurance planning services and acts as a liaison between artists and those seeking their services, and as an arts advocate in legislative and policy matters. Graphics services are offered to artists and nonprofit arts groups at nominal rates, and the Arts Library holds a wide reference collection on arts issues. The *Arts Directory* covers almost 200 arts organizations, and the *Facilities Guide* provides information about space available for exhibitions and presentations. The council administers an Artists in the Schools program.

ARTS COUNCIL OF INDIANAPOLIS (ACI)

47 South Pennsylvania
Suite 703
Indianapolis, IN 46204
317-631-3301
FAX: 317-624-2559

CONTACT: NORMAN BRANDENSTEIN, DIRECTOR OF SERVICES

TECHNICAL ASSISTANCE PROGRAMS AND SERVICES

Programs of Special Interest: The council maintains the unjuried Indianapolis Artist Registry. Direct funding programs and community project opportunities which provide indirect funding for artists are currently under review. Contact the council for further information.

Please read carefully!
Do not contact any listed organization unless you fulfill all eligibility requirements.

ARTS COUNCIL OF SANTA CLARA COUNTY

4 North Second Street, Suite 505
San Jose, CA 95113
408-998-2787
CONTACT: LAWRENCE THOO, ASSOCIATE DIRECTOR

PROFILE OF FINANCIAL SUPPORT TO ARTISTS
Total Funding/Value of In-Kind Support: $12,000 for FY 1993
(fellowship program only)
Competition for Funding: Total applications, n/a; total individuals
funded/provided with in-kind support, 6
Grant Range: $2,000

➤ **ARTIST FELLOWSHIPS**
Purpose: To recognize the importance of individual artists to the
community
Eligibility:
    Residency: Santa Clara County, one year prior to application
    Age: 18 or older
    Special Requirements: Previous recipients ineligible for one cy-
    cle; no undergraduate students enrolled in degree granting pro-
    gram; no graduate students in program related to specific
    discipline of application
    Art Forms: Disciplines rotate: visual and literary arts in even-
    numbered years; media/new genre and performing arts in odd-
    numbered years
Type of Support: $2,000 awards in FY 1993
Scope of Program: Up to 6 awards in FY 1993
Application/Selection Process:
    Deadline: Contact for exact dates
    Preferred Initial Contact: Call or write for application/guidelines
    Application Procedure: Submit application form, samples of
    work, financial statement, project budget
    Selection Process: Peer panel of artists, council staff, board of
    trustees
    Notification Process: Letter within 3 months
    Formal Report of Grant Required: No

TECHNICAL ASSISTANCE PROGRAMS AND SERVICES
Programs of Special Interest: The council cosponsors the annual
Hands on Arts festival for children. A registry of individual Santa
Clara County artists is in development. Arts Connect is a fee-for-
service program which provides arts activities at children's care

Please read carefully!
Do not contact any listed organization unless you fulfill all eligibility requirements.

facilities in Santa Clara County; the program serves the two major shelter and residential care organizations for abused or neglected children, and the county Office of Education's Alternative Schools.

ARTS FOR GREATER ROCHESTER, INC. (AGR)

335 East Main Street, Suite 200
Rochester, NY 14604
716-546-5602
CONTACT: GRANTS COORDINATOR

PROFILE OF FINANCIAL SUPPORT TO ARTISTS
Total Funding/Value of In-Kind Support: $51,250 in 1993
Competition for Funding: n/a
Grant Range: Up to $5,000

DIRECT SUPPORT PROGRAMS
➤ AGR COMMUNITY ARTS GRANTS

Purpose: To assist nonprofit community organizations and arts groups to sponsor arts-related projects of community interest that are open to the public
Eligibility:
    Citizenship: U.S.
    Residency: Monroe County
    Age: 18 or older
    Special Requirements: Artists must apply through a Monroe County nonprofit organization
    Art Forms: All disciplines
Type of Support: Up to $5,000 for specific project
Scope of Program: 34 grants, totalling $51,250, awarded to organizations in 1993
Application/Selection Process:
    Deadline: Late August, annually; contact for exact date
    Preferred Initial Contact: Attend application seminar; call or write for information
    Application Procedure: Sponsor submits application form, financial statement, project budget, artist's resumé, samples of work
    Selection Process: Peer panel of artists and community representatives
    Notification Process: Letter 3-4 months after deadline
    Formal Report of Grant Required: Yes

Please read carefully!
Do not contact any listed organization unless you fulfill all eligibility requirements.

TECHNICAL ASSISTANCE PROGRAMS AND SERVICES

Programs of Special Interest: AGR's Volunteer Lawyers for the Arts program provides legal assistance to Monroe County artists with annual incomes below $15,000 per year and nonprofit organizations who bring in less than $75,000 per year. AGR maintains an artist slide registry and a reference library, and offers group insurance for artists. The organization also administers an arts-in-education program and provides networking opportunities through weekly breakfasts and an annual "artist to artist" event. The AGR Exhibit Space showcases work of artist members. AGR sponsors the annual Lilac Festival and sponsors a summer concert series at Hamlin Beach State Park.

ARTS FOUNDATION OF MICHIGAN (AFM)

2164 Penobscot Building
Detroit, MI 48226
313-964-2244
CONTACT: KIMBERLY ADAMS, EXECUTIVE DIRECTOR

PROFILE OF FINANCIAL SUPPORT TO ARTISTS

Total Funding/Value of In-Kind Support: $202,000 for 1992

Competition for Funding: Total applications, 300; total individuals funded/provided with in-kind support, 50

Grant Range: $500-$10,000

DIRECT SUPPORT PROGRAMS

➤ **CREATIVE ARTISTS GRANTS**

Purpose: To enable Michigan artists to create significant new work or complete works-in-progress by providing funds that may be used for living expenses, materials, rent, and other expenses involved in producing original art; project must be accessible to the public

Eligibility:
   Residency: Michigan
   Special Requirements: Originating artists only; no students; previous grantees ineligible for 2 years
   Art Forms: All disciplines

Type of Support: Up to $7,000

Scope of Program: 25 awards in FY 1993; average grant approximately $5,000

Application/Selection Process:
   Deadline: Deadline varies each year; call for updated information

Please read carefully!
Do not contact any listed organization unless you fulfill all eligibility requirements.

Preferred Initial Contact: Call or write for guidelines
Application Procedure: Submit letter of intent; eligible artists invited to apply
Selection Process: Peer panel of artists, board of trustees
Notification Process: Letter
Formal Report of Grant Required: Yes

➤ GENERAL GRANTS PROGRAM

Purpose: To support unmet needs of artists on a discipline-by-discipline basis; focus changes yearly
Eligibility:
    Residency: Michigan
    Special Requirements: Professional artists only; must apply with nonprofit sponsoring organization; project must be accessible to the public; limit 1 per year to an artist or sponsoring organization
    Art Forms: All disciplines (includes architecture, ceramics, dance, film, glassmaking, graphic design, literature, metalsmithing, music, painting, photography, printmaking, sculpture, theater, video, weaving)
Type of Support: $500-$2,500 grants
Scope of Program: 11 grants totalling $17,150 in FY 1992
Application/Selection Process:
    Deadline: Varies annually; call for detailed information
    Preferred Initial Contact: Call or write for information
    Application Procedure: Sponsoring organization submits application form, proof of nonprofit status, financial statement, project narrative and budget
    Selection Process: Board of trustees
    Notification Process: Letter
    Formal Report of Funding Required: Yes

TECHNICAL ASSISTANCE PROGRAMS AND SERVICES

Programs of Special Interest: The Competition Program supplies funds for cash prizes to Michigan organizations sponsoring arts competitions. The Gallery Program curates exhibitions in State of Michigan office buildings. Artist Update Newsletter provides technical assistance, deadlines and other items of interest to the individual artist.

Please read carefully!
Do not contact any listed organization unless you fulfill all eligibility requirements.

ARTS INTERNATIONAL (AI)

Institute of International Education
809 United Nations Plaza
New York, NY 10017
212-984-5370
FAX: 212-984-5574

PROFILE OF FINANCIAL SUPPORT TO ARTISTS
Total Funding/Value of In-Kind Support: n/a
Competition for Funding: n/a
Grant Range: n/a

DIRECT SUPPORT PROGRAMS
➤ THE TRAVEL GRANTS PILOT

Purpose: To enable artists to engage in mutually beneficial collaborative activities with colleagues in Africa, Latin America and the Caribbean, and South or Southeast Asia.

Eligibility:

Citizenship: U.S. or permanent resident

Residency: Open

Age: Open

Special Requirements: Professional artists only; students and student groups ineligible; scholars, curators, presenters, administrators and critics ineligible; previous recipients ineligible for one year; program does not support travel costs related only to solo exhibitions or performances

Art Forms: All disciplines

Type of Support: Average grants, $500 to $2,500; $5,000 maximum; the program supports significant international travel including participation in international conferences, exhibitions, performance series and other events that are important to an artist's professional development.

Scope of Program: 50 grants totalling $150,000 in 1992

Application/Selection Process:

Deadline: Two deadlines vary annually; contact for exact dates

Preferred Initial Contact: Write or call for information

Application Procedure: Submit application form, project description, artist's statement, resumé, work samples

Selection Process: Peer panel review

Notification Process: Letter 9 weeks after deadline

Formal Report of Grant Required: Yes

➤ KADE COLLABORATIVE WORKS FELLOWSHIPS

Purpose: To encourage the co-creation of new work across cultural and national boundaries

Eligibility:
 Citizenship: U.S. and France/Germany
 Residency: Open
 Age: Open
 Special Requirements: Project must be a collaborative one between U.S., French and/or German artists
 Art Forms: All disciplines

Type of Support: $1,000 to $5,000 grants

Scope of Program: n/a

Application/Selection Process:
 Deadline: Open
 Preferred Initial Contact: Write for application/guidelines
 Application Procedure: Submit two-page proposal and budget summary
 Selection Process: Staff/advisory committee review
 Notification Process: Letter within 8-12 weeks
 Formal Report of Grant Required: Yes

ASIAN CINEVISION

32 East Broadway
New York, NY 10002
212-925-8685
FAX: 212-925-8157
CONTACT: PETER CHOW, EXECUTIVE DIRECTOR

EQUIPMENT ACCESS

Video: Production for VHS, 3/4"; post-production (off-line) for S-VHS and 3/4"

Comments: Selected video artists may have access to equipment and facilities at low rates.

TECHNICAL ASSISTANCE PROGRAMS AND SERVICES

Programs of Special Interest: Asian Cinevision holds annual Asian-American film and video festivals and maintains a video archive of Asian-American films and videos.

Please read carefully!
Do not contact any listed organization unless you fulfill all eligibility requirements.

ASIAN CULTURAL COUNCIL

1290 Avenue of the Americas, Room 3450
New York, NY 10104

PROFILE OF FINANCIAL SUPPORT TO ARTISTS

Total Funding/Value of In-Kind Support: $200,000 in 1992 (figures reflect Japan-U.S. program only)

Competition for Funding: Total applications, 250; total individuals funded/provided with in-kind support, 10 (U.S. recipients)

Grant Range: $500-$17,000

DIRECT SUPPORT PROGRAM

➤ **JAPAN-UNITED STATES ARTS PROGRAM**

Purpose: To provide grants to individuals and institutions in Japan and the United States for exchange activities which encourage the understanding of Japanese art and culture

Eligibility:
  Citizenship: U.S. or Japan
  Residency: Open
  Age: Open
  Special Requirements: Graduate students are eligible; undergraduate students and previous recipients are ineligible
  Art Forms: Architecture, art history, crafts, dance, film, music, painting, photography, sculpture, theater and video

Type of Support: Project support including cost of supplies and materials, stay in Japan of 1-6 months, round-trip air fare, allowances for local travel and maintenance, interpreter's fees

Scope of Program: 18-20 awards annually (includes U.S. and Japanese applicants); of U.S. recipients, 2 are visual artists on average

Application/Selection Process:
  Deadline: February 1, annually
  Preferred Initial Contact: Write for information
  Application Procedure: Send preliminary letter outlining project; if project fits within the program's guidelines, the artist is asked to fill out a short application form
  Selection Process: Board of trustees
  Notification Process: Letter after board meeting
  Formal Report of Grant Required: Yes

Please read carefully!
Do not contact any listed organization unless you fulfill all eligibility requirements.

ASSOCIATION OF INDEPENDENT VIDEO AND FILMMAKERS (AIVF)

625 Broadway, 9th Floor
New York, NY 10012
212-473-3400
FAX: 212-677-8732

TECHNICAL ASSISTANCE PROGRAMS AND SERVICES

Programs of Special Interest: AIVF's magazine, the *Independent*, is a national publication devoted exclusively to independent production. The Festival Bureau maintains information on over 400 film and video festivals in the U.S. and around the world. AIVF's resource files contain sample proposals, contracts, and press kits, and information on funders, distributors, exhibitors, and television markets. The association maintains a library and sells hard-to-find books and pamphlets on topics ranging from feature film production to copyright law. AIVF publishes significant guides on festivals and distribution. Seminars and workshops address business, technological, and aesthetic issues. AIVF offers group health, life, and disability insurance. (Some AIVF services are for members only; individual memberships are $45; student memberships are $25.)

ATHENS CENTER FOR FILM AND VIDEO

P.O. Box 388
Athens, OH 45701
614-593-1330

EQUIPMENT ACCESS

Film: Production and post-production for 16mm
Video: Production and post-production (off-line) for 3/4"
Comments: The Athens Post Production Center gives independent media artists in Ohio, West Virginia, Kentucky, Indiana, Michigan, and the surrounding region access to equipment and facilities at a low cost. Projects must not be commercial or for academic credit. A reservation form must be filled out in advance.

TECHNICAL ASSISTANCE PROGRAMS AND SERVICES

Programs of Special Interest: The Athens International Film and Video Festival includes a competition for independent film and video artists and producers.

Please read carefully!
Do not contact any listed organization unless you fulfill all eligibility requirements.

BAY AREA VIDEO COALITION (BAVC)

1111 17th Street
San Francisco, CA 94107
415-861-3282
FAX: 415-861-4316

PROFILE OF FINANCIAL SUPPORT TO ARTISTS
Total Funding/Value of In-Kind Support: n/a
Competition for Funding: n/a
Grant Range: n/a

DIRECT SUPPORT PROGRAMS
➤ **EQUIPMENT ACCESS AWARDS**

Purpose: To be a creative catalyst for video artists

Eligibility:
  Citizenship: n/a
  Residency: Open
  Special Requirements: Must be a member of BAVC
  Art Forms: Video, other art forms which use video

Type of Support: Access to equipment

Scope of Program: 4-6 recipients in 1993

Application/Selection Process:
  Deadline: Varies annually; contact for exact date
  Preferred Initial Contact: Write or call for guidelines
  Application Procedure: Submit one-page project description
  along with 10-minute sample VHS tape
  Selection Process: Panel of media artists and arts professionals
  Notification Process: Outlined in guidelines
  Formal Report of Grant Required: No

➤ **THE INTERACT PROGRAM: THE JOHN D. AND CATHERINE T.
MACARTHUR FOUNDATION FELLOWSHIPS IN INTERACTIVE
VIDEODISC PRODUCTION**

Purpose: To produce interactive videodiscs for community organizations by training independent producers in multi-media production

Eligibility:
  Citizenship: Open
  Residency: Open
  Special Requirements: Must have background working with community organizations and 1 useful skill necessary to produce an interactive video (e.g., video production, graphic design)
  Art Forms: Level III interactive videodisc

Please read carefully!
Do not contact any listed organization unless you fulfill all eligibility requirements.

Type of Support: Fellowship to work 10-15 hours per week over a 10-week period on a team producing interactive videodiscs

Scope of Program: 16 awards in 1992

Application/Selection Process:
    Deadline: Varies annually; contact for exact date
    Preferred Initial Contact: Write for application information
    Application Procedure: Submit answers to application questions, resumé
    Selection Process: Panel review
    Notification Process: Letter
    Formal Report of Grant Required: No

EQUIPMENT ACCESS

CONTACT: FACILITY MANAGER, OPERATIONS SUPERVISOR, EDUCATIONAL COORDINATOR, OR EXECUTIVE DIRECTOR

Video: Production and post-production for 1", Betacam SP, 3/4", VHS, Hi-8; capabilities include digital audio suite, video toaster, quicktime

Comments: BAVC offers subsidized equipment access to BAVC members working on noncommercial projects. BAVC's principal interest is in supporting independent video producers who create noncommercial innovative or experimental work. Applications for subsidized access can be approved on the same day they are submitted to any of the contacts listed above if an appointment is scheduled in advance.

TECHNICAL ASSISTANCE PROGRAMS AND SERVICES

Programs of Special Interest: BAVC maintains a job and networking bulletin board and a media library; offers workshops on business, production, and post-production subjects (fees involved); has a production insurance program for producers; and acts as a nonprofit umbrella for local independent producers. Project consultation is available to subsidized access program members for $20/hour. BAVC's journal, Video Networks, publishes national resource directories on distributors, festivals, funders, etc.

BLACK AMERICAN CINEMA SOCIETY

3617 Mont Clair Street
Los Angeles, CA 90018
213-737-3292
FAX: 213-737-2842

PROFILE OF FINANCIAL SUPPORT TO ARTISTS

Total Funding/Value of In-Kind Support: $6,750 in 1993

Competition for Funding: Total applications, n/a; total individuals funded/provided with in-kind support, 6

Grant Range: $250-$3,000

DIRECT SUPPORT PROGRAMS

➤ **BLACK FILMMAKERS GRANTS PROGRAM**

Purpose: To give cash awards to black film and video artists for completed or near-complete film or video

Eligibility:
    Special Requirements: Must be a black artist; independent filmmakers and student producers (college level and above) are eligible; no scholarship funds available
    Art Forms: Film, video

Type of Support: $250-$3,000 award; work screened at annual festival

Scope of Program: 6 awards annually

Application/Selection Process:
    Deadline: February, annually; contact for exact date
    Preferred Initial Contact: Call or write for application/guidelines (available in January)
    Application Procedure: Submit application form, sample of work, script (if work is in progress)
    Selection Process: Jury
    Notification Process: Recipients by phone, nonrecipients by mail
    Formal Report of Grant Required: No

TECHNICAL ASSISTANCE PROGRAMS AND SERVICES

Programs of Special Interest: BACS annually presents a week-long festival of classic and contemporary black films. The Western States Black Research Center, home of the Black American Cinema Society, exists to preserve and disseminate the unique history and cultural heritage of Americans of African descent. The center's collection includes rare and historically significant books, documents, films,

Please read carefully!
Do not contact any listed organization unless you fulfill all eligibility requirements.

music, fine art and memorabilia and is available for a wide variety of research; some fees involved.

BLACK FILM INSTITUTE (BFI)

University of the District of Columbia
800 Mount Vernon Place, NW
Washington, DC 20001
202-727-2396
FAX: 202-727-9267
CONTACT: TONY GITTENS, DIRECTOR

TECHNICAL ASSISTANCE PROGRAMS AND SERVICES
Programs of Special Interest: BFI exhibits independent and other films and videos focusing on black and Third World artists.

LYN BLUMENTHAL MEMORIAL FUND FOR INDEPENDENT VIDEO

P.O. Box 3514
Church Street Station
New York, NY 10007

PROFILE OF FINANCIAL SUPPORT TO ARTISTS
Total Funding/Value of In-Kind Support: n/a
Competition for Funding: Total applications, n/a; total individuals funded/provided with in-kind support, 3-5 annually
Grant Range: $1,000-$3,000

DIRECT SUPPORT PROGRAM
➤ **VIDEO PRODUCTION GRANTS/VIDEO CRITICISM GRANTS**
Purpose: To encourage projects that make inventive and strategic uses of small-format media technologies (video 8, VHS) with low budgets ($6,000 or less); to award small grants for original essays on video criticism to encourage writing on independent and experimental video work
Eligibility:
　　Citizenship: n/a
　　Residency: U.S.

Please read carefully!
Do not contact any listed organization unless you fulfill all eligibility requirements.

Age: Open

Special Requirements: For production grants: final form must be videotape; grants must be applied to production and post-production costs only; projects must be completed within 12 months of receiving the grant. For criticism grants: essay must be at least 5,000-6,000 words; essay must be completed within six months of receipt of the award

Art Forms: Video, writing

Type of Support: $1,000-$3,000 grants (production); $1,000 grants (criticism), text will be published and distributed

Scope of Program: $10,000 available for production grants; $3,000 available for criticism grants

Application/Selection Process:

Deadline: March 15, 1994 for video production; after that, awards expected to alternate between video production (even-numbered years) and video criticism (odd-numbered years), but this may change; contact directly for details

Preferred Initial Contact: Write for basic information and for application/guidelines

Application Procedure: Submit application form, work sample, project description, resumé (production grants); submit proposal including outline of essay (criticism grants)

Selection Process: Board review

Notification Process: Letter approximately 3 months after deadline

Formal Report of Grant Required: Yes

BOSTON FILM•VIDEO FOUNDATION (BF•VF)

1126 Boylston Street
Boston, MA 02215
617-536-1540
FAX: 617-536-3576

PROFILE OF FINANCIAL SUPPORT TO ARTISTS

Total Funding/Value of In-Kind Support: $52,000 for FY 1993

Competition for Funding: Total applications, 160; total individuals funded/provided with in-kind support, 14

Grant Range: Up to $7,000 in cash and in-kind support

DIRECT SUPPORT PROGRAMS

➤ **NEW ENGLAND FILM/VIDEO FELLOWSHIP PROGRAM**

Purpose: To foster the production of independent film and video by New England media makers through completion of works-in-progress or support of new works

Please read carefully!
Do not contact any listed organization unless you fulfill all eligibility requirements.

Eligibility:
    Residency: Connecticut, Maine, Massachusetts, New Hampshire, Rhode Island, Vermont, 1 year
    Age: 18 or older
    Special Requirements: Artist must have complete creative control over project; commercial and instructional projects ineligible; no students; previous recipients ineligible for 2 years
    Art Forms: Film, video

Type of Support: Up to $7,000 in cash, equipment usage, or a combination of the two for specific phase (i.e. production or post-production) of proposed project; grantees must supply a copy of their completed work to the BF•VF Archives

Scope of Program: $45,000 cash, $7,000 in noncash equipment access in FY 1993

Application/Selection Process:
    Deadline: Early April, annually; contact for exact date
    Preferred Initial Contact: Call or write for application/guidelines
    Application Procedure: Submit application form, samples of work, resumé, project budget
    Selection Process: Panel of artists, curators, critics, media activists, administrators
    Notification Process: 3 months after deadline
    Formal Report of Grant Required: n/a

EQUIPMENT ACCESS

CONTACT: MICHAEL KING, EQUIPMENT/FACILITIES MANAGER

Film: Production and post-production for 16mm

Video: Production for Hi-8, Video 8, VHS, S-VHS, 3/4"; post-production for VHS (off-line), 3/4" (off-line and on-line)

Comments: BF•VF offers access to all equipment facilities during office hours; selected members may apply to use location and in-house equipment independently, with 24-hour access; equipment membership is $100.

TECHNICAL ASSISTANCE PROGRAMS AND SERVICES

Programs of Special Interest: BF•VF conducts workshops on film and video production and post-production as well as grantwriting, marketing, and other business and legal issues for independent media makers. Workshop fees range from $15 to $500. Members have access to technical expertise on fundraising, distribution, and other issues. Selected members may apply by invitation for BF•VF fiscal sponsorship of their independent projects. BF•VF is working with a consortium of regional cable access centers to develop new options for screening independent media works, and collaborates regularly

Please read carefully!
Do not contact any listed organization unless you fulfill all eligibility requirements.

with other arts and cultural organizations to present films and videos throughout New England. BF•VF is the co-sponsor of the New England Film/Video Festival and the Boston International Festival of Women's Cinema.

BRITISH COLUMBIA MINISTRY OF TOURISM AND MINISTRY RESPONSIBLE FOR CULTURE— CULTURAL SERVICES BRANCH (CSB)

800 Johnson Street, 5th Floor
Victoria, British Columbia
Canada V8V 1X4
604-356-1718
CONTACT: WALTER K. QUAN, CO-ORDINATOR, ARTS AWARDS PROGRAMS

TECHNICAL ASSISTANCE PROGRAMS AND SERVICES

Programs of Special Interest: The government of the Province of British Columbia, through the Cultural Services Branch of the Ministry of Tourism and Ministry Responsible for Culture, provides a wide variety of programs of consultative and financial assistance. Individuals supported through the CSB must be Canadian citizens or landed immigrants and should have lived in the Province of British Columbia for at least 12 months prior to application. Organizations supported through the CSB must be nonprofit arts organizations, incorporated under the Societies Act of the Province of British Columbia. Eligible artists should contact the Cultural Services Branch for specific program guidelines, eligibility criteria and application forms.

BRONX COUNCIL ON THE ARTS (BCA)

1738 Hone Avenue
Bronx, NY 10461
718-931-9500
FAX: 718-409-6445
CONTACT: ED FRIEDMAN OR BEN SPIERMAN

PROFILE OF FINANCIAL SUPPORT TO ARTISTS

Total Funding/Value of In-Kind Support: $45,000 for FY 1992

Please read carefully!
Do not contact any listed organization unless you fulfill all eligibility requirements.

Competition for Funding: Total applications, 90; total individuals funded/provided with in-kind support, 10

Grant Range: $1,500

DIRECT SUPPORT PROGRAMS

➤ **BRONX RECOGNIZES ITS OWN (BRIO)**

Purpose: To assist the career development of Bronx artists

Eligibility:

Citizenship: Open

Residency: Bronx County

Age: 18 or older

Special Requirements: No degree-seeking students; previous grantees ineligible for 1 year

Art Forms: Architecture, choreography, crafts, fiction, film, interpretive performance, music composition, nonfiction literature, painting, performing art/emergent forms, photography, playwriting/screenwriting, poetry, printmaking/drawing/artists' books, sculpture, video

Type of Support: $1,500; recipients must perform public service activity

Scope of Program: 10 awards in 1992

Application/Selection Process:

Deadline: March, annually; contact for exact dates

Preferred Initial Contact: Call or write for application/guidelines

Application Procedure: Submit application form, samples of work, resumé

Selection Process: Peer panel of artists

Notification Process: Letter in April

Formal Report of Grant Required: Yes

➤ **COMMUNITY ARTS GRANT PROGRAM**

CONTACT: ED FRIEDMAN, DIRECTOR OF ARTS SERVICES

Purpose: To fund ongoing programs of local community-based organizations that meet high standards of artistic quality and provide needed community service, programs developed by arts and community organizations that reach unserviced or underserved areas of the Bronx, and programs that serve or sponsor individual artists

Eligibility:

Special Requirements: Individual artists must find nonprofit organization to apply on their behalf

Art Forms: All disciplines

Type of Support: $300-$3,000 awards to organization

Scope of Program: $72,000 total funding in 1992

Application/Selection Process:

Deadline: Late July/early August, annually; contact for exact dates

Please read carefully!
Do not contact any listed organization unless you fulfill all eligibility requirements.

Preferred Initial Contact: Call or write for application/guidelines
Application Procedure: Sponsoring organization submits application form, financial statement, project budget, samples of artist's work, artist's resumé
Selection Process: Individuals from outside of BCA
Notification Process: Letter 5 months after deadline
Formal Report of Grant Required: Yes

TECHNICAL ASSISTANCE PROGRAMS AND SERVICES
Programs of Special Interest: The council provides seminars in such areas as management, fundraising, marketing and public relations, and offers the arts constituency graphic and public relations services, fundraising assistance, computer services, and special mailing privileges. BCA conducts arts-in-education programs and holds summer neighborhood festivals.

THE MARY INGRAHAM BUNTING INSTITUTE OF RADCLIFFE COLLEGE

34 Concord Avenue
Cambridge, MA 02138
617-495-8212
FAX: 617-495-8136
CONTACT: ALEXANDRA CHISHOLM, FELLOWSHIP COORDINATOR

PROFILE OF FINANCIAL SUPPORT TO ARTISTS
Total Funding/Value of In-Kind Support: $86,000 for FY 1991-92
Competition for Funding: Total applications, 138; total individuals funded/provided with in-kind support, 4
Grant Range: $30,000

DIRECT SUPPORT PROGRAMS
➤ BUNTING FELLOWSHIP/RESIDENCY PROGRAM
Purpose: To support women who wish to advance their careers through independent work in academic and professional fields and in the creative arts
Eligibility:
    Special Requirements: Women only; artists must demonstrate significant professional accomplishments (participation in group or one-person shows) and must reside in Cambridge/Boston area *during* residency
    Art Forms: Visual arts, film/video, performing arts, literary arts (scholars in any field also eligible)

Please read carefully!
Do not contact any listed organization unless you fulfill all eligibility requirements.

Type of Support: 1-year residency including $30,000 stipend, studio space, access to most Harvard/Radcliffe resources; fellows present work-in-progress at public colloquia or in exhibitions

Scope of Program: 2 to 3 awards per year, on average, in visual/media arts

Application/Selection Process:
    Deadline: October 15, annually
    Preferred Initial Contact: Call or write for application/guidelines which are available in June
    Application Procedure: Submit application form, $40 fee, samples of work, resumé, references
    Selection Process: Peer panel of artists, interdisciplinary final selection committee
    Notification Process: Letter in April

TECHNICAL ASSISTANCE PROGRAMS AND SERVICES

Programs of Special Interest: The Affiliation Program offers appointees the use of studio space and other resources available to Bunting Fellows for 1 year; applicants must meet same eligibility requirements as Bunting Fellows.

THE BUSH FOUNDATION

E-900 First National Bank Building
332 Minnesota Street
St. Paul, MN 55101
612-227-5222
CONTACT: SALLY DIXON, DIRECTOR, BUSH ARTIST FELLOWSHIPS

PROFILE OF FINANCIAL SUPPORT TO ARTISTS

Total Funding/Value of In-Kind Support: $495,000 in 1993

Competition for Funding: Total applications, 485; total individuals funded/provided with in-kind support, 15

Grant Range: $33,000

DIRECT SUPPORT PROGRAMS

➤ **BUSH ARTIST FELLOWSHIPS**

Purpose: To allow Minnesota, North Dakota, South Dakota, and western Wisconsin artists a significant period of uninterrupted time for work in their chosen art form

Eligibility:
    Residency: Minnesota, North Dakota, South Dakota, western Wisconsin

Please read carefully!
Do not contact any listed organization unless you fulfill all eligibility requirements.

Age: 25 or older
Special Requirements: No students or nonprofessionals; previous grantees ineligible for 5 years
Art Forms: Visual arts, performance art, film/video, choreography, music composition, literature, playwriting, screenwriting
Type of Support: $26,000 total stipend for 12-18 months' work on projects outlined in applicant's proposal, plus up to $7,000 for production and travel costs
Scope of Program: Up to 15 awards
Application/Selection Process:
    Deadline: October, annually; contact for specific dates
    Preferred Initial Contact: Call or write for application/guidelines
    Application Procedure: Submit application, samples of work, names of two references
    Selection Process: Peer panel of artists, interdisciplinary final panel
    Notification Process: Letter 1 week after panel deliberations
    Formal Report of Grant Required: Yes

CALIFORNIA ARTS COUNCIL (CAC)

2411 Alhambra Boulevard
Sacramento, CA 95817
916-227-2550
TDD: 916-227-2571
FAX: 916-227-2628

PROFILE OF FINANCIAL SUPPORT TO ARTISTS
Total Funding/Value of In-Kind Support: $1,833,000 for FY 1992-93
Competition for Funding: n/a
Grant Range: $2,500 (fellowships)

DIRECT SUPPORT PROGRAMS
➤ **ARTISTS FELLOWSHIP PROGRAM**
Purpose: To recognize and honor the work and careers of California artists who are primary creators of their art
Eligibility:
    Residency: California, 1 year
    Special Requirements: Professional artist with at least 5 years experience; no students enrolled in degree-granting programs; previous grantees ineligible for 4 years

Please read carefully!
Do not contact any listed organization unless you fulfill all eligibility requirements.

Art Forms: Disciplines rotate on 4-year cycle among visual arts (1993-94), performing arts (originating artists only) (1994-95), media arts/new genres (1995-96), literature (1996-97)

Type of Support: $2,500

Scope of Program: 20 fellowships in FY 1992-93

Application/Selection Process:
Deadline: Fall, 1993; contact for exact date
Application Procedure: Submit application form, resumé, artist's statement (optional), samples of work
Selection Process: Peer panel of artists and arts professionals
Notification Process: Letter in June
Formal Report of Grant Required: Yes

➤ **ARTIST IN RESIDENCE PROGRAM**
CONTACT: CAROL SHIFFMAN, PROGRAM MANAGER

Purpose: To offer long-term interaction of professional artists with the public in workshops sponsored by schools, nonprofit arts organizations, government units, and tribal councils

Eligibility:
Special Requirements: Professional artists with at least 3 years experience; artist must apply with sponsor; no full-time students in degree programs
Art Forms: All disciplines

Type of Support: 3- to 11-month residencies; artists earn $1,300 per month for 80 hours project time

Scope of Program: 175 residencies FY 1992-93

Application/Selection Process:
Deadline: Deadlines vary; contact for exact date
Preferred Initial Contact: Call or write for application/guidelines; 30-minute Artist in Residence video available
Application Procedure: Submit application form, artist's statement, sponsor organization statement, project description and budget, supporting materials (e.g., reviews, performance programs), letters of support, samples of work
Selection Process: Peer panel of artists and arts professionals
Notification Process: 4-6 months after deadline

TECHNICAL ASSISTANCE PROGRAMS AND SERVICES

Programs of Special Interest: The California Arts Council will also offer a Public Art and Design program, which has been temporarily suspended due to budget constraints, to "identify, encourage and support leadership in the field of public art and design."

CALIFORNIA COMMUNITY FOUNDATION

606 South Olive Street
Suite 2400
Los Angeles, CA 90014
213-413-4042
FAX: 213-383-2046
CONTACT: SUSAN FONG, PROGRAM OFFICER

PROFILE OF FINANCIAL SUPPORT TO ARTISTS
Total Funding/Value of In-Kind Support: $110,000 for FY 1992
Competition for Funding: Total applications, 626; total individuals funded/provided with in-kind support, 19
Grant Range: Up to $15,000

DIRECT SUPPORT PROGRAMS
➤ **J. PAUL GETTY TRUST FUND FOR THE VISUAL ARTS**
Purpose: To nurture the accomplishments of mid-career artists
Eligibility:
  Residency: Los Angeles County
  Age: Generally over 30
  Special Requirements: Artists must be 30 years old or have at least 10 years experience in field; no students
  Art Forms: Painting, sculpture, photography, crafts, printmaking, drawing, artists' books, experimental and independent film and video, performance art with original visual art as integral component, conceptual art, new genres
Type of Support: $15,000 fellowship
Scope of Program: 5 awards for 1992
Application/Selection Process:
  Deadline: Third week in October, annually; contact for exact date
  Preferred Initial Contact: Call or write for application/guidelines
  Application Procedure: Submit application form, samples of work, resumé, supporting materials (e.g., reviews, references)
  Selection Process: Outside advisory panel, staff
  Notification Process: Phone call and follow-up letter
  Formal Report of Grant Required: Yes
➤ **BRODY ARTS FUND**
Purpose: To strengthen and encourage emerging artists representing communities often outside the mainstream
Eligibility:
  Residency: Los Angeles County
  Age: No undergraduate students or younger

Please read carefully!
Do not contact any listed organization unless you fulfill all eligibility requirements.

Special Requirements: No students; preference given to ethnic and other minorities (e.g., disabled, gay)
Art Forms: Disciplines rotate on a 3-year cycle among literature/media arts (1994), visual arts (1995), performing arts (1996)
Type of Support: Up to $5,000
Scope of Program: 14 awards in 1992
Application/Selection Process:
Deadline: March, annually; contact for exact date
Preferred Initial Contact: Call or write for application/guidelines
Application Procedure: Submit application form, samples of work, resumé, supporting materials (e.g., reviews, references)
Selection Process: Multi-disciplinary panels, staff
Notification Process: Phone call and follow-up letter in May
Formal Report of Grant Required: Yes

TECHNICAL ASSISTANCE PROGRAMS AND SERVICES
Programs of Special Interest: The California Community Foundation maintains the Funding Information Center, a collection focusing on regional grant and fellowship opportunities. Grantseekers should call for reservations for an orientation workshop (orientations take place on Thursday mornings). The Center is open Monday through Friday, from 10 am to 5 pm.

THE CANADA COUNCIL/
CONSEIL DES ARTS DU CANADA (CC/CAC)

P.O. Box 1047
Ottawa, Ontario
Canada K1P 5V8
613-598-4365
FAX: 613-598-4390
CONTACT: LISE ROCHON, INFORMATION OFFICER, COMMUNICATIONS SECTION

PROFILE OF FINANCIAL SUPPORT TO ARTISTS
Total Funding/Value of In-Kind Support: n/a
Competition for Funding: n/a
Grant Range: n/a

DIRECT SUPPORT PROGRAMS

➤ **FILM—ARTS GRANTS "A"/ARTS GRANTS "B"**

CONTACT: MONIQUE BÉLANGER, ARTS AWARDS SERVICE

Phone: 613-598-4312

Purpose: Arts Grants "A" support the creative work of professional Canadian artists who have made a nationally or internationally recognized contribution to their discipline over a number of years and are still active in their profession; Arts Grants "B" support the creative work of Canadian artists who have completed their basic training or are recognized as a professional and meet the eligibility criteria for their discipline

Eligibility:

Citizenship: Canada (permanent residents of Canada also eligible)

Special Requirements: Funding for production and post-production ineligible (see Film Production Grants in this listing); film directors must have directed at least one independent film; scriptwriters must have had one independent work professionally produced; preference is given to film artists whose work demonstrates an innovative, original or experimental approach to form and content; projects involving conventional or commercial approaches to filmmaking are not a priority of the program; instructional, commissioned and undergraduate projects are ineligible; industrial films and pilots for commercial or educational television also ineligible; films to be produced, co-produced or sponsored by another Canadian federal or provincial agency are ineligible

Art Forms: Film

Type of Support: Arts Grants "A" up to $31,000 for living expenses (up to $2,500 per month) and project costs, plus up to $2,800 travel allowance; Arts Grants "B" up to $17,000 for living expenses (up to $1,500 per month), project costs, and travel costs; grants for collaborations are: up to $23,500 for 2 artists; up to $28,500 for 3 artists)

Scope of Program: n/a

Application/Selection Process:

Deadline: Arts Grants "A": October 1, annually; Arts Grants "B": October 1 and April 1, annually

Preferred Initial Contact: Call or write for guidelines; submit project description and resumé before applying

Application Procedure: Submit application form, samples of work, references, project budget, resumé, financial statement

Selection Process: Peer panel of artists

Notification Process: Letter 3-5 months after deadline

Formal Report of Grant Required: n/a

Please read carefully!
Do not contact any listed organization unless you fulfill all eligibility requirements.

➤ **FILM—SHORT-TERM GRANTS/TRAVEL GRANTS**

CONTACT: MONIQUE BÉLANGER, ARTS AWARDS SERVICE

Phone: 613-598-4312

Purpose: Short-Term Grants support Canadian artists who meet the eligibility criteria of their discipline and need a short period of time in which to pursue their own creative work; Travel Grants assist professional artists who need to travel on occasions important to their career

Eligibility:
   Citizenship: Canada (permanent residents of Canada also eligible)
   Age: 18 or older
   Special Requirements: Film directors must have directed at least one independent film; scriptwriters must have had one independent work professionally produced; preference is given to film artists whose work demonstrates an innovative, original or experimental approach to form and content; projects involving conventional or commercial approaches to filmmaking are not a priority of the program; instructional, commissioned and undergraduate projects are ineligible; industrial films and pilots for commercial or educational television also ineligible; films to be produced, co-produced or sponsored by another Canadian federal or provincial agency are ineligible
   Art Forms: Film

Type of Support: Short-Term Grants up to $4,000 for living expenses (up to $1,500 per month) or project costs, plus travel allowance up to $2,800; Travel Grants up to $2,800

Scope of Program: 11 Short-Term Grants, 8 Travel Grants in FY 1991-92

Application/Selection Process:
   Deadline: May 15 and September 15, annually
   Preferred Initial Contact: Call or write for guidelines; submit project description and resumé before applying
   Application Procedure: Submit application form, samples of work, references, project budget, resumé, financial statement
   Selection Process: Peer panel of artists
   Notification Process: Letter 6-8 weeks after deadline
   Formal Report of Grant Required: n/a

➤ **FILM PRODUCTION GRANTS**

CONTACT: MARTINE SAUVAGEAU, MEDIA ARTS OFFICER (FILM)

Phone: 613-598-4358

Purpose: To foster and promote the development of film as a medium of personal artistic expression; the grants are intended to support experimentation with form, content, and technical process within a wide range of genres, including experimental, documentary, dramatic, animation, etc.

Eligibility:

Citizenship: Canada (permanent residents of Canada also eligible)

Special Requirements: Independent filmmakers must have directed at least one film; professional artists must have produced a body of work in video; filmmakers must have total editorial control over the proposed project; dramatic feature-length film is limited to low-budget works of an innovative or experimental nature whose other funding sources don't compromise the filmmaker's artistic control; applicants who have directed film in 8 mm or Super 8 and wish to undertake their first 16 mm production should apply to the Explorations Program of the Canada Council (contact the council directly for details); first-time directors who have worked in other areas of filmmaking also should apply to the Explorations program; film students are ineligible

Art Forms: Film

Type of Support: Up to $50,000 to cover total or partial production costs of a project; applicants whose budgets exceed this amount must indicate where other sources of funds will be obtained

Scope of Program: 65 grants in FY 1991-92

Application/Selection Process:

Deadline: March 15, July 15 and November 15, annually

Preferred Initial Contact: Call or write for guidelines

Application Procedure: Submit application form, project budget, samples of work, letters of appraisal

Selection Process: Jury of filmmakers and film experts

Formal Report of Grant Required: Yes

➤ **VIDEO—ARTS GRANTS "A"/ARTS GRANTS "B"**

CONTACT: ANNE-MARIE HOGUE, ARTS AWARDS SERVICE

Phone: 613-598-4318

Purpose: Arts Grants "A" support the creative work of professional Canadian artists who have made a nationally or internationally recognized contribution to their discipline over a number of years and are still active in their profession; Arts Grants "B" support the creative work of Canadian artists who have completed their basic training or are recognized as a professional and meet the eligibility criteria for their discipline

Eligibility:

Citizenship: Canada (permanent residents of Canada also eligible)

Age: 18 or older

Special Requirements: Funding for production and post-production ineligible (see Video Production Grants in this listing); artists must already have to their credit one or more non-industrial video production(s), or be otherwise recognized as a professional in the field; video artists who have produced only educational or commercial videos are not eligible; preference given to candidates who approach video in an original, innovative or experimental way; video artists interested in criticism must have published critical works about video in media arts periodicals and arts magazines; journalists and reviewers who have published only in trade magazines or newpapers are not eligible

Art Forms: Video

Type of Support: Arts Grants "A" up to $39,000 for living expenses (up to $2,500 per month) and project costs; Arts Grants "B" up to $17,000 for living expenses (up to $1,500 per month), project costs, and travel costs; grants for collaborations are $23,000 for 2 artists, $28,500 for 3 artists

Scope of Program: 1 Arts Grants "A", 5 Arts Grants "B" in FY 1991-92

Application/Selection Process:
    Deadline: Arts Grants "A": October 1, annually; Arts Grants "B": October 1 and April 1, annually
    Preferred Initial Contact: Call or write for guidelines; submit project description and resumé before applying
    Application Procedure: Submit application form, samples of work, references, project budget, resumé, financial statement
    Selection Process: Peer panel of artists
    Notification Process: Letter 3-5 months after deadline
    Formal Report of Grant Required: n/a

➤ **VIDEO—SHORT-TERM GRANTS/TRAVEL GRANTS**
CONTACT: ANNE-MARIE HOGUE, ARTS AWARDS SERVICE
Phone: 613-598-4318

Purpose: Short-Term Grants support professional Canadian artists who meet the eligibility criteria of their discipline and need a short period of time in which to pursue their own creative work; Travel Grants assist professional artists who need to travel on occasions important to their career

Eligibility:
    Citizenship: Canada (permanent residents also eligible)
    Age: 18 or older
    Special Requirements: Artists must already have to their credit one or more non-industrial video production(s), or be otherwise recognized as a professional in the field; video artists who have produced only educational or commercial videos are not eligible; preference given to candidates who approach video in an original, innovative or experimental way; video artists interested in criticism must have published critical works about video in media arts periodicals and arts magazines; journalists and reviewers who

have published only in trade magazines or newpapers are not eligible

Art Forms: Video

Type of Support: Short-Term Grants up to $4,000 for living expenses (up to $1,500 per month) or project costs, plus travel allowance up to $2,800; Travel Grants up to $2,800

Scope of Program: 5 Short-Term Grants, 5 Travel Grants in FY 1991-92

Application/Selection Process:
  Deadline: April 15 and October 1, annually
  Preferred Initial Contact: Call or write for guidelines; submit project description and resumé before applying
  Application Procedure: Submit application form, samples of work, references, project budget, resumé, financial statement
  Selection Process: Peer panel of artists
  Notification Process: Letter 6-8 weeks after deadline

➤ **VIDEO PRODUCTION GRANTS**

CONTACT: YASMINE KARINI, MEDIA ARTS OFFICER (VIDEO, AUDIO, COMPUTER-INTEGRATED MEDIA)

Phone: 613-598-4356

Purpose: To encourage and promote the development of video as a medium of artistic expression by providing support for experimentation with form, content or technology in a variety of genres, including experimental, documentary, dramatic, narrative, conceptual, computer graphics, animation, etc.

  Citizenship: Canada (permanent residents also eligible)
  Special Requirements: Independent directors who have already directed videos and films may apply for a production grant; director must have total artistic control over the proposed project; first-time video producers should apply to the Explorations Program of the Canada Council (contact the council directly for details); projects commissioned by educational institutions or by social affairs agencies are ineligible, as are promotional, corporate or industrial videos; films to be produced, co-produced or sponsored by another Canadian federal or provincial agency are ineligible
  Art Forms: Video

Type of Support: Up to $35,000 for living expenses (including a portion for pre-production period), salaries and fees for technicians, actors and other participants, necessary travel expenses, equipment rental, technical services and the purchase of tapes

Scope of Program: 20 grants in FY 1991-92

Application/Selection Process:
  Deadline: March 1 and September 15, annually

Please read carefully!
Do not contact any listed organization unless you fulfill all eligibility requirements.

Application Procedure: Submit application form, samples of work, letters of appraisal, project budget
Selection Process: Jury of video artists and experts
Formal Report of Grant Required: n/a

CANADIAN FILMMAKERS DISTRIBUTION CENTRE (CFMDC)

67A Portland Street
Toronto, Ontario
Canada M5V-2M9
416-593-1808
FAX: 416-593-8661
CONTACT: AL MATTES, DIRECTOR

TECHNICAL ASSISTANCE PROGRAMS AND SERVICES

Programs of Special Interest: CFMDC is a nonprofit, membership-based, cooperative distribution center with a collection of over 1,400 films, including historically important titles as well as new works. CFMDC promotes and distributes films, most of which have been produced by Canadian artists, throughout Canada and abroad. Filmmakers retain all rights to their work and receive a return of 70% of the revenue of all sales and rentals; remaining revenue is applied to operating the centre and maintaining the film collection. CFMDC facilitates visits by filmmakers to show and talk about their work or hold filmmaking workshops; visiting artists are usually paid a fee or honorarium. Along with opportunities for rental and purchase of films, CFMDC provides in-house screening rooms for curators and journalists, and preview services for galleries, curators, educational institutions, etc. All films at the centre are works made under the complete control of the filmmaker and fall in the following categories: experimental, animation, documentary and drama. Membership fee is $30 annually.

THE CENTER FOR NEW TELEVISION

1440 North Dayton
Chicago, IL 60622
312-951-6868
FAX: 312-951-5717

PROFILE OF FINANCIAL SUPPORT TO ARTISTS

Total Funding/Value of In-Kind Support: $115,300 in 1992 (estimate)

Please read carefully!
Do not contact any listed organization unless you fulfill all eligibility requirements.

Competition for Funding: Total applications, 322; total individuals funded/provided with in-kind support, 45

Grant Range: Up to $6,000

DIRECT SUPPORT PROGRAMS

➤ **NEA/AFI GREAT LAKES REGIONAL FELLOWSHIP PROGRAM: FILM AND VIDEO PRODUCTION GRANTS**

Purpose: To assist independent film and video artists whose personal work shows promise or excellence

Eligibility:
> **Residency:** Illinois, Indiana, Ohio, Michigan, 1 year
> **Special Requirements:** Full-time students ineligible; commercial and instructional projects and projects associated with a degree program ineligible; applicant must have overall control and primary creative responsibility for project; previous grantees must have completed projects or production stages for which they received funding
> **Art Forms:** Film, video

Type of Support: New Project Grants, up to $6,000 may be used for any stage of production of new projects with total budgets up to $100,000; Work in Progress Grants, up to $6,000 for projects where at least half the shooting is completed or the editing is underway; Encouragement Grants, up to $3,000 for new projects with total cash budgets up to $30,000 (Encouragement Grants targeted to emerging artists); recipients supply 1 copy of their finished work to the CNTV library for a 1-time screening and/or broadcast

Scope of Program: $50,000 awarded in 1993; $20,000 in New Project Grants, $20,000 in Work in Progress Grants, $10,000 in Encouragement Grants

Application/Selection Process:
> **Deadline:** May, annually; contact for exact date
> **Preferred Initial Contact:** Call or write for application/guidelines
> **Application Procedure:** Submit application form, $4 for return postage, samples of work, resumé, project description and budget
> **Selection Process:** Peer panel of artists and arts professionals
> **Notification Process:** Letter in October
> **Formal Report of Grant Required:** Yes

➤ **RETIREMENT RESEARCH FOUNDATION NATIONAL MEDIA AWARDS**

CONTACT: RAY BRADFORD, PROJECT DIRECTOR

Purpose: To identify and promote the visibility of outstanding films, videotapes, and television programs for and about aging or aged people and to encourage excellence in media productions on issues related to aging

Please read carefully!
Do not contact any listed organization unless you fulfill all eligibility requirements.

Eligibility:
>   **Special Requirements:** Work must have been produced in the U.S. and must deal primarily with concerns that are of specific interest to aging or aged people or those working in the field of aging; work that primarily promotes a particular organization, institution, or product is ineligible; completed work only
>   **Art Forms:** Independent films and videos, television and theatrical film fiction, television nonfiction, training films and videos

Type of Support: $500-$5,000 awards; recipients asked to donate a copy of their work to the Retirement Research Foundation National Media Awards Library for in-house use only and to attend an awards ceremony in Chicago or to designate a representative to attend

Scope of Program: 9-12 awards totalling $33,000 available annually

Application/Selection Process:
>   **Deadline:** First week of February, annually; contact for exact date
>   **Preferred Initial Contact:** Call or write for application/guidelines
>   **Application Procedure:** Submit application form, sample of work
>   **Selection Process:** CNTV staff, media professionals, specialists on aging, Retirement Research Foundation representatives
>   **Notification Process:** 2-3 months after deadline

➤   **NEW TELEVISION AWARDS**
CONTACT: CHRISTINE MROZ, PROJECT SERVICES DIRECTOR

Purpose: To provide access to facilities in order to encourage independent videomakers to produce and complete projects

Eligibility:
>   **Residency:** Illinois, Indiana, Michigan, Ohio residents
>   **Special Requirements:** Project must be an independent production
>   **Art Forms:** Video

Type of Support: Access to the center's equipment

Scope of Program: $45,000 worth of equipment access in 1992

Application/Selection Process:
>   **Deadline:** Fall, annually; contact for exact date
>   **Preferred Initial Contact:** Call or write for application/guidelines
>   **Application Procedure:** Submit application form, sample of work
>   **Selection Process:** Board committee
>   **Notification Process:** Letter
>   **Formal Report of Grant Required:** Yes

Equipment Access

Video: Production for Hi-8, 3/4"; post-production for 3/4" (on-line and off-line), VHS (off-line)

Comments: CNTV equipment and facilities are available at low rates to independents and artists who are not working for a client. The videomaker must exercise complete creative control over the project and be a member of CNTV. Individual access memberships are $60.

TECHNICAL ASSISTANCE PROGRAMS AND SERVICES

Programs of Special Interest: Staff consultation on project development, equipment acquisition and maintenance, and other subjects is available to members for $25/hour.

CHANGE, INC.

P.O. Box 705
Cooper Station
New York, NY 10276
CONTACT: DENISE LE BEAU, BOARD MEMBER

DIRECT SUPPORT PROGRAMS

➤ **EMERGENCY ASSISTANCE**
Special Note: At the time of this printing (Spring, 1994) Change's grants have been suspended since September, 1992; artists may have difficulty in communicating with the organization until funding has been restored; the organization expects to resume normal operation

Purpose: To assist artists in need of emergency financial aid

Eligibility:
Special Requirements: Professional artists only; students ineligible; applicants must require emergency financial aid; no previous recipients
Art Forms: All disciplines

Type of Support: Cash grant

Application/Selection Process: Request guidelines by mail to see if Change has resumed operation

CHICAGO DEPARTMENT OF CULTURAL AFFAIRS

Cultural Grants
78 East Washington Street
Chicago, IL 60602
312-744-1742
TDD: 312-744-2947
FAX: 312-744-2089
CONTACT: MARY E. YOUNG, DIRECTOR OF CULTURAL GRANTS

PROFILE OF FINANCIAL SUPPORT TO ARTISTS

Total Funding/Value of In-Kind Support: $392,900 for FY 1992
(includes project support to small arts organizations)
Competition for Funding: Total applications, 640; total individuals
funded/provided with in-kind support, 340
Grant Range: $1,000-$4,000

DIRECT SUPPORT PROGRAMS

➤ **COMMUNITY ARTS ASSISTANCE PROGRAM**
CONTACT: COMMUNITY ARTS ASSISTANCE STAFF
Phone: 312-744-6630

Purpose: To promote Chicago's new and emerging multi-ethnic
artists and nonprofit arts organizations by funding technical
assistance, professional, or organizational development projects that
address a specific need or problem
Eligibility:
    Citizenship: U.S. (permanent residents also eligible)
    Residency: Chicago, 6 months
    Age: 21 or older
    Art Forms: All disciplines
Type of Support: Up to $1,500 for project
Scope of Program: 288 grants in FY 1992 (includes grants
to organizations)
Application/Selection Process:
    Deadline: January, annually; contact for exact date
    Preferred Initial Contact: Call or write for application/guidelines
    Application Procedure: Submit application form, samples of
    work, and proof of residency
    Selection Process: Panel of artists and arts professionals
    Notification Process: Letter 4-5 months after deadline
Formal Report of Funding Required: Yes

Please read carefully!
Do not contact any listed organization unless you fulfill all eligibility requirements.

➤ **NEIGHBORHOOD ARTS PROGRAM (NAP)**
CONTACT: NEIGHBORHOOD ARTS STAFF MEMBER
Phone: 312-744-6630
Purpose: To encourage and support the presentation of high-quality instructional arts projects that benefit youth, elderly, and disabled participants in Chicago's low- and moderate-income neighborhoods
Eligibility:
    Citizenship: U.S. (permanent residents also eligible)
    Residency: Chicago, 6 months
    Age: 21 or older
    Special Requirements: 1 project per applicant per funding year
    Art Forms: All disciplines
Type of Support: Up to $4,000 for project materials, artists' salaries, and support services
Scope of Program: 52 grants in FY 1992
Application/Selection Process:
    Deadline: August, annually; contact for exact date
    Preferred Initial Contact: Call or write for application/guidelines
    Application Procedure: Submit application forms, samples of work, proof of residency
    Selection Process: Panel of artists and arts professionals
    Notification Process: Letter 4-5 weeks after deadline
    Formal Report of Funding Required: Yes

TECHNICAL ASSISTANCE PROGRAMS AND SERVICES

Programs of Special Interest: Arts Resource Workshops and Special Events, conducted by professional consultants, are offered to artists, students, and arts administrators for nominal fees or free. The Arts Technical Assistance Guide outlines local and regional nonprofit arts organizations that provide technical assistance and funding opportunities for artists and arts administrators.

CITIZEN EXCHANGE COUNCIL

12 West 31st Street
New York, NY 10001-4415
212-643-1985
CONTACT: LEA CHECRONI-FREID, DIRECTOR OF ARTS AND MEDIA PROGRAMS, OR CHRISTOPHER MINARICH, PROGRAM ASSISTANT

PROFILE OF FINANCIAL SUPPORT TO ARTISTS
Total Funding/Value of In-Kind Support: $200,000 in 1993

Please read carefully!
Do not contact any listed organization unless you fulfill all eligibility requirements.

Competition for Funding: Total applications, n/a; total individuals funded/provided with in-kind support, 35-40 will be funded in 1993

Grant Range: Up to $5,000, average $500-$2,500

DIRECT SUPPORT PROGRAM
➤ ARTSLINK COLLABORATIVE PROJECTS

Purpose: To encourage collaborations and professional training between arts professionals and organizations in the U.S. and Eastern and Central Europe and the former Soviet Union.

Eligibility:

Citizenship: U.S., or permanent resident

Residency: Open

Age: Open

Special Requirements: Scholars, curators, presenters, administrators, critics, students and amateur groups ineligible; recipients ineligible to reapply for one year

Art Forms: Media, visual and performing artists

Type of Support: Grants to individuals and groups of no more than 5 artists; assistance in travelling to Eastern Europe, Central Europe, the former Soviet Union and the Baltics to work on mutually beneficial projects with counterparts; artists may have partners already in the region or be seeking counterparts; no support available for travel costs related only to solo exhibitions or performances or to participation in performing arts festivals abroad

Scope of Program: $200,000 available for 35-40 collaborative projects in 1993

Application/Selection Process:

Deadline: Early April, annually; contact for exact date

Preferred Initial Contact: Write or call for application/guidelines

Application Procedure: Submit application form, project description, artist's statement, work samples, resumé, letter of invitation from host organization

Selection Process: Peer panel review

Notification Process: Letter by July

Formal Report of Grant Required: Yes

CITY OF CINCINNATI HUMAN SERVICES DIVISION

Cincinnati Arts Allocation Committee
City Hall, Room 158
801 Plum Street
Cincinnati, OH 45202
513-352-1595
FAX: 513-352-5241
CONTACT: CAROLYN GUTJAHR, CAAC STAFF PERSON

PROFILE OF FINANCIAL SUPPORT TO ARTISTS

Total Funding/Value of In-Kind Support: $43,948 in 1992

Competition for Funding: Total applications, 51; total individuals funded/provided with in-kind support, 33

Grant Range: $500-$3,000

DIRECT SUPPORT PROGRAMS

➤ **INDIVIDUAL ARTIST GRANT PROGRAM**

Purpose: To provide support for emerging and established artists, to encourage excellence and professionalism in the arts, to encourage development and presentation of art which benefits the City of Cincinnati and its residents, to encourage arts programming for city residents, to encourage art as a means to increase understanding among diverse cultures in Cincinnati, to encourage development of innovative arts projects or programs

Eligibility:
  Residency: Legal resident of City of Cincinnati
  Art Forms: All disciplines

Type of Support: Project or operating support; average grant $1,400 in 1992

Scope of Program: $43,948 in 1992; no set guidelines for number of applications funded

Application/Selection Process:
  Deadline: February 15, annually
  Preferred Initial Contact: Call or write for information; applications available after January 1
  Application Procedure: Submit completed application form, samples of recent work, artist profile
  Selection Process: Cincinnati Arts Allocation Committee review; final approval by City Council with public review session included
  Notification Process: Letter after approval by City Council
  Formal Report of Grant Required: Yes

Please read carefully!
Do not contact any listed organization unless you fulfill all eligibility requirements.

TECHNICAL ASSISTANCE PROGRAMS AND SERVICES
Programs of Special Interest: Limited information and referral services and grant workshops are available to artists.

CITY OF RALEIGH ARTS COMMISSION (CORAC)

311 South Blount Street
Raleigh, NC 27601
919-831-6234
TDD: 800-735-2962
FAX: 919-828-8036
CONTACT: ELAINE LORBER, EXECUTIVE DIRECTOR

PROFILE OF FINANCIAL SUPPORT TO ARTISTS
Total Funding/Value of In-Kind Support: $8,000 in FY 1992-93
Competition for Funding: Total applications, 14; total individuals funded/provided with in-kind support, 8
Grant Range: $250-$1,000

DIRECT SUPPORT PROGRAMS
➤ **CAREER DEVELOPMENT GRANTS FOR ARTISTS**
Purpose: To recognize and provide financial support for committed, accomplished artists, enabling them to advance their careers
Eligibility:
 Residency: Wake County, 1 year
 Age: 18 or older
 Special Requirements: Previous grantees ineligible for 3 years
 Art Forms: All disciplines
Type of Support: $250-$1,000 for specific professional development projects (e.g., expenses for training, travel, space, supplies)
Scope of Program: 8 awards in 1992-93
Application/Selection Process:
 Deadline: Fall, annually; contact for exact dates
 Preferred Initial Contact: Call for application/guidelines
 Application Procedure: Confer with executive director before applying; submit application form, project proposal and budget, resumé, letters of recommendation, references, samples of work, supporting materials (optional)
 Selection Process: Judge, panel review
 Notification Process: Letter 6-7 weeks after deadline
 Formal Report of Grant Required: Yes

Please read carefully!
Do not contact any listed organization unless you fulfill all eligibility requirements.

COLORADO COUNCIL ON THE ARTS

750 Pennsylvania Street
Denver, CO 80203-3699
303-894-2619
CONTACT: DANIEL A. SALAZAR, DIRECTOR,
INDIVIDUAL ARTISTS PROGRAMS

PROFILE OF FINANCIAL SUPPORT TO ARTISTS

Total Funding/Value of In-Kind Support: $160,000 for FY 1994
(figures reflect CoVisions program only)
Competition for Funding: n/a
Grant Range: Up to $5,000

DIRECT SUPPORT PROGRAMS

➤ **COLORADO VISIONS (COVISIONS)—RECOGNITION AWARDS**

Purpose: To acknowledge outstanding artistic accomplishment among Colorado artists

Eligibility:
    Citizenship: n/a
    Residency: Colorado, one year
    Special Requirements: n/a
    Art Forms: Visual arts, media arts, folk arts, performing arts, literature

Type of Support: $4,000 awards; additional $1,000 available for presentation of work in the community

Scope of Program: $70,000 available in FY 1995

Application/Selection Process:
    Deadline: Fall, annually; contact for exact dates (disciplines will be grouped into separate deadlines)
    Preferred Initial Contact: Call or write for application/guidelines
    Application Procedure: Submit application form, samples of work, resumé, SASE for return of materials
    Selection Process: Peer panel review by out-of-state experts
    Notification Process: Letter by January for all disciplines except literature (which receives notification by April)
    Formal Report of Grant Required: Yes

➤ **COLORADO VISIONS (COVISIONS)—PROJECT GRANTS**

Purpose: To encourage the creation and public presentation of new works of high artistic merit by Colorado artists and arts organizations

Eligibility:
    Citizenship: n/a
    Residency: Colorado, 1 year

Please read carefully!
Do not contact any listed organization unless you fulfill all eligibility requirements.

Special Requirements: n/a

Art Forms: Visual arts, media arts, folk arts, performing arts, literature

Type of Support: Up to $5,000 grant (projects must include public presentation)

Scope of Program: $90,000 available in FY 1995

Application/Selection Process:

Deadline: June, annually; contact for exact date

Preferred Initial Contact: Call or write for application/guidelines

Application Procedure: Submit project proposal, budget, work samples, SASE for return of materials

Selection Process: Multi-disciplinary panel review

Notification Process: Letter by September

Formal Report of Grant Required: Yes

TECHNICAL ASSISTANCE PROGRAMS AND SERVICES

Programs of Special Interest: The Art in Public Places Program commissions and purchases artwork for state-owned buildings (contact Simon Zelkind, Director; 303-894-2618). The unjuried Colorado Artists Register (CAR) houses slides of professional Colorado artists; registered artists automatically receive a monthly CAR newsletter, a listing of opportunities for visual artists (contact Suzy Roesler, Director, Colorado Artists Register, P.O. Drawer H, Boulder, CO 80306; 303-441-4391). Colorado artists accepted to the CCAH Resource List are eligible for 1-week to 5-month residencies in schools through the Artist in Residence Program (contact Patty Ortiz, Artists in Residence Program Director, Young Audiences, Inc., 1415 Larimer Street, Denver, CO 80202; 303-825-3650).

COMMONWEALTH COUNCIL FOR ARTS AND CULTURE (CCAC)/COMMONWEALTH OF NORTHERN MARIANA ISLANDS

P.O. Box 5553, CHRB
Saipan, MP 96950
011-670-322-9982/9983
FAX: 011-670-322-9028
CONTACT: MARGARITA D.L.G. WONENBERG, EXECUTIVE DIRECTOR

PROFILE OF FINANCIAL SUPPORT TO ARTISTS

Total Funding/Value of In-Kind Support: n/a

Please read carefully!

Do not contact any listed organization unless you fulfill all eligibility requirements.

Competition for Funding: n/a

Grant Range: $200-$2,000

DIRECT SUPPORT PROGRAMS

➤ **GRANTS-IN-AID**

Eligibility:
  Citizenship: U.S.
  Residency: Northern Mariana Islands
  Art Forms: Dance, media arts, music (performance, composition), photography, theater, visual arts (general, painting, sculpture, printmaking), literature, folk arts

Type of Support: $200-$2,000

Scope of Program: 6-9 awards per year

Application/Selection Process:
  Deadline: May 1 and November 1, annually
  Preferred Initial Contact: Call or write the CCAC main office on Saipan or CCAC board representatives for application/guidelines
  Notification Process: Letter within 60 days

THE COMMUNITY FILM WORKSHOP (CFW)

1130 South Wabash Avenue
Suite 302
Chicago, IL 60605
312-427-1245

PROFILE OF FINANCIAL SUPPORT TO ARTISTS

Total Funding/Value of In-Kind Support: $20,000 for 1993

Competition for Funding: Total applications, 30; total individuals funded/provided with in-kind support, 4

Grant Range: $2,000-$5,000 worth of equipment access

DIRECT SUPPORT PROGRAMS

➤ **BUILD ILLINOIS FILMMAKERS GRANTS**

Purpose: To encourage the production of independent films by offering grants to be applied to rentals of CFW's production and post-production equipment and facilities to emerging independent film-makers

Eligibility:
  Residency: Illinois

Please read carefully!
Do not contact any listed organization unless you fulfill all eligibility requirements.

Special Requirements: Must be CFW member; students and projects associated with a degree program ineligible; commercial and instructional projects are ineligible; previous grantees must have completed funded projects; minority applicants encouraged to apply

Art Forms: Film

Type of Support: Up to $5,000 worth of equipment/facilities rental for 16mm production and post-production

Scope of Program: 4 awards in 1993

Application/Selection Process:
   Deadline: December 1, annually
   Preferred Initial Contact: Call or write for application/guidelines
   Application Procedure: Submit application form, $30 membership fee (if not a member of CFW), project description and budget, resumé, samples of work
   Selection Process: Independent jury of artists and arts professionals
   Notification Process: January
   Formal Report of Grant Required: Yes

CONNECTICUT COMMISSION ON THE ARTS

227 Lawrence Street
Hartford, CT 06106
203-566-4770
FAX: 203-566-6462
CONTACT: LINDA DENTE, PROGRAM MANAGER

PROFILE OF FINANCIAL SUPPORT TO ARTISTS
Total Funding/Value of In-Kind Support: $100,000 for FY 1992-93
Competition for Funding: Total applications, 300; total individuals funded/provided with in-kind support, 20
Grant Range: $5,000

DIRECT SUPPORT PROGRAMS
➤ ARTIST GRANTS
Purpose: To provide financial support for artists to develop new work or to complete works in progress
Eligibility:
   Residency: Connecticut, 4 years
   Special Requirements: No students; previous recipients ineligible for 4 years
   Art Forms: Visual arts (sculpture, printmaking, painting, photography, crafts, performance art/new genres) in odd-numbered years;

film, video, poetry, playwriting, fiction, music composition, chore-ography in even-numbered years

Type of Support: $5,000

Scope of Program: 20 awards in FY 1992-93

Application/Selection Process:

  Deadline: End of January, annually

  Preferred Initial Contact: Call or write for application/guidelines

  Application Procedure: Submit application form, 10 slides of work, resumé, project budget

  Selection Process: Peer panel of artists

  Notification Process: Letter in July

  Formal Report of Grant Required: Yes

TECHNICAL ASSISTANCE PROGRAMS AND SERVICES

Programs of Special Interest: The commission holds an annual com-petition for Connecticut film and video artists. The winning entries are broadcast on Connecticut Public Television. Artist residencies are available through the Arts-in-Education program. Connecticut Volun-teer Lawyers for the Arts provides a variety of free services for eligible artists and holds an annual Arts Law conference.

CONTEMPORARY ARTS CENTER

900 Camp Street
P.O. Box 30498
New Orleans, LA 70190
504-523-1216
FAX: 504-528-3828

CONTACT: PATRICIA MARTINEZ,
ASSISTANT FOR THE PERFORMANCE DEPARTMENT

PROFILE OF FINANCIAL SUPPORT TO ARTISTS

Total Funding/Value of In-Kind Support: $43,000 in FY 1992-93

Competition for Funding: Total applications, 102; total individuals funded/provided with in-kind support, 10

Grant Range: $1,500-$6,000

DIRECT SUPPORT PROGRAMS

➤ **REGIONAL ARTISTS PROJECTS (RAP)**

Purpose: To provide funding for experimental or multi-cultural pro-jects that would not be considered in other arts discipline categories because they are new or nontraditional forms

Please read carefully!
Do not contact any listed organization unless you fulfill all eligibility requirements.

Eligibility:
  Citizenship: U.S.
  Residency: Louisiana, Mississippi, Alabama, Arkansas
  Art Forms: Film, video, visual arts, dance, music, literature, interdisciplinary
Type of Support: $1,500-$6,000 project support
Scope of Program: $43,000 in FY 1992-93
Application/Selection Process:
  Deadline: March, annually; contact for exact date
  Preferred Initial Contact: Write for application/guidelines; guidelines available in December
  Application Procedure: Submit application form, project description, biographical information, samples of work
  Selection Process: Peer panel of artists
  Notification Process: Letter by end of September
  Formal Report of Grant Required: Yes

TECHNICAL ASSISTANCE PROGRAMS AND SERVICES
Programs of Special Interest: The center offers information services in a wide range of areas, including equipment/facilities, employment, competitions, marketing, fellowships, and project support.

CORPORATION FOR PUBLIC BROADCASTING (CPB)

901 E Street, NW
Washington, DC 20004-2006
202-879-9734
FAX: 202-783-1019
CONTACT: TELEVISION PROGRAM FUND

PROFILE OF FINANCIAL SUPPORT TO ARTISTS
Total Funding/Value of In-Kind Support: n/a
Competition for Funding: n/a
Grant Range: n/a

DIRECT SUPPORT PROGRAMS
➤ **CONTENT SPECIFIC SOLICITATIONS**
Purpose: To solicit from diverse sources high quality programs of a specific nature that may be broadly or narrowly defined and range from one-hour documentaries on a particular theme to miniseries concepts
Eligibility:
  Citizenship: U.S., or U.S. co-producer required
  Residency: Open

Please read carefully!
Do not contact any listed organization unless you fulfill all eligibility requirements.

Special Requirements: Organizations and independent producers are eligible; student, instructional, and industrial projects ineligible; programs must be able to command a national public broadcasting audience and have the potential to be broadcast by a majority of PBS stations; other requirements vary
Art Forms: Film, video
Type of Support: Grant for project support
Scope of Program: n/a
Application/Selection Process:
Deadline: Varies annually; announced when requests for proposals are issued
Preferred Initial Contact: Call or write to be placed on mailing list for solicitations
Application Procedure: Complete application per guidelines; applications/guidelines will be issued as solicitations are created
Selection Process: Panel review
Notification Process: Letter; final decision about 3 months after deadline
Formal Report of Grant Required: Yes

➤ **MULTI-CULTURAL PROGRAMMING SOLICITATION**
Purpose: To support programming by producers from the 5 ethnic minorities (African-American, Asian-American, Native American, Latino, and Pacific Islander) and on subjects that could be of special interest to their indigenous communities
Eligibility:
Citizenship: U.S., or U.S. co-producer required
Residency: Open
Special Requirements: Organizations and independent producers are eligible; producer and director of independent production teams must be ethnic minorities; priority to projects that have significant representation of minority personnel
Art Forms: Film, video
Type of Support: Grant for project support
Scope of Program: $2,000,000 available for each fiscal year
Application/Selection Process:
Deadline: Varies annually; announced when requests for proposals are issued
Preferred Initial Contact: Call or write to be placed on mailing list for solicitations
Application Procedure: Complete application per guidelines; applications/guidelines will be issued as solicitations are created
Selection Process: Outside readers, panel review
Notification Process: Letter approximately 3 months after deadline
Formal Report of Grant Required: Yes

Please read carefully!
Do not contact any listed organization unless you fulfill all eligibility requirements.

➤ **GENERAL PROGRAM REVIEW**

Purpose: To support television projects throughout any stage of research and development, scripting, preproduction, or post-production

Eligibility:
    Citizenship: U.S., or U.S. co-producer required
    Residency: Open
    Special Requirements: Organizations and independent producers are eligible; emphasis on multi-cultural and children's programs; programs must be appropriate for national PBS schedule; projects may be submitted only once; student, instructional and industrial films are not appropriate
    Art Forms: Film, video

Type of Support: Up to $250,000

Scope of Program: Proposals reviewed continuously; funding is limited

Application/Selection Process:
    Deadline: Ongoing
    Preferred Initial Contact: See application procedure
    Application Procedure: Submit a two-page description of the project, a cover letter stating any other sources of funding, and biographies of key personnel involved; please do not submit scripts or sample tapes
    Selection Process: Staff and director of Program Fund; panel of program managers, independent producers, and specialists in certain disciplines; PBS program staff
    Notification Process: Letter or phone call
    Formal Report of Grant Required: Yes

➤ **PROGRAM CHALLENGE FUND**

Purpose: To insure that high-visibility, prime-time limited series are available each year for the national PBS schedule

Eligibility:
    Citizenship: U.S., or U.S. co-producer required
    Residency: Open
    Special Requirements: Organizations and independent producers are eligible; priority to series with potential for above-average viewership and critical attention; series may be documentary or drama and should cover subjects of significance
    Art Forms: Film, video

Type of Support: Grant for project support

Scope of Program: $10,000,000 available annually

Application/Selection Process:
    Deadline: Open

Please read carefully!
Do not contact any listed organization unless you fulfill all eligibility requirements.

Preferred Initial Contact: Call any senior programming staffer at PBS or CPB for general information
Application Procedure: Send proposal or letter to senior programming staff at CPB or PBS
Selection Process: Outside readers, staff review
Notification Process: Phone call or letter
Formal Report of Grant Required: Yes

TECHNICAL ASSISTANCE PROGRAMS AND SERVICES
Programs of Special Interest: Employment Outreach Project; contact Ms. Shelley Danzy, Coordinator, at 202-879-9794. The Employment Outreach Project (EOP) provides job information and resource services to people seeking careers in public broadcasting. The EOP Talent Bank contains resumés from people across the country and emphasizes identifying members of groups traditionally underrepresented in broadcasting. The EOP Job Line publicizes opportunities at public radio and television stations (call 202-393-1045).

COUNCIL FOR INTERNATIONAL EXCHANGE OF SCHOLARS (CIES)

3007 Tilden Street, NW
Suite 5M
Washington, DC 20008-3009
202-686-7877
See Fulbright Awards listing.

CREATIVE TIME, INC.

131 West 24th Street
New York, NY 10011
212-206-6674

PROFILE OF FINANCIAL SUPPORT TO ARTISTS
Total Funding/Value of In-Kind Support: n/a
Competition for Funding: n/a
Grant Range: $200-$10,000

DIRECT SUPPORT PROGRAM
➤ **CITYWIDE PROJECT SERIES**
Purpose: To present art in unusual public settings in and around New York City.

Please read carefully!
Do not contact any listed organization unless you fulfill all eligibility requirements.

Eligibility:
Residency: Open nationally, but project must take place in New York City
Special Requirements: Professional artists only; students ineligible
Art Forms: All disciplines
Type of Support: Project grants of $200-$10,000; publicity and production support
Scope of Program: 10-12 projects annually
Application/Selection Process:
Deadline: Open; proposals reviewed every 3-6 months
Preferred Initial Contact: Send SASE for guidelines
Application Procedure: Submit project description, resumé, technical assessment of site, project budget, samples of work, SASE for return of materials
Selection Process: Peer panel review
Notification Process: n/a
Formal Report of Grant Required: No

CULTURAL COUNCIL OF SANTA CRUZ COUNTY

7960 Soquel Drive, Suite 1
Aptos, CA 95003
408-688-5399
FAX: 408-688-2208
CONTACT: ROBIN LARSEN, PROGRAM MANAGER FOR GRANTS AND MARKETING

PROFILE OF FINANCIAL SUPPORT TO ARTISTS
Total Funding/Value of In-Kind Support: $33,000 in FY 1992-93
Competition for Funding: Total applications, 38; total individuals funded/provided with in-kind support, 32 (figures include both organizations and individuals applying with a nonprofit sponsor)
Grant Range: Up to $1,500

DIRECT SUPPORT PROGRAM
➤ **PROJECT GRANTS**
Purpose: To support well-planned, quality, short-term arts projects that respond to and serve the cultural needs and interests of the people of Santa Cruz County.
Eligibility:
Citizenship: Open
Residency: Santa Cruz county and surrounding area

Please read carefully!
Do not contact any listed organization unless you fulfill all eligibility requirements.

Special Requirements: Individual artists may apply only if sponsored by a nonprofit organization; project must take place in Santa Cruz County
Art Forms: All disciplines
Type of Support: Up to $1,500 cash grant; $1,000 average grant
Scope of Program: $33,000 in FY 1992-93
Application/Selection Process:
  Deadline: October, annually; contact for specific date
  Preferred Initial Contact: Call for information
  Application Procedure: Submit application form; applicants are invited to interview with program committee
  Selection Process: Committee recommendation, board decision
  Notification Process: Letter within one month of interview
  Formal Report of Grant Required: Yes

TECHNICAL ASSISTANCE PROGRAMS AND SERVICES
Programs of Special Interest: Cultural Council of Santa Cruz County conducts an Open Studio Tour which links individual artists to the community through a self-guided tour of 300 artists' workplaces for three weekends each October. A museum quality catalog is published and an exhibition of participating artists' work is held. The council presents rotating exhibitions of artwork by Santa Cruz County artists. Workshops, lecture/demos and ongoing classes are offered through the Santa Cruz Art League, 526 Broadway, Santa Cruz, CA 95060; 408-426-5787.

CUMMINGTON COMMUNITY OF THE ARTS

Rural Route #1
P.O. Box 145
Cummington, MA 01026
413-634-2172
CONTACT: RICK REIKEN, RESIDENTIAL DIRECTOR

PROFILE OF FINANCIAL SUPPORT TO ARTISTS
Total Funding/Value of In-Kind Support: $120,000 for FY 1992
Competition for Funding: Total applications, 1,500; total individuals funded/provided with in-kind support, 120
Grant Range: n/a

Please read carefully!
Do not contact any listed organization unless you fulfill all eligibility requirements.

DIRECT SUPPORT PROGRAMS
➤ **ARTIST RESIDENCIES**

Purpose: To encourage artistic innovation and development, a commitment that favors emerging artists and writers, particularly those that offer alternative voices based on sex, race, age, or class

Eligibility:
  Special Requirements: Previous residents ineligible for up to 3 years
  Art Forms: Visual arts, fiction, playwriting, poetry, music composition, film/video, photography, performance art/choreography

Type of Support: 2-week to 3-month residencies including room, studio; residents pay $600-$700 per month and maintain the community; work exchange residencies are available

Scope of Program: 120 residencies

Application/Selection Process:
  Deadline: April 1, annually, for summer residencies; for non-summer residencies (September through May) applicant must apply 2 months prior to desired residency
  Preferred Initial Contact: Call or write for application/guidelines
  Application Procedure: Submit application form, $10 fee, samples of work, references, resumé, supporting materials (optional)
  Selection Process: Peer panel of artists
  Notification Process: Letter

DALLAS MUSEUM OF ART

1717 North Harwood
Dallas, TX 75201
214-922-1234
TDD: 214-922-1355
FAX: 214-954-0174
CONTACT: DEBRA WITTRUP, PROGRAM DIRECTOR

PROFILE OF FINANCIAL SUPPORT TO ARTISTS

Total Funding/Value of In-Kind Support: $18,000 in 1992

Competition for Funding: Total applications, 300; total individuals funded/provided with in-kind support, 5-10 annually

Grant Range: Up to $6,000

Please read carefully!
Do not contact any listed organization unless you fulfill all eligibility requirements.

DIRECT SUPPORT PROGRAM

➤ **OTIS AND VELMA DAVIS DOZIER TRAVEL GRANT**

Purpose: To recognize exceptional talent in professional artists who wish to expand their artistic horizons through domestic or foreign travel

Eligibility:

Residency: Texas, currently and for past 3 years

Age: 30 years of age or older

Special Requirements: Professional artists only; financial need will be a consideration, but not the determining factor in granting the award; grant must be used during the same calendar year

Art Forms: Visual arts, including film and video

Type of Support: Maximum of $6,000

Scope of Program: 1 or 2 awards per year, on average

Application/Selection Process:

Deadline: March 1, annually

Preferred Initial Contact: Write for guidelines

Application Procedure: Send examples of recent work, updated resumé (including birth date and residency information for past 3 years), description of and budget for travel, one-page statement and mailing address/daytime phone

Selection Process: Jury

Notification Process: Call to recipients, letter to all applicants; announcement in May at DMA Annual Meeting

Formal Report of Grant Required: Yes

➤ **ARCH AND ANNE GILES KIMBROUGH FUND**

Purpose: To recognize exceptional talent and promise in young visual artists

Eligibility:

Residency: Texas, currently and for past 3 years

Age: Under 30 years of age

Special Requirements: Grants must be used during same calendar year and are not available for college or art school tuition

Art Forms: Visual arts, including film and video

Type of Support: Maximum of $3,500

Scope of Program: 3 to 5 awards per year, on average

Application/Selection Process:

Deadline: March 1, annually

Preferred Initial Contact: Write for guidelines

Application Procedure: Send examples of recent work, updated resumé (including birth date and residency information for past 3 years), two letters of recommendation, a short statement accompanied by project budget outlining purpose to

Please read carefully!
Do not contact any listed organization unless you fulfill all eligibility requirements.

which award would be applied, and mailing address/daytime phone
Selection Process: Jury
Notification Process: Call to recipients, letter to all applicants; announcement in May at DMA Annual Meeting
Formal Report of Grant Required: Yes

➤ **CLARE HART DEGOLYER MEMORIAL FUND**

Purpose: To recognize exceptional talent and promise in young visual artists
Eligibility:
  Residency: Southwestern U.S. for past 4 years (Arizona, Colorado, New Mexico, Oklahoma, Texas)
  Age: Artist must be between 15 and 25 years of age
  Special Requirements: Grants must be used during same calendar year and are not available for college or art school tuition
  Art Forms: Visual arts, including film and video
Type of Support: Maximum of $1,500
Scope of Program: 1 or 2 awards per year, on average
Application/Selection Process:
  Deadline: March 1, annually
  Preferred Initial Contact: Write for guidelines
  Application Procedure: Send examples of recent work, updated resumé (including birth date and residency information for past 4 years), two letters of recommendation, a short statement accompanied by project budget outlining purpose to which award would be applied, and mailing address/daytime phone
  Selection Process: Jury
  Notification Process: Call to recipients, letter to all applicants; announcement in May at DMA Annual Meeting
  Formal Report of Grant Required: Yes

DANE COUNTY CULTURAL AFFAIRS COMMISSION

City-County Building, Room 421
210 Martin Luther King, Jr. Boulevard
Madison, WI 53709
608-266-5915
FAX: 608-266-2643

PROFILE OF FINANCIAL SUPPORT TO ARTISTS
Total Funding/Value of In-Kind Support: $172,000 in 1993
Competition for Funding: n/a
Grant Range: $100-$6,000

Please read carefully!
Do not contact any listed organization unless you fulfill all eligibility requirements.

DIRECT SUPPORT PROGRAMS

➤ **ARTS PROJECT GRANTS/MINI GRANTS**

Purpose: Arts Project Grants support individuals and nonprofit groups seeking supplementary funds for arts projects such as public exhibitions, workshops, commissioned art, and community art residencies; Mini Grants assist individuals and nonprofit organizations in emergency situations or with unique opportunities

Eligibility:
   Residency: Dane County
   Special Requirements: Project must take place in Dane County; grants must be matched in cash and in-kind support (part of match must be cash); applications for projects with 3 or more participating individuals must be submitted by a nonprofit sponsor; degree credit students may not apply for projects directly related to their academic studies
   Art Forms: All disciplines

Type of Support: Matching grant for up to 50% of project budget; Mini Grants up to $500

Scope of Program: 80 project grants in 1992

Application/Selection Process:
   Deadline: February 1, June 1, September 1, annually; open deadline for Mini Grants
   Preferred Initial Contact: Discuss proposal with commission staff
   Application Procedure: Submit application form, project narrative and budget, resumé, samples of work, letters of support (strongly recommended)
   Selection Process: Advisory panel
   Notification Process: Letter within 3 months
   Formal Report of Grant Required: Yes

➤ **ARTS IN SCHOOLS GRANTS**

Purpose: To support cultural programs offering artistic experiences for students in Dane County schools; eligible programs include workshops, lecture-demonstrations, and residencies with an emphasis on the creative process

Eligibility:
   Special Requirements: Grants must be matched in cash and in-kind support (at least 25% of cash must come from school, school district, parent-teacher organizations, or private underwriters)
   Art Forms: All disciplines

Type of Support: Matching grant for up to 50% of project budget

Scope of Program: n/a

Application/Selection Process:
   Deadline: June 1, annually

Please read carefully!
Do not contact any listed organization unless you fulfill all eligibility requirements.

Application Procedure: Submit application form, project narrative and budget, samples of work, resumé, letters of support
Selection Process: Advisory panel
Notification Process: Letter
Formal Report of Grant Required: Yes

TECHNICAL ASSISTANCE PROGRAMS AND SERVICES
Programs of Special Interest: The Dane County Cultural Resources Directory profiles 260 local arts and historical organizations and lists local media contacts.

D.C. COMMISSION
ON THE ARTS AND HUMANITIES

410 8th Street, NW
Stables Art Center, 5th Floor
Washington, DC 20004
202-724-5613
TDD: 202-727-3148
FAX: 202-727-4135
CONTACT: JANN DARSIE, PROGRAM COORDINATOR

PROFILE OF FINANCIAL SUPPORT TO ARTISTS
Total Funding/Value of In-Kind Support: $550,462 for FY 1993
Competition for Funding: Total applications, 475; total individuals funded/provided with in-kind support, 119
Grant Range: $2,000-$5,000

DIRECT SUPPORT PROGRAMS
➤ ARTS EDUCATION PROJECTS/CITY ARTS
PROJECTS/GRANTS-IN-AID
Purpose: Arts Education Projects grant funds to professional artists, arts professionals, educators, and persons with demonstrated experience in community service for projects which target youth, pre-K through 21 years of age; City Arts Projects grant funds to professional artists, arts professionals, educators, and persons with demonstrated experience in community service for projects which target special persons traditionally underserved or separated from the mainstream, due to geographic location, economic constraints or disability; Grants-in-Aid provides fellowships to artists
Eligibility:
Residency: District of Columbia

Please read carefully!
Do not contact any listed organization unless you fulfill all eligibility requirements.

Age: 18 and older

Art Forms: Visual arts, media, crafts, interdisciplinary, multidisciplinary, dance, literature, music, theater

Type of Support: Individuals may receive up to $5,000 in all programs

Scope of Program: For FY 1993, individuals received 31 Arts Education Project grants, 21 City Arts grants, and 67 Grants-in-Aid fellowships

Application/Selection Process:

Preferred Initial Contact: Call or write for application/guidelines

Application Procedure: Submit application form, samples of work, resumé, project budget

Selection Process: Peer panel of artists, arts professionals and administrators

Notification Process: Letter

Formal Report of Grant Required: Yes

TECHNICAL ASSISTANCE PROGRAMS AND SERVICES

Programs of Special Interest: The Art in Public Places program acquires and commissions work.

DEKALB COUNCIL FOR THE ARTS, INC. (DCA)

P.O. Box 875
Decatur, GA 30031
404-371-8826
CONTACT: THEA BEASLEY, OFFICE MANAGER

PROFILE OF FINANCIAL SUPPORT TO ARTISTS

Total Funding/Value of In-Kind Support: $7,600 for FY 1993

Competition for Funding: Total applications, 21; total individuals funded/provided with in-kind support, 7

Grant Range: Up to $2,000

DIRECT SUPPORT PROGRAMS

➤ **INDIVIDUAL ARTISTS PROGRAM**

Purpose: To provide artists with financial assistance that will enable them to provide the citizens of DeKalb County with an arts service

Eligibility:

Residency: DeKalb County, 1 year

Art Forms: All disciplines

Please read carefully!
Do not contact any listed organization unless you fulfill all eligibility requirements.

Type of Support: Up to $2,000

Scope of Program: 7 awards, totalling $7,600, in FY 1993

Application/Selection Process:

Deadline: January, annually; contact for exact date

Preferred Initial Contact: Call or write for application/guidelines

Application Procedure: Submit application form, samples of work, resumé, financial statement, project budget

Selection Process: Peer panel of artists, organization staff, board of directors

Notification Process: Letter 6 months after deadline

Formal Report of Grant Required: Yes

TECHNICAL ASSISTANCE PROGRAMS AND SERVICES

Programs of Special Interest: The Guide to the Arts in Dekalb lists area cultural and arts organizations, individual artists, and DCA members. Staff is available to provide general information to artists on issues such as marketing and funding. Free and low-cost workshops are offered on grantwriting and copyright and tax issues.

DELAWARE STATE ARTS COUNCIL

Division of the Arts
820 North French Street
Wilmington, DE 19801
302-577-3540
FAX: 302-577-6561
CONTACT: BARBARA R. KING, VISUAL ARTS/INDIVIDUAL ARTIST FELLOWSHIP COORDINATOR

PROFILE OF FINANCIAL SUPPORT TO ARTISTS

Total Funding/Value of In-Kind Support: $57,000 for FY 1993

Competition for Funding: Total applications, 80; total individuals funded/provided with in-kind support, 15

Grant Range: $2,000-$5,000

DIRECT SUPPORT PROGRAMS

➤ **INDIVIDUAL ARTIST FELLOWSHIPS**

Purpose: To enable artists to set aside time, purchase materials, and work in their fields with fewer financial constraints

Eligibility:

Citizenship: U.S. or permanent resident

Please read carefully!
Do not contact any listed organization unless you fulfill all eligibility requirements.

Residency: Delaware, 1 year
Special Requirements: No students; previous recipients in "established professional" category ineligible; previous recipients in "emerging professional" category ineligible for 3 years; to apply, visual artists must establish or already maintain a file in the council's Artists Slide Registry (this does not apply to media artists)
Art Forms: All disciplines
Type of Support: $5,000 for established professional; $2,000 for emerging professional
Scope of Program: 9 established professional, 6 emerging professional awards in FY 1993
Application/Selection Process:
  Deadline: March 1, annually
  Preferred Initial Contact: Call or write for application/guidelines
  Application Procedure: Submit application form, samples of work, resumé, supporting materials
  Selection Process: Individuals from outside of organization
  Notification Process: Letter in July
  Formal Report of Grant Required: Yes

TECHNICAL ASSISTANCE PROGRAMS AND SERVICES

Programs of Special Interest: The Arts in Education program publishes a directory of artists approved for residencies. The council maintains an Arts Resource Library and a Job Bank of job announcements and career resources in the arts.

EBEN DEMAREST TRUST

Mellon Bank, N.A., Room 3845
One Mellon Bank Center
Pittsburgh, PA 15258
412-234-4695
CONTACT: HELEN COLLINS, ASSOCIATE VICE PRESIDENT,
MELLON BANK

PROFILE OF FINANCIAL SUPPORT TO ARTISTS

Total Funding/Value of In-Kind Support: $9,100 for FY 1991-92

Competition for Funding: Total applications, 4; total individuals funded/provided with in-kind support, 1

Grant Range: $9,100

Please read carefully!
Do not contact any listed organization unless you fulfill all eligibility requirements.

DIRECT SUPPORT PROGRAMS

➤ **EBEN DEMAREST TRUST**

Purpose: To allow a gifted artist or archeologist to pursue his or her work without dependence on public sale or approval of the work

Eligibility:

Citizenship: Preference to U.S. citizens

Age: Preference to mature artists

Special Requirements: Artist's income must be less than income accruing from the trust; application must be sponsored by an arts organization; no students

Art Forms: All arts disciplines and archeology

Type of Support: $9,100 grant in FY 1991-92

Scope of Program: 1 award per year

Application/Selection Process:

Deadline: June 1, annually

Preferred Initial Contact: Arts organization requests forms or writes letter on behalf of artist

Application Procedure: Arts organization submits letter/forms, references, financial statement; unsolicited applications from individuals not accepted

Selection Process: Board of directors

Notification Process: Phone call or letter in mid-June

DIVERSE WORKS

1117 East Freeway
Houston, TX 77002
713-223-8346
CONTACT: DEBORAH GROTFELDT, ASSISTANT DIRECTOR

PROFILE OF FINANCIAL SUPPORT TO ARTISTS

Total Funding/Value of In-Kind Support: $45,000 for 1993

Competition for Funding: Total applications, 200; total individuals funded/provided with in-kind support, 16

Grant Range: $2,000-$5,000 average

DIRECT SUPPORT PROGRAMS

➤ **NEW FORMS REGIONAL INITIATIVE**

Purpose: To provide funds for works that challenge traditional art disciplines and explore new forms of art and culture

Eligibility:

Residency: New Mexico, Texas, Arizona, Oklahoma

Please read carefully!
Do not contact any listed organization unless you fulfill all eligibility requirements.

Special Requirements: Individual artists and collaborating artists may apply; projects must challenge traditional definitions of art or culture; no students

Art Forms: Projects may involve one or more of the following disciplines: visual arts, video, film, dance, music, theater, performance art, installations, text, sound art, environmental art

Type of Support: $2,000-$5,000 average

Scope of Program: 13 awards, totalling $45,000, in 1993

Application/Selection Process:

Deadline: April, annually; contact for exact date

Preferred Initial Contact: Call or write for application/guidelines

Application Procedure: Submit application form, resumé, sample of work

Selection Process: Panel review

Notification Process: Letter by mid-August

Formal Report of Grant Required: Yes

ALDEN B. DOW CREATIVITY CENTER

Northwood University
Midland, MI 48640-2398
517-837-4478
CONTACT: CAROL B. COPPAGE, DIRECTOR

PROFILE OF FINANCIAL SUPPORT TO ARTISTS

Total Funding/Value of In-Kind Support: n/a

Competition for Funding: n/a

Grant Range: n/a

DIRECT SUPPORT PROGRAMS

➤ **RESIDENCY FELLOWSHIP PROGRAM**

Purpose: To provide individuals in all professions an opportunity to pursue innovative ideas having the potential for impact in their fields

Eligibility:

Residency: Open

Citizenship: Open; foreign speaking applicants must apply in English

Art Forms: All arts, sciences and humanities

Type of Support: 10-week summer residency, including round-trip travel to center, room, board, project expenses, and stipend

Please read carefully!
Do not contact any listed organization unless you fulfill all eligibility requirements.

Scope of Program: 4 residencies per year

Application/Selection Process:
   Deadline: December 31, annually
   Preferred Initial Contact: Call or write for application/guidelines
   Application Procedure: Submit application form, samples of work, resumé, project budget; finalists make expenses-paid visit to Midland for interview
   Selection Process: Board of directors, professionals in applicant's field
   Notification Process: April 1
   Formal Report of Grant Required: Yes

DOWNTOWN COMMUNITY TELEVISION CENTER (DCTV)

87 Lafayette Street
New York, NY 10013
212-966-4510
FAX: 212-219-0248

PROFILE OF FINANCIAL SUPPORT TO ARTISTS

Total Funding/Value of In-Kind Support: n/a

Competition for Funding: Total applications, 100; total individuals funded/provided with in-kind support, 10

Grant Range: n/a

DIRECT SUPPORT PROGRAM

➤ **ARTIST-IN-RESIDENCE PROGRAM**

Purpose: To support small independent projects by emerging video makers

Eligibility:
   Citizenship: n/a
   Residency: New York State
   Age: Open
   Special Requirements: Students eligible
   Art Forms: Video (includes video combined with other media or expression such as sculpture, performance, etc.)

Type of Support: $500 equipment access at DCTV

Scope of Program: 10 recipients annually (5 awards given twice each year)

Application/Selection Process:
   Deadline: February 28 and August 31, annually

Please read carefully!
Do not contact any listed organization unless you fulfill all eligibility requirements.

Preferred Initial Contact: Send SASE for information
Application Procedure: Submit project proposal, sample tape
Selection Process: Jury of independent media producers
Notification Process: Phone call
Formal Report of Grant Required: No

EQUIPMENT ACCESS

Video: Production for S-VHS, VHS, Video-8, Hi-8; post-production for S-VHS, VHS, 3/4"

Comments: The Community Projects program offers free or low-cost use of equipment to members interested in producing tapes that would impact their communities in a positive way. Applications for Community Projects are accepted on an ongoing basis. Use of production equipment for other approved projects is available at low rates. Post-production facilities are available to the public on a first-come, first-served basis.

TECHNICAL ASSISTANCE PROGRAMS AND SERVICES

Programs of Special Interest: DCTV regularly screens works by new videomakers. Producers can submit tapes at any time for consideration. Call 212-941-1298 for information about screenings and tape submissions. Internships are available in all areas of the center, and interns receive free access to workshops and to equipment (for work on individual projects). DCTV also hosts festivals including the Act of Video Festival, Lookout Lesbian and Gay Video Fest, and Youth Festival. Works-in-Progress meetings provide support for producers, including critiques of their work. Membership is $30 annually.

DURHAM ARTS COUNCIL (DAC)

120 Morris Street
Durham, NC 27701
919-560-2720
CONTACT: MARGARET J. DeMOTT, DIRECTOR OF ARTIST SERVICES

PROFILE OF FINANCIAL SUPPORT TO ARTISTS

Total Funding/Value of In-Kind Support: $12,800 for FY 1992-93

Competition for Funding: Total applications, 89; total individuals funded/provided with in-kind support, 17

Grant Range: $250-$1,000

Please read carefully!
Do not contact any listed organization unless you fulfill all eligibility requirements.

DIRECT SUPPORT PROGRAMS
➤ **EMERGING ARTISTS PROGRAM**
CONTACT: ELLA FOUNTAIN PRATT, DIRECTOR AND GRANTS OFFICER
Phone: 919-560-2742
Purpose: To support developing professionals by funding a project pivotal to the advancement of their work and careers as artists
Eligibility:
    Residency: Chatham, Durham, Granville, Orange, or Person counties, 1 year
    Age: 18 or older
    Special Requirements: No degree-seeking students; previous grantees ineligible for 1 year
    Art Forms: All disciplines
Type of Support: Up to $1,000 for projects such as promotion/ presentation, travel, securing services, supplies, or training
Scope of Program: 17 awards, totalling $12,800 in FY 1992-93
Application/Selection Process:
    Deadline: September, annually; contact for exact date
    Preferred Initial Contact: Call or write for application/guidelines
    Application Procedure: Submit application form, samples of work, resumé, project budget, references (optional)
    Selection Process: Anonymous judges, organizational committee
    Notification Process: Phone or letter
    Formal Report of Grant Required: Yes

TECHNICAL ASSISTANCE PROGRAMS AND SERVICES
Programs of Special Interest: Through the Creative Arts in Public Schools (CAPS) program, DAC and Durham schools provide in-class arts residencies and teacher workshops. CenterFest, an outdoor arts festival, exhibits the work of over 200 artists. Artist Services offers artists workshops on taxes, copyright, slide preparation, grantwriting.

DUTCHESS COUNTY ARTS COUNCIL (DCAC)

39 Market Street
Poughkeepsie, NY 12601
914-454-3222
CONTACT: SHERRE WESLEY, EXECUTIVE DIRECTOR

PROFILE OF FINANCIAL SUPPORT TO ARTISTS
Total Funding/Value of In-Kind Support: $12,500 in FY 1992-93

Please read carefully!
Do not contact any listed organization unless you fulfill all eligibility requirements.

Competition for Funding: Total applications, 16; total individuals funded/provided with in-kind support, 5

Grant Range: Up to $5,000

DIRECT SUPPORT PROGRAMS

➤ **INDIVIDUAL ARTISTS FELLOWSHIP PROGRAM**

Purpose: To provide support to individuals who are in the developmental phase of a career as a creative artist

Eligibility:
   Citizenship: U.S.
   Residency: Dutchess County, 2 years
   Age: 18 or older
   Special Requirements: No students enrolled in degree programs
   Art Forms: Eligible disciplines change yearly

Type of Support: Up to $3,000; recipients perform a public service activity

Scope of Program: 2 awards in 1992

Application/Selection Process:
   Deadline: May, annually; contact for exact date
   Preferred Initial Contact: Call or write for application/guidelines
   Application Procedure: Submit application form, resumé, proof of residency, samples of work
   Selection Process: Peer panel of artists, board of directors
   Notification Process: Letter
   Formal Report of Grant Required: Yes

➤ **SPECIAL CONSTITUENCY ART AND COMMUNITY AWARD**

Purpose: To recognize the achievement of people of various minority ethnicities, creeds, physical capabilities, ages and sexual orientations, and acknowledge their cultural contribution to the community

Eligibility:
   Residency: Dutchess county, two years
   Art Forms: All disciplines

Type of Support: $5,000 annually; may be split between more than one person

Scope of Program: 1 artist in 1993

Application/Selection Process:
   Deadline: September, annually; contact for exact date
   Preferred Initial Contact: Call or write for application/guidelines
   Application Procedure: Submit application form, work samples
   Selection Process: Special Constituency panel; board of directors
   Notification Process: Letter
   Formal Report of Grant Required: Yes

Please read carefully!
Do not contact any listed organization unless you fulfill all eligibility requirements.

➤ **PROJECT GRANTS: DUTCHESS ART FUND/NYSCA DECENTRALIZATION GRANTS**

Purpose: To support art and cultural projects of Dutchess County and Ulster County nonprofit organizations

Eligibility:

Citizenship: U.S.

Residency: Dutchess County, Ulster County

Special Requirements: Individual artists must be sponsored by a Dutchess County or Ulster County nonprofit organization; project must take place in Dutchess or Ulster County and be open to the public

Art Forms: Dance, music, opera/musical theater, theater, visual arts, design arts, crafts, photography, media arts, literature, folk arts, humanities, multi-disciplinary

Type of Support: Up to $5,000 for specific project

Scope of Program: In FY 1992-93, $25,000 allocated for Dutchess and $13,000 for Ulster; 2 individual projects funded with grants averaging $1,500

Application/Selection Process:

Deadline: September, annually; contact for exact date

Preferred Initial Contact: Sponsor attends an application workshop or discusses project with DCAC staff

Application Procedure: Sponsor submits application form, board list, financial statement, proof of nonprofit status, project budget, support documentation (e.g, samples of artist's work, reviews), artist's resumé

Selection Process: Panel of community leaders, artists, and arts professionals, board of directors

Notification Process: Letter

Formal Report of Grant Required: Yes

TECHNICAL ASSISTANCE PROGRAMS AND SERVICES

Programs of Special Interest: DCAC provides artist referrals, maintains an arts resource library and an artist registry, and publishes several directories, including the *Mid-Hudson Directory of Arts and Cultural Resources*. Workshops address topics such as arts-in-education, grantwriting and marketing. The council also offers a telephone hotline, which publicizes arts events, and a quarterly newspaper.

EL PASO ARTS RESOURCE DEPARTMENT (ARD)

2 Civic Center Plaza, 6th Floor
El Paso, TX 79901
915-541-4481 (Voice & TDD)
FAX: 915-541-4902
CONTACT: ALEJANDRINA DREW, DIRECTOR

PROFILE OF FINANCIAL SUPPORT TO ARTISTS

Total Funding/Value of In-Kind Support: $3,616 in FY 1992

Competition for Funding: Total applications, 2; total individuals funded/provided with in-kind support, 2

Grant Range: n/a

DIRECT SUPPORT PROGRAMS

➤ **INDIVIDUAL PROJECT SUPPORT PROGRAM**

Purpose: To provide funding for local, community-based arts/cultural projects that have specific goals, objectives, and short-term time horizons. Funding is available for individuals (under an umbrella organization), emerging groups and established organizations.

Eligibility:

Residency: City of El Paso

Special Requirements: Local artist must apply with nonprofit, government, or educational umbrella organization; applicant must have matching funds (up to 50% may be in-kind support); no commercial projects

Art Forms: All disciplines

Type of Support: Matching grant for specific project

Scope of Program: 1 grant, totalling $1,515, in FY 1992

Application/Selection Process:

Deadline: January 15, annually

Preferred Initial Contact: Write or call for information

Application Procedure: All applicants must attend a funding workshop; submit application form, project budget, umbrella contract, proof of umbrella's nonprofit status, umbrella's list of board and staff, samples of artist's works (optional), artist's resumé (optional), additional support material (optional)

Selection Process: Review and scoring by multi-disciplinary panel

Notification Process: Letter

Formal Report of Grant Required: Yes

➤ **EMERGENCY FUNDING PROGRAM**

Purpose: To provide limited funding for artists and groups in El Paso in the event of an emergency or an extraordinary opportunity that may arise outside the regular funding cycle

Eligibility:

Residency: City of El Paso residents only

Special Requirements: Local artists must have a nonprofit sponsor; 50% cash matching funds required.

Art Forms: All disciplines

Type of Support: Matching grant for a project emergency or extraordinary opportunity

Scope of Program: 1 grant, totalling $2,101, in FY 1992

Application/Selection Process:

Deadline: 15th of each month

Application Procedure: All applicants must attend a funding workshop; submit application form, project budget, umbrella contract, proof of umbrella's nonprofit status, umbrella's list of board and staff, samples of artist's works (optional), artist's resumé (optional), additional support material (optional)

Selection Process: Organization staff, advisory board

Notification Process: Letter

Formal Report of Grant Required: Yes

TECHNICAL ASSISTANCE PROGRAMS AND SERVICES

Programs of Special Interest: ARD's directory of local artists and arts organizations is distributed nationally to U.S. and Mexican presenters.

EMPOWERMENT PROJECT (EP)

3403 Highway 54 West
Chapel Hill, NC 27516
919-967-1963
CONTACT: DAVID KASPER, EXECUTIVE DIRECTOR

California Center:
1653 18th Street, #3
Santa Monica, CA 90404
310-828-8807
CONTACT: JAKE BUCKWALTER, FACILITY MANAGER

EQUIPMENT ACCESS

Video: Post-production (on-line and off-line) for 3/4", VHS, S-VHS, Hi-8 formats with interformat capability

Please read carefully!
Do not contact any listed organization unless you fulfill all eligibility requirements.

Comments: EP offers low-cost video post-production, duplication and computer facilities and services at its main location in North Carolina. Applications are accepted for partial subsidies in the form of reduced facility rates. Equipment includes a Video Toaster. A 90-seat screening auditorium is available for video exhibitions as is equipment for location screenings. The original California center continues operating as a low-cost video post-production facility.

TECHNICAL ASSISTANCE PROGRAMS AND SERVICES
Programs of Special Interest: The Empowerment Project functions as a media center for independent videographers, filmmakers, artists and activists. EP coordinates and supports progressive organizing efforts, and produces and distributes its own documentary films and videos. The North Carolina location also functions as a learning center for developing media skills and exploring appropriate uses of new media technology. There is a library of instructional materials as well as media-related periodicals and reference works. Individual instruction and consulting is available, and a database of information is being developed which will allow EP to act as a clearinghouse for media information and contacts, and as a referral service to connect people with media projects and organizing efforts. Wordprocessing, database, print graphics and publishing facilities are available. EP expects to offer organized workshops and seminars by late 1993.

EZTV

8547 Santa Monica Boulevard
West Hollywood, CA 90069
310-657-1532
FAX: 310-657-6558
CONTACT: MICHAEL MASUCCI, DIRECTOR

EQUIPMENT ACCESS
Video: Production for VHS, S-VHS, 3/4", Video 8, Hi-8; post-production (off-line) for VHS, S-VHS, 3/4"

TECHNICAL ASSISTANCE PROGRAMS AND SERVICES
Programs of Special Interest: EZTV exhibits video art and maintains a resource center.

Please read carefully!
Do not contact any listed organization unless you fulfill all eligibility requirements.

FILM ARTS FOUNDATION (FAF)

346 Ninth Street
Second Floor
San Francisco, CA 94103
415-552-8760
CONTACT: GAIL SILVA, DIRECTOR

PROFILE OF FINANCIAL SUPPORT TO ARTISTS

Total Funding/Value of In-Kind Support: $59,000 in FAF grants for
FY 1993

Competition for Funding: Total applications, 299; total individuals
funded/provided with in-kind support, 22

Grant Range: $1,000-$4,000

DIRECT SUPPORT PROGRAMS

➤ **FAF GRANTS PROGRAM**

Purpose: To aid experimental and independent media artists who
have little recourse to traditional funding sources, or whose projects are
at a stage where a small grant can have a significant impact

Eligibility:

Residency: 10-county San Francisco Bay Area (San Francisco,
Marin, Sonoma, Napa, Solano, Alameda, Contra Costa, San
Mateo, Santa Clara, Santa Cruz counties), 1 year

Special Requirements: Applicant must have artistic control of
project; no commercial projects; previous grantees ineligible for 2
years

Art Forms: Film, video

Type of Support: $3,000 Personal Works awards for new, short
personal works that can be completely realized within this budget
(funded projects must be available for Film Arts Festival); $1,000
Development awards for projects in the development and fundraising stages; $4,000 Completion/Distribution awards for films or
tapes that can be completed or distributed with this amount

Scope of Program: 14 Personal Works awards, 5 Development
awards, 3 Completion/Distribution awards in 1993

Application/Selection Process:

Deadline: May, annually; contact for exact date

Preferred Initial Contact: Call or write for application/guidelines

Application Procedure: Submit application form, resumé, project
description and budget; semi-finalists submit samples of work

Selection Process: Independent panel of artists and arts professionals

Notification Process: Letter 2-3 months after deadline

Formal Report of Grant Required: Yes

Please read carefully!
Do not contact any listed organization unless you fulfill all eligibility requirements.

EQUIPMENT ACCESS
Film: Production and post-production for Super 8, 16mm
Comments: Members receive low-cost access to equipment and editing facility for noncommercial projects ($35 membership fee).

TECHNICAL ASSISTANCE PROGRAMS AND SERVICES
Programs of Special Interest: FAF maintains a resource library whose collection focuses on distribution, fundraising, grantwriting, copyright and media law, and film/video festivals; a videotape library of members' works; a Resumé File of information relating to members' backgrounds and interests; and listings of projects seeking interns and of members who are seeking internships. FAF exhibits independent film and video, and holds the annual Film Arts Festival. Seminars and workshops cover the art, technical processes, and business of independent film and video (fees involved). The Group Legal Plan includes initial office or telephone consultation at no charge for up to 30 minutes, and reduced rates thereafter. Association health plan options are available. The Project Sponsorship program makes available nonprofit fiscal agent services to selected noncommercial film/video projects. Staff assistance is available for developing project proposals, fundraising, and exhibition/distribution plans. FAF's monthly newsletter, *Release Print*, provides comprehensive coverage of regional independent film and video activities. (Membership required for most FAF services.)

FILM IN THE CITIES (FITC)

NOTICE: At the time of this printing, Film in the Cities is no longer operating. The grant programs it has administered will be run by other agencies, as yet undetermined. Please contact the organizations listed under each program title for further details.

DIRECT SUPPORT PROGRAMS
➤ **REGIONAL FILM/VIDEO GRANTS PROGRAM**
National Endowment for the Arts, Media Arts Program
Nancy Hanks Center
1100 Pennsylvania Avenue, NW
Room 720
Washington, DC 20506
202-682-5452
Purpose: To assist independent film and video artists whose personal work shows promise of excellence

Please read carefully!
Do not contact any listed organization unless you fulfill all eligibility requirements.

Eligibility:
   Residency: Minnesota, Iowa, Wisconsin, North Dakota, South Dakota
   Special Requirements: Artist must have creative control over project; commercial projects and projects associated with a degree program ineligible; no full-time students
   Art Forms: Film, video
Type of Support: Production Grants, up to $16,000; Completion Grants, up to $7,000; Encouragement Grants, up to $3,000
Scope of Program: $110,000+ available in 1993: $15,000 in Encouragement Grants and the remainder in Production and Completion Grants
Application/Selection Process:
   Deadline: May, annually; contact for exact date
   Preferred Initial Contact: Call or write for application/guidelines
   Application Procedure: Submit application form, samples of work, project description and budget, resumé, screening notes
   Selection Process: Independent panel of artists and arts professionals
   Notification Process: Letter 4 months after deadline
   Formal Report of Grant Required: Yes

➤ **MCKNIGHT SCREENWRITING FELLOWSHIP PROGRAM**
The McKnight Foundation
121 South Eighth Street
Suite 600
Minneapolis, MN 55402
612-333-4220

Purpose: To assist Minnesota screenwriters whose work demonstrates the ability to translate personal artistic vision into well-crafted dramatic, narrative screenplays
Eligibility:
   Citizenship: Open
   Residency: Minnesota only
   Age: Open
   Special Requirements: All applicants must provide documentation of one of the following for a screenplay they have authored: a public staged reading, a screenplay sale or option, a professional workshop production, or a public screening or broadcast of a film or video from a screenplay the applicant has written; commercial projects, organizational projects, and work associated with a degree program are ineligible; no full-time students
   Art Forms: Screenwriting
Type of Support: $5,000 fellowship
Scope of Program: 5 awards of $5,000 given biennially
Application/Selection Process:
   Deadline: Fall of odd-numbered years; contact for exact dates

Please read carefully!
Do not contact any listed organization unless you fulfill all eligibility requirements.

Preferred Initial Contact: Call or write for application/guidelines
Application Procedure: Submit one feature-length/hour-long screenplay or three half-hour screenplays with brief description; resumé; artist's statement (optional)
Selection Process: Independent 3-person panel
Notification Process: Letter within 4 months after deadline
Formal Report of Grant Required: Yes

FILM/VIDEO ARTS (F/VA)

817 Broadway at 12th Street
Second Floor
New York, NY 10003
212-673-9361
FAX: 212-475-3467

EQUIPMENT ACCESS

Film: Production and post-production for 16mm

Video: Production for Hi-8; post-production for VHS, 3/4", Hi-8, S-VHS, Betacam

Comments: Low rates on equipment access are available to artists working on noncommercial projects. Duplication and transfer services available.

TECHNICAL ASSISTANCE PROGRAMS AND SERVICES

Programs of Special Interest: F/VA screens independent works, provides financial assistance for film speaker's fees to nonprofit organizations in New York State and offers beginning and advanced courses in production, editing, and fundraising. F/VA also has an Equipment Rental and General Liability Insurance program for low-budget productions.

FLORIDA DIVISION OF CULTURAL AFFAIRS/ FLORIDA ARTS COUNCIL

Department of State
The Capitol
Tallahassee, FL 32399-0250
904-487-2980
TDD: 904-488-5779
FAX: 904-922-5259

PROFILE OF FINANCIAL SUPPORT TO ARTISTS

Total Funding/Value of In-Kind Support: $195,000 for FY 1992-93

Competition for Funding: Total applications, 483; total individuals funded/provided with in-kind support, 38

Grant Range: $5,000

DIRECT SUPPORT PROGRAMS

➤ **FELLOWSHIP PROGRAM**

Purpose: To enable Florida artists to improve their artistic skills and enhance their careers

Eligibility:
   Residency: Florida, 1 year
   Age: 18 or older
   Special Requirements: Originating, professional artists only; no students pursuing degrees; previous grantees ineligible for 5 years
   Art Forms: Choreography, folk arts, literature (fiction, poetry, children's literature), media arts, music composition, theater (design, playwriting, mime), visual arts (includes photography)and crafts

Type of Support: $5,000

Scope of Program: 38 awards in 1992-93

Application/Selection Process:
   Deadline: Varies; contact the council for details
   Preferred Initial Contact: Call or write for application/guidelines
   Application Procedure: Submit application form, samples of work, support materials (optional)
   Selection Process: Panel of arts professionals
   Notification Process: Letter to all applicants
   Formal Report of Grant Required: Yes

TECHNICAL ASSISTANCE PROGRAMS AND SERVICES

Programs of Special Interest: The *Florida Artists Directory* lists artists interested in Arts in Education residencies (minimum residency, 10 days). The Florida Visiting Artists Program supports 9-

Please read carefully!
Do not contact any listed organization unless you fulfill all eligibility requirements.

to 10-month artist residencies in community colleges (contact Nancy Smith) and is designed to provide artists with opportunities to travel throughout Florida. The Art in State Buildings Program acquires and commissions art for new state buildings, and the Capitol Complex Exhibition Program features work of Florida visual artists in the Capitol Complex. The *Florida Visual Artists Resource Directory* provides information on visual artists residing in Florida.

RICHARD A. FLORSHEIM ART FUND

4202 Fowler Avenue
USF 3033
Tampa, FL 33620-3033
813-949-6886
CONTACT: AUGUST FREUNDLICH, PRESIDENT

PROFILE OF FINANCIAL SUPPORT TO ARTISTS
Total Funding/Value of In-Kind Support: $200,000 in 1992
Competition for Funding: Total applications, n/a; total individuals funded/provided with in-kind support, 35
Grant Range: $1,000-$20,000

DIRECT SUPPORT PROGRAM
➤ **INDIVIDUAL ARTIST GRANTS**
Purpose: To address the situation faced by senior American artists of merit whose previous recognition may have been eclipsed, but who continue to be productive in their work
Eligibility:
    Citizenship: U.S.
    Residency: Open
    Age: Over 55 generally preferred
    Special Requirements: Senior American artists and/or institutions may apply
    Art Forms: Visual arts (includes film/video)
Type of Support: $1,000-$20,000 grants in partial support of museum purchases, exhibitions, catalogs, monographs; the Fund encourages individuals and institutions to seek additional sponsoring monies for proposed projects
Scope of Program: Approximately $200,000 for 35 grants in 1992
Application/Selection Process:
    Deadline: October 1 and March 1, annually
    Preferred Initial Contact: Write for application/guidelines

Please read carefully!
Do not contact any listed organization unless you fulfill all eligibility requirements.

Application Procedure: Submit application form
Selection Process: Board of Trustees
Notification Process: By letter approximately 60 days after deadline
Formal Report of Grant Required: n/a

FRAMELINE

P.O. Box 14792
San Francisco, CA 94114
415-861-5245
FAX: 415-861-1404

PROFILE OF FINANCIAL SUPPORT TO ARTISTS
Total Funding/Value of In-Kind Support: $5,500 in 1992

Competition for Funding: Total applications, 61; total individuals funded/provided with in-kind support, 5

Grant Range: Up to $5,000

DIRECT SUPPORT PROGRAMS
➤ FRAMELINE FILM/VIDEO COMPLETION FUND

Purpose: To support works-in-progress by lesbian and gay video and film artists

Eligibility:
　　Citizenship: Open
　　Residency: Open
　　Special Requirements: All independent producers and nonprofit corporations eligible; project must make unique statement about lesbians and gay men or about issues of concern to lesbians and gay men; project must be in final stages of completion at time of award notification
　　Art Forms: Film, video

Type of Support: Up to $5,000 for project completion (average $1,000-$2,000); work must be made available for screening at the San Francisco International Lesbian and Gay Film Festival

Scope of Program: $5,500 awarded in 1992

Application/Selection Process:
　　Deadline: October, annually; contact for exact date
　　Preferred Initial Contact: Call or write for application/guidelines
　　Application Procedure: Submit application form, $25 application fee, project description or synopsis, project budget, biographies of all personnel, sample of work-in-progress
　　Selection Process: Panel of artists and arts professionals

Please read carefully!
Do not contact any listed organization unless you fulfill all eligibility requirements.

Notification Process: 2 months after deadline
Formal Report of Grant Required: Yes

TECHNICAL ASSISTANCE PROGRAMS AND SERVICES

Programs of Special Interest: Frameline presents the annual San Francisco International Lesbian and Gay Film Festival, distributes films and videos by and about gays and lesbians, and co-hosts other lesbian and gay screenings locally, nationally and internationally. Frameline provides information services on working with theaters, organizations, and festivals.

FULBRIGHT AWARDS

PROFILE OF FINANCIAL SUPPORT TO ARTISTS

Total Funding/Value of In-Kind Support: n/a

Competition for Funding: Total applications, 7,200; total individuals funded/provided with in-kind support, 1,700 (figures approximate)

Grant Range: Varies according to program

Fulbright Awards are administered by two different organizations: the Council for International Exchange of Scholars (CIES) which serves faculty and professionals, and the Institute for International Education (IIE) which serves students and emerging artists.

➤ **FULBRIGHT AWARDS FOR FACULTY AND PROFESSIONALS**
Council for International Exchange of Scholars (CIES)
3007 Tilden Street, NW
Suite 5M
Washington, DC 20008-3009
202-686-7877

Purpose: To promote mutual understanding through scholarly and professional exchange

Eligibility:
  Citizenship: U.S.
  Residency: Persons who have lived outside the U.S. for the full 10-year period immediately preceding application are not eligible
  Special Requirements: Must be a practicing professional or have an advanced degree
  Art Forms: All areas of the visual arts (painting, sculpture, photography, performance, film/video, etc.)

Type of Support: Stipend for maintenance in-country overseas, travel for grantee; other supplemental support (tuition for dependents, housing, etc.) may apply; benefits vary by country and type of award

Scope of Program: A total of 1,000 grants in 135 countries are offered each year to faculty and professionals; the number of opportunities for grants to artists fluctuates by competition; an average competition receives about 3,300 applications

Application/Selection Process:
Deadline: August 1, annually
Preferred Initial Contact: Call for awards/application booklet
Application Procedure: Candidates apply for a specific advertised award opening in a specific country; submit application form, project statement, resumé, 4 letters of recommendation, sample of professional work as applicable
Selection Process: Peer review by independent review committees in the U.S.; selection by binational Fulbright Commissions/U.S. Embassies/Host Institutions abroad
Notification Process: Letter
Formal Report of Grant Required: Yes

➤ **FULBRIGHT AND OTHER GRANTS FOR GRADUATE STUDY AND RESEARCH ABROAD**
Institute of International Education
U.S. Student Programs
809 United Nations Plaza
New York, NY 10017-3580
212-984-5330

Purpose: To enable the government of the United States to increase mutual understanding between the people of the United States and the people of other countries; in addition to grants for academic study and research, grants for practical training in the creative and performing arts are also available

Eligibility:
Citizenship: U.S.
Residency: Open
Age: n/a
Special Requirements: B.A. or equivalent by beginning date of grant
Art Forms: All disciplines

Type of Support: Support includes travel, maintenance and health insurance; funding varies according to program and country of assignment; other grants will be utilized if appropriate for an applicant

Scope of Program: Approximately 700 awards in 1992

Application/Selection Process:
Deadline: October 31, annually
Preferred Initial Contact: Write or call for information

Application Procedure: Submit application form
Selection Process: National Screening Committee; Fulbright Commission or award sponsor in host country; J. William Fullbright Foreign Scholarship Board
Notification Process: Letter by January 31
Formal Report of Grant Required: Yes

THE FUNDING EXCHANGE

666 Broadway, Suite 500
New York, NY 10012

PROFILE OF FINANCIAL SUPPORT TO ARTISTS
Total Funding/Value of In-Kind Support: $200,000 for FY 1992
Competition for Funding: Total applications, 400; total individuals funded/provided with in-kind support, 35
Grant Range: $5,000-$10,000 average

DIRECT SUPPORT PROGRAMS
➤ THE PAUL ROBESON FUND
CONTACT: ROBERT McCULLOUGH, PROGRAM COORDINATOR

Purpose: To support independent socio-political issue film and video documentaries and radio productions that comment on the ills of our society, addressing such issues as sexism, racism, homophobia, AIDS, environmental issues, homelessness, etc. All productions should reach a broad audience, respect the intelligence of the viewers, and combine intellectual clarity with creative use of the medium

Eligibility:
  Special Requirements: Must be affiliated with a tax-exempt organization; priority to projects on issues where there are local or national organizing efforts and issues that have received minimal coverage, and to distribution initiatives that seek to increase the use of social issue films, videos and radio by institutional users, public interest and community-based groups, cable and satellite programmers; no purely personal projects or strictly sociological/anthropological explorations; support given to projects that have little recourse to other funding sources due to the controversial nature of themes; experimental or non-traditional approaches to documentary film, video and radio production are of particular interest to the fund; media artists who are women, gay and lesbian, physically challenged, or from communities of color are particularly encouraged to apply

Please read carefully!
Do not contact any listed organization unless you fulfill all eligibility requirements.

Art Forms: Film, video (preproduction and distribution), radio productions (preproduction, production and distribution); animators may apply if their theme is appropriate for the Fund

Type of Support: $5,000-$10,000

Scope of Program: $200,000 granted in FY 1992

Application/Selection Process:
  Deadline: December 1, annually
  Preferred Initial Contact: Write for application/guidelines only between September 1 and December 1—do not contact the organization regarding the Robeson Fund outside of those dates; no phone calls please
  Application Procedure: Submit application form (includes project budget and description, fundraising and distribution strategy, project bios)
  Selection Process: Staff, board
  Notification Process: 4 months after deadline

GEORGIA COUNCIL FOR THE ARTS (GCA)

530 Means Street, NW
Suite 115
Atlanta, GA 30318
404-651-7920
FAX: 404-651-7922
TDD: 404-255-0056

CONTACT: RICHARD WATERHOUSE, VISUAL ARTS AND DANCE MANAGER

PROFILE OF FINANCIAL SUPPORT TO ARTISTS

Total Funding/Value of In-Kind Support: $118,000 for FY 1993

Competition for Funding: Total applications, 223; total individuals funded/provided with in-kind support, 70

Grant Range: $500-$5,000

DIRECT SUPPORT PROGRAMS

➤ **INDIVIDUAL ARTIST GRANTS**

Purpose: To provide income for artists whose work demonstrates artistic merit and whose careers will potentially benefit from the completion of a particular project

Eligibility:
  Residency: Georgia, 1 year
  Special Requirements: No full-time students; previous grantees ineligible for 2 years
  Art Forms: All disciplines

Please read carefully!
Do not contact any listed organization unless you fulfill all eligibility requirements.

Type of Support: Up to $5,000 for a specific project that includes a public service component

Scope of Program: 70 awards in FY 1993

Application/Selection Process:
  Deadline: April 1, annually
  Preferred Initial Contact: Call or write for application/guidelines
  Application Procedure: Submit application form, samples of work, resumé, project budget
  Selection Process: Multidisciplinary panel
  Notification Process: Letter in June
  Formal Report of Grant Required: Yes

TECHNICAL ASSISTANCE PROGRAMS AND SERVICES

Programs of Special Interest: The Artist-in-Education (AIE) Program (contact 404-651-7931) provides 3- to 18-week residencies in Georgia schools; GCA maintains the Georgia Artists Registry, and the Georgia Touring Roster lists artists approved for Georgia Touring Grants activities. The services of Georgia Volunteer Lawyers for the Arts are available to eligible artists.

GERMAN ACADEMIC EXCHANGE SERVICE/ DEUTSCHER AKADEMISCHER AUSTAUCHDIENST (DAAD)

950 Third Avenue, 3rd Floor
New York, NY 10022
212-758-3223
FAX: 212-755-5780

PROFILE OF FINANCIAL SUPPORT TO ARTISTS

Total Funding/Value of In-Kind Support: n/a
Competition for Funding: n/a
Grant Range: n/a

DIRECT SUPPORT PROGRAM
➤ **ARTIST IN BERLIN PROGRAM**

Purpose: To promote the exchange of artists' experiences and the concern for current cultural issues in other countries

Eligibility:
  Citizenship: Open internationally
  Residency: Open
  Age: Open

Please read carefully!
Do not contact any listed organization unless you fulfill all eligibility requirements.

Special Requirements: Accomplished artists only
Art Forms: Film/video, literature, music composition; (visual arts—including video art—by nomination only)
Type of Support: Residency in Berlin for 1 year, including studio and housing, stipend to cover living expenses, round-trip transportation (including spouse and children), health insurance (cost deducted from stipend)
Scope of Program: 20 residencies annually; 5 to media artists
Application/Selection Process:
Deadline: January 1, annually
Preferred Initial Contact: Write or call for guidelines
Application Procedure: Submit application form, samples of work, artistic and professional background, listing of previous prizes won and experiences abroad
Selection Process: International jury
Notification Process: Letter by May
Formal Report of Grant Required: n/a

JOHN SIMON GUGGENHEIM MEMORIAL FOUNDATION

90 Park Avenue
New York, NY 10016
212-687-4470

PROFILE OF FINANCIAL SUPPORT TO ARTISTS

Total Funding/Value of In-Kind Support: $4,375,000 for FY 1991 (includes grants to nonartists)
Competition for Funding: Total applications 3,400 (includes nonartists); total individuals funded/provided with in-kind support, 167 (about 60 artists)
Grant Range: $10,000-$30,000

DIRECT SUPPORT PROGRAMS
➤ GUGGENHEIM FELLOWSHIP

Purpose: To further the development of scholars and artists by assisting them to engage in research in any field of knowledge and creation in any of the arts
Eligibility:
Citizenship: U.S., Canada, Latin America, the Caribbean (permanent residents also eligible)

Please read carefully!
Do not contact any listed organization unless you fulfill all eligibility requirements.

Special Requirements: Artists must have already demonstrated exceptional creative ability
Art Forms: All disciplines
Type of Support: $26,000 average grant
Scope of Program: About 60 artists funded in 1991
Application/Selection Process:
Deadline: October 1 (U.S. & Canada), December 1 (Latin America and the Caribbean)
Preferred Initial Contact: Write for application/guidelines
Application Procedure: Submit application form, samples of work, references, 3 supplementary statements regarding career and proposed use of funds
Selection Process: Juries of artists and arts professionals, Committee of Selection
Notification Process: 5-6 months after deadline
Formal Report of Grant Required: Yes

HALLWALLS CONTEMPORARY ARTS CENTER

700 Main Street
Buffalo, NY 14202
716-854-5828

TECHNICAL ASSISTANCE PROGRAMS AND SERVICES
Programs of Special Interest: Besides ongoing opportunities for artists in all media (painting, sculpture, installation, performance art, video, film) to exhibit and present their work, and to be paid fees for doing so, Hallwalls maintains a slide registry for visual artists and independent producers. Video artists and independent producers: contact Ms. Chris Hill, Video Curator. Visual artists: send slides or contact Sara Kellner, Exhibitions Curator. Performance artists: contact Ronald Ehmke, Performance Curator. No deadlines, no formal application form, selection is by curatorial staff.

Please read carefully!
Do not contact any listed organization unless you fulfill all eligibility requirements.

HAWAII STATE FOUNDATION ON CULTURE AND THE ARTS (SFCA)

335 Merchant Street
Room 202
Honolulu, HI 96813
808-586-0300
FAX: 808-586-0308
CONTACT: ALAN NAKAMURA, INFORMATION SPECIALIST

TECHNICAL ASSISTANCE PROGRAMS AND SERVICES
Programs of Special Interest: The Hawaii State Foundation on Culture and the Arts offers a bimonthly newsletter, *Hawaii Artreach*, which includes national opportunities in the arts and humanities.

HEADLANDS CENTER FOR THE ARTS

944 Fort Barry
Sausalito, CA 94965
415-331-2787
FAX: 415-331-3857
CONTACT: JENNIFER DOWLEY, EXECUTIVE DIRECTOR

PROFILE OF FINANCIAL SUPPORT TO ARTISTS
Total Funding/Value of In-Kind Support: n/a
Competition for Funding: n/a
Grant Range: n/a

DIRECT SUPPORT PROGRAMS
➤ **REGIONAL, NATIONAL AND INTERNATIONAL RESIDENCIES**
Purpose: To provide time for the incubation and investigation of new ideas and to nurture exchange among artists of all mediums
Eligibility:
   Residency: San Francisco Bay Area (regional residencies); Minnesota, North Carolina, Ohio, Philadelphia (national residencies); Italy, Sweden, Norway (international residencies)
   Special Requirements: No students; previous grantees ineligible for 5 years
   Art Forms: All disciplines

Please read carefully!
Do not contact any listed organization unless you fulfill all eligibility requirements.

Type of Support: Long-term regional residencies, 11-month residency including studio space and $2,500 stipend; short-term regional residencies, 4-week to 3-month residencies including studio space, housing, $500 monthly stipend; national and international residencies, 2- to 5-month residency including studio space, housing, $500 monthly stipend, travel expenses, dinner served 5 nights/week for live-in residents

Scope of Program: 5 long-term regional residencies, 3 short-term regional residencies, 5 national and international residencies in 1992

Application/Selection Process:
    Deadline: Varies depending on state's or country's program
    Preferred Initial Contact: Call or write for application/guidelines
    Application Procedure: Submit application form, samples of work, resumé, references; prospective residents interviewed when possible
    Selection Process: Organization staff, board of directors, peer panel of artists
    Notification Process: Recipients by phone; nonrecipients by letter
    Formal Report of Grant Required: No

HELENA PRESENTS

15 North Ewing
Helena, MT 59601
406-443-0287
CONTACT: GALEN MCKIBBEN OR SUZANNE WILCOX, 406-933-8384

PROFILE OF FINANCIAL SUPPORT TO ARTISTS
Total Funding/Value of In-Kind Support: $27,500 for 1992
Competition for Funding: Total applications, 132; total individuals funded/provided with in-kind support, 14
Grant Range: $1,000-$5,000

DIRECT SUPPORT PROGRAMS
➤ **ARTISTS PROJECTS REGIONAL INITIATIVE**
Purpose: To fund artists' projects that are innovative and adventurous and that explore new definitions of art forms or cultural definitions
Eligibility:
    Residency: Colorado, Idaho, Montana, Nevada, Utah, Wyoming, 1 year
    Special Requirements: No students enrolled in degree programs; previous grantees ineligible for 1 cycle; projects that are solely

traditional in intent are ineligible; intercultural projects must involve artists active in the ethnic traditions to be explored
Art Forms: Dance, music/sound, theater, visual arts, video, film, text, performance art, installations, environmental art, environmental performance works, interdisciplinary, multi-disciplinary
Type of Support: $1,000-$5,000 (most grants $3,500 and under); public presentation of work required
Scope of Program: 14 grants totalling $27,500 in 1992
Application/Selection Process:
   Deadline: February 1, annually
   Preferred Initial Contact: Write or call for application and guidelines; the program is co-administered by the Colorado Dance Festival, P.O. Box 356, Boulder, CO 30306; 303-442-7666
   Application Procedure: Submit application form, project description and budget, biographies or resumés for key artistic personnel, samples of work, 2 reviews or 2 letters of support
   Selection Process: Interdisciplinary, culturally diverse panel of artists and arts professionals
   Notification Process: Approximately 7 months after deadline
   Formal Report of Grant Required: Yes

IDAHO COMMISSION ON THE ARTS (ICA)

304 West State Street
Boise, ID 83720
208-334-2119
FAX: 208-334-2488
CONTACT: JACQUELINE S. CRIST, ARTIST SERVICES DIRECTOR

PROFILE OF FINANCIAL SUPPORT TO ARTISTS
Total Funding/Value of In-Kind Support: $46,000 in 1992 (not including technical assistance funding)
Competition for Funding: Total applications, 92; total individuals funded/provided with in-kind support, 8
Grant Range: Up to $5,000

DIRECT SUPPORT PROGRAMS
➤ **FELLOWSHIP AWARDS**
Purpose: To recognize outstanding work of exceptionally talented individual artists
Eligibility:
   Citizenship: U.S.

Please read carefully!
Do not contact any listed organization unless you fulfill all eligibility requirements.

Residency: Idaho, 1 year
Age: 18 or older
Special Requirements: No degree-seeking students
Art Forms: Disciplines alternate between literature, dance, music, theater, media arts (odd-numbered years) and visual arts, crafts, design arts (even-numbered years)
Type of Support: $5,000 fellowships
Scope of Program: 6 awards in 1992
Application/Selection Process:
    Deadline: Mid-March, 1993; contact for exact dates thereafter
    Preferred Initial Contact: Call or write for application/guidelines
    Application Procedure: Submit application form, samples of work, resumé
    Selection Process: Peer panel of artists and arts professionals
    Notification Process: Phone call to recipients, letter to all applicants
    Formal Report of Grant Required: Yes

➤ **WORKSITES AWARDS**

Purpose: Worksites are awarded to artists seeking to work with a master, or to artists seeking an artist colony residency, time to develop new work or work-in-progress, or travel to investigate ideas relevant to existing work or work-in-progress
Eligibility:
    Citizenship: U.S.
    Residency: Idaho, 1 year
    Age: 18 or older
    Special Requirements: No degree-seeking students; previous recipients ineligible for 5 years
    Art Forms: Disciplines alternate between media arts, literature, dance, music, theater (odd-numbered years) and visual arts, crafts, design arts (even-numbered years)
Type of Support: Up to $5,000
Scope of Program: 2 awards in 1992
Application/Selection Process:
    Deadline: Mid-March, 1993; contact for exact dates thereafter
    Preferred Initial Contact: Call or write for application/guidelines
    Application Procedure: Submit application form, samples of work, resumé
    Selection Process: Peer panel of artists and arts professionals
    Notification Process: Phone call to recipients, letter to all applicants
    Formal Report of Grant Required: Yes

Please read carefully!
Do not contact any listed organization unless you fulfill all eligibility requirements.

➤ **SUDDEN OPPORTUNITY AWARDS**

Purpose: To support a professional opportunity that is uniquely available during a limited time

Eligibility:
   Citizenship: U.S.
   Residency: Idaho, 1 year
   Age: 18 or older
   Special Requirements: No degree-seeking students
   Art Forms: All disciplines

Type of Support: Up to $1,000

Scope of Program: $8,000 available in 1993

Application/Selection Process:
   Deadline: Quarterly; contact for exact dates
   Preferred Initial Contact: Call or write for application/guidelines
   Application Procedure: Submit application form, samples of work, resumé
   Selection Process: Staff review and commission decision
   Notification Process: Phone call to recipients, letter to all applicants
   Formal Report of Grant Required: Yes

TECHNICAL ASSISTANCE PROGRAMS AND SERVICES

Programs of Special Interest: Funds available on a limited basis for attendance at conferences and workshops and for management consultant fees for organizations; requests may be for one-half of the cost of the activities, and awards are generally between $100 and $500; grant-writing assistance available for organizations and individuals

ILLINOIS ARTS COUNCIL (IAC)

100 West Randolph
Suite 10-500
Chicago, IL 60601
800-237-6994 (in Illinois) or 312-814-6750
TDD: 312-814-4831
FAX: 312-814-1471
CONTACT: B. ROSE PARISI, ARTISTS SERVICES COORDINATOR

PROFILE OF FINANCIAL SUPPORT TO ARTISTS

Total Funding/Value of In-Kind Support: $411,500 for FY 1992

Competition for Funding: Total applications, 1,335; total individuals funded/provided with in-kind support, 133

Grant Range: $700-$10,000

Please read carefully!
Do not contact any listed organization unless you fulfill all eligibility requirements.

DIRECT SUPPORT PROGRAMS

➤ **ARTISTS FELLOWSHIP PROGRAM**

Purpose: To recognize Illinois artists of exceptional talent for their outstanding work and commitment within the arts

Eligibility:

    Citizenship: U.S. or permanent resident alien status

    Residency: Illinois, one year

    Special Requirements: No students; previous grantees ineligible for 1-2 years

    Art Forms: Disciplines alternate on a two-year cycle: Choreography, crafts, media arts, playwriting/screenwriting, visual arts in even-numbered years; ethnic and folk arts, interdisciplinary/performance art, music composition, photography, poetry and prose in odd-numbered years

Type of Support: $5,000-$10,000 fellowships; $500 finalist awards

Scope of Program: 72 fellowship awards; 33 finalist awards in FY 1992

Application/Selection Process:

    Deadline: September 1, annually

    Preferred Initial Contact: Call or write for application/guidelines

    Application Procedure: Submit application form, samples of work, proof of residency

    Selection Process: Panel of out-of-state artists and arts professionals, IAC board

    Notification Process: Letter 3-4 months after deadline

    Formal Report of Funding Required: Yes

TECHNICAL ASSISTANCE PROGRAMS AND SERVICES

Programs of Special Interest: IAC maintains the unjuried Illinois Artists Registry. The Arts-in-Education Residency program administers 5-day to 8-month school and community residencies.

IMAGE FILM/VIDEO CENTER

75 Bennett Street, NW
Suite M-1
Atlanta, GA 30309
404-352-4225
CONTACT: NANCY KIRACOFE, OPERATIONS MANAGER

EQUIPMENT ACCESS

Film: Production and post-production for Super 8, 16mm

Video: Production for VHS, S-VHS; post-production for VHS, 3/4"

Comments: IMAGE offers equipment access at low cost to independent media artists working on noncommercial projects. A $35 membership fee ($20 for senior citizens and students) and a $25 access fee are required. The On-Line Program provides access to local commercial production and post-production equipment and facilities at low cost. Members interested in the On-Line Program must submit a $25 application fee.

TECHNICAL ASSISTANCE PROGRAMS AND SERVICES

Programs of Special Interest: IMAGE acts as a fiscal agent for member independent producers and exhibits independent films and videos. The annual Atlanta Film and Video Festival features over 30 independent works and distributes cash awards and equipment prizes ($25 entry fee, January deadline; contact Claire Reynolds, Events Coordinator). IMAGE also sponsors the annual Southeastern Screenwriting Competition; winning screenplays are sent to story editors at major production companies in Los Angeles and New York ($25 entry fee, July deadline; residents of VA, FL, KY, SC, NC, GA, AL, MS, LA, and DC are eligible). IMAGE conducts workshops and seminars on topics such as film and video technology, production, fundraising, and budgeting (fees involved).

INDEPENDENT FEATURE PROJECT (IFP)

New York Branch:
Independent Feature Project
132 West 21st Street, 6th Floor
New York, NY 10011
212-243-7777
FAX: 212-243-3882
CONTACT: CATHERINE TAIT, EXECUTIVE DIRECTOR

Los Angeles Branch:
Independent Feature Project/West
5550 Wilshire Boulevard, Suite 204
Los Angeles, CA 90036
213-937-4379
FAX: 213-937-4038
CONTACT: DAWN HUDSON, EXECUTIVE DIRECTOR

Please read carefully!
Do not contact any listed organization unless you fulfill all eligibility requirements.

Minneapolis Branch:
Independent Feature Project/North
119 North 4th Street, Suite 202
Minneapolis, MN 55401
612-338-0871
FAX: 612-338-6673
CONTACT: JANE MINTON-FORS, EXECUTIVE DIRECTOR

San Francisco Branch:
Independent Feature Project, Northern California
P.O. Box 460278
San Francisco, CA 94146
415-431-5890
FAX: 415-431-4349
CONTACT: JEFFREY HARDY, EXECUTIVE DIRECTOR

Chicago Branch:
Independent Feature Project, Midwest
116 West Illinois Street, 2nd Floor
Chicago, IL 60610
312-467-4437
CONTACT: JIM VINCENT, PRESIDENT

Miami Branch:
Independent Feature Project, South
1205 Washington Avenue
Miami Beach, FL 33139
305-531-7621
FAX: 305-674-3224
CONTACT: SUSAN SCHEIN, EXECUTIVE DIRECTOR

TECHNICAL ASSISTANCE PROGRAMS AND SERVICES

Programs of Special Interest: IFP is a nonprofit, membership organization that provides information, support, and education programs to independent filmmakers. Services include seminars, workshops, screenings, advice, and referrals.

Please read carefully!
Do not contact any listed organization unless you fulfill all eligibility requirements.

INDIANA ARTS COMMISSION (IAC)

402 West Washington, Room 072
Indianapolis, IN 46204
317-232-1268
TDD: 317-233-3001
FAX: 317-232-5595
CONTACT: BOB BURNETT, INDIVIDUAL ARTIST MANAGER

PROFILE OF FINANCIAL SUPPORT TO ARTISTS

Total Funding/Value of In-Kind Support: $110,000 in FY 1993

Competition for Funding: Total applications, 191; total individuals funded/provided with in-kind support, 31

Grant Range: Up to $5,000

DIRECT SUPPORT PROGRAMS

➤ **INDIVIDUAL ARTIST FELLOWSHIPS (IAF)**

Purpose: To assist artists with activities significant to their professional growth and recognition, or with the creation or completion of a project

Eligibility:

　Residency: Indiana, 1 year

　Special Requirements: High school and undergraduate students ineligible

　Art Forms: Visual arts (including crafts, design arts, folk arts), media arts eligible in odd-numbered years; performing arts (including dance, theater, folk arts), literature eligible in even-numbered years

Type of Support: $2,000 Associate Fellowship; $5,000 Master Fellowship

Scope of Program: 30 fellowships in FY 1993

Application/Selection Process:

　Deadline: April 1, annually

　Preferred Initial Contact: Call or write for application/guidelines

　Application Procedure: Submit application form, samples of work

　Selection Process: Panel of artists and arts professionals, board of directors

　Notification Process: Letter

　Formal Report of Grant Required: Yes

➤ **ARTS PROJECTS AND SERIES (APS)**

Purpose: The Arts Projects and Series (APS) program awards grants to not-for-profit organizations for high-quality arts projects and ongoing programs. Artist initiated projects are accepted.

Please read carefully!
Do not contact any listed organization unless you fulfill all eligibility requirements.

Eligibility:
    Citizenship: Open
    Residency: Open, but project must benefit Indiana residents
    Special Requirements: Artist must be sponsored by a not-for-profit organization; applicant must be able to match on a dollar-for-dollar basis any award from IAC; the match can be a combination of cash and in-kind goods and services
    Art Forms: All disciplines
Type of Support: Applicants are eligible to receive up to one-half of their project budget; the average award is between $2,000 and $3,000
Scope of Program: 1 individual project funded in FY 1993
Application/Selection Process:
    Deadline: February 1, annually, for projects occurring in the following fiscal year (July 1 - June 30)
    Preferred Initial Contact: Call or write for application guidelines
    Application Procedure: Submit application (original and 14 copies) and appropriate artistic documentation (tapes, slides, photographs, etc.)
    Selection Process: Peer panel review process; meetings are open to the public
    Notification Process: By letter
    Formal Report of Grant Required: Yes

TECHNICAL ASSISTANCE PROGRAMS AND SERVICES

Programs of Special Interest: The Arts in Education (AIE) program places professional artists in educational settings throughout Indiana for 1- to 8-month residencies; the Visiting Artist Program (VAP) brings artists to educational settings to offer adults and children introductory arts experiences (contact Education Program Specialist). The Presenter Touring Program (PTP) brings Indiana artists to under-funded, underrepresented urban and rural areas of the state to present performances, exhibitions, or readings (contact Media Arts Program Specialist). IAC maintains an unjuried Artists Registry and publishes an annual Fairs and Festivals Directory. IAC Program Managers are available to consult with grant applicants.

INSTITUTE OF INTERNATIONAL EDUCATION

U.S. Student Programs
809 United Nations Plaza
New York, NY 10017-3580
212-984-5330
See Fulbright Awards listing.

Please read carefully!
Do not contact any listed organization unless you fulfill all eligibility requirements.

INSTITUTE OF PUERTO RICAN CULTURE/ INSTITUTO DE CULTURA PUERTORRIQUENA

Apartado Postal 4184
San Juan, PR 00902-4184
809-724-0700, ext. 4407
FAX: 809-724-8393
CONTACT: EVELYN GUERRIOS, COORDINATOR, OR JUAN TOMASINI,
ADMINISTRATIVE ASSISTANT

PROFILE OF FINANCIAL SUPPORT TO ARTISTS

Total Funding/Value of In-Kind Support: $36,500 in FY 1992-93
(fellowships only)

Competition for Funding: Total applications, n/a; total individuals
funded/provided with in-kind support, 8

Grant Range: n/a

DIRECT SUPPORT PROGRAM

➤ **BASIC ASSISTANCE PROGRAM FOR THE ARTS**

Purpose: To support the different streams of cultural development in
Puerto Rico and to encourage collaborative efforts to promote the
arts.

Eligibility:
   Citizenship: U.S.
   Residency: Puerto Rico only
   Special Requirements: Students ineligible; previous recipients
   ineligible for 3 years;
   Art Forms: All disciplines; disciplines rotate annually

Type of Support: Cash grants

Scope of Program: 8 fellowships, totalling $36,500, awarded in FY
1992-93 in media arts and design

Application/Selection Process:
   Deadline: April 15, annually
   Preferred Initial Contact: Call for application/guidelines
   Application Procedure: Submit application form, work samples
   Selection Process: Peer panel review, executive director, board of
   directors
   Notification Process: Artists are notified by a written Confidential
   Inquiry which must be accepted or rejected
   Formal Report of Grant Required: Yes

INTERMEDIA ARTS

425 Ontario Street, SE
Minneapolis, MN 55414
612-627-4444
CONTACT: AL KOSTERS, DIRECTOR OF ARTIST PROGRAMS

PROFILE OF FINANCIAL SUPPORT TO ARTISTS

Total Funding/Value of In-Kind Support: $114,000 in FY 1991-92

Competition for Funding: Total applications, 225 (regional programs), 59 (Minnesota programs); total individuals funded/provided with in-kind support, 15 (regional), 11 (Minnesota)

Grant Range: $500-$12,000

DIRECT SUPPORT PROGRAMS

➤ **MCKNIGHT INTERDISCIPLINARY ARTISTS FELLOWSHIP**

Purpose: To provide support for artists who have a track record of pursuing personal interdisciplinary work

Eligibility:
    Citizenship: U.S.
    Residency: Iowa, Kansas, Minnesota, Nebraska, North Dakota, South Dakota, Wisconsin, 1 of 2 years prior to application deadline
    Special Requirements: No full-time students or projects for a degree program; noncommercial work only
    Art Forms: All disciplines

Type of Support: $8,000-$12,000

Scope of Program: $70,000 available annually; 8 artists funded in FY 1991-92 out of 126 applications

Application/Selection Process:
    Deadline: Late fall, annually; call for exact dates
    Preferred Initial Contact: Write for application/guidelines
    Application Procedure: Detailed in application workshops
    Selection Process: Independent panel review
    Notification Process: Letter
    Formal Report of Grant Required: Yes

➤ **DIVERSE VISIONS REGIONAL GRANTS PROGRAM**

Purpose: To support artists who are attempting to explore new definitions of, or boundaries between, cultures, arts disciplines, or traditions in their work

Eligibility:
    Citizenship: U.S.
    Residency: Iowa, Kansas, Minnesota, North Dakota, Nebraska, South Dakota, Wisconsin, 1 of 2 years prior to application deadline

---

Please read carefully!
Do not contact any listed organization unless you fulfill all eligibility requirements.

Special Requirements: No full-time students or projects for a degree program; noncommercial work only
Art Forms: All disciplines
Type of Support: Up to $5,000 for emerging artists
Scope of Program: $30,000 available annually; 7 artists funded in FY 1991-92 out of 99 applications
Application/Selection Process:
  Deadline: Spring, annually; call for exact dates
  Preferred Initial Contact: Write for application/guidelines
  Application Procedure: Detailed in application workshops
  Selection Process: Panel review
  Notification Process: Letter 3 to 5 months after deadline
  Formal Report of Grant Required: Yes

➤ **JEROME INSTALLATION ART COMMISSIONS**

CONTACT: MASON RIDDLE, VISUAL ARTS CURATOR

Purpose: To commission emerging artists to create art installations specifically for the Intermedia Arts Gallery
Eligibility:
  Citizenship: U.S.
  Residency: Minnesota
  Special Requirements: No full-time students or projects for a degree program; noncommercial work only
  Art Forms: Open
Type of Support: $2,200 commission; up to $200 in additional materials and equipment support
Scope of Program: 3 awards per year; 35 applications in FY 1991-92
Application/Selection Process:
  Deadline: Winter, annually; call for exact dates
  Preferred Initial Contact: Write for application/guidelines
  Application Procedure: Submit application form, additional materials as requested
  Selection Process: Panel review
  Notification Process: Letter
  Formal Report of Grant Required: Yes

➤ **EXTENSIONS: MENTOR PROGRAM FOR ARTISTS OF COLOR**

Purpose: Program matches more established artists of color with emerging artists of color to encourage experimentation in new art forms and re-interpretations of traditional art forms
Eligibility:
  Citizenship: U.S.
  Residency: Minnesota
  Special Requirements: Emerging artists must be 16 years or older; mentorship period is three months and works toward final project

Please read carefully!
Do not contact any listed organization unless you fulfill all eligibility requirements.

to be showcased for the public at the Intermedia Arts Gallery; selected mentors present one lecture for the public at the gallery

Art Forms: All disciplines

Type of Support: $1,000 for mentor artists; $350 for emerging artists

Scope of Program: 4 mentors selected each year to work with 1-2 emerging artists each

Application/Selection Process:
  Deadline: Late fall/early winter annually; write for exact dates
  Preferred Initial Contact: Write for application/guidelines
  Application Procedure: Submit application form and additional materials as requested
  Selection Process: Curator and Project Coordinator review
  Notification Process: Letter
  Formal Report of Grant Required: Yes

EQUIPMENT ACCESS

Video: Production for VHS, 3/4"; post-production for VHS, S-VHS, 3/4"

Comments: Intermedia Arts Artist Affiliate Members ($75 fee) receive low-cost access to equipment and facilities.

TECHNICAL ASSISTANCE PROGRAMS AND SERVICES

Programs of Special Interest: Intermedia Arts acts as a fiscal agent for individual artist projects.

INTERNATIONAL CENTER FOR 8MM FILM AND VIDEO (IC8FV)

P.O. Box 335
Rowley, MA 01969
508-948-7985

TECHNICAL ASSISTANCE PROGRAMS AND SERVICES

Programs of Special Interest: IC8FV acts as an information center for artists who use 8mm, Super 8, or Single 8 film or small format video. Its co-founders direct artists to technical information and other resources.

INTERNATIONAL DOCUMENTARY ASSOCIATION

1551 South Robertson Boulevard
Suite 201
Los Angeles, CA 90035
310-284-8422
FAX: 310-785-9334

TECHNICAL ASSISTANCE PROGRAMS AND SERVICES

Programs of Special Interest: The International Documentary Association is a nonprofit association which seeks to promote nonfiction film and video and support the efforts of documentary film and videomakers. IDA serves as a fiscal sponsor to enable documentarians to apply for nonprofit status grants and charitable contributions. The association publishes a journal ten times per year, *International Documentary*, which contains articles, interviews and a calendar of events. IDA also publishes a membership directory. Monthly screenings present members' completed work and works-in-progress. Professional seminars and workshops are offered featuring prominent members of the film and television community. IDA Awards annually honor distinguished achievement in the field. IDA also sponsors the IDA/David L. Wolper Student Documentary Achievement Award, a $1,000 cash prize which is presented annually to recognize exceptional creative achievement in nonfiction film and video production at the university level and to bring greater public and industry awareness to the work of students in the documentary field. The organization sponsors health insurance for members and also provides discounts on services from production suppliers. Membership is $60 for individuals ($25 for students).

IOWA ARTS COUNCIL (IAC)

Capitol Complex
New Historical Building
Des Moines, IA 50319
515-281-6787
TDD: 800-735-2942 (Relay Service)
FAX: 515-242-6498
CONTACT: BRUCE WILLIAMS, DIRECTOR, CREATIVE ARTISTS AND VISUAL ARTS

PROFILE OF FINANCIAL SUPPORT TO ARTISTS

Total Funding/Value of In-Kind Support: n/a

Please read carefully!
Do not contact any listed organization unless you fulfill all eligibility requirements.

Competition for Funding: Total applications, 52; total individuals funded/provided with in-kind support, 29 (figures reflect artists project grant program only)

Grant Range: n/a

DIRECT SUPPORT PROGRAMS

➤ **MINI-GRANTS**

Purpose: To provide grants for project support, training, or technical assistance to individual artists, and to support emergency or educational grants to organizations

Eligibility:
  Citizenship: U.S.
  Residency: Iowa
  Special Requirements: Professional artists only
  Art Forms: All disciplines

Type of Support: Up to $500 for project support, professional development (e.g., attendance at workshops, seminars), and artist arts education projects

Scope of Program: $20,000 total budget for FY 1993

Application/Selection Process:
  Deadline: 60 days before beginning date
  Preferred Initial Contact: Call or write for application/guidelines
  Application Procedure: Submit application, resumé, project budget, samples of work
  Selection Process: Organization staff
  Notification Process: Letter within 30 days of application
  Formal Report of Grant Required: Yes

➤ **INDIVIDUAL ARTIST PROJECT GRANTS**

Purpose: To support projects designed and managed by artists

Eligibility:
  Residency: Iowa or bordering towns, 1 year
  Age: 18 or older
  Special Requirements: No students; previous grantees ineligible for 1-2 years
  Art Forms: All disciplines

Type of Support: Grants of at least $500 (average $2,000)

Scope of Program: 29 recipients in 1992

Application/Selection Process:
  Deadline: January, annually; call by December 1 for exact dates
  Preferred Initial Contact: Call or write for application/guidelines
  Application Procedure: Submit application form, samples of work, resumé, financial statement, project budget
  Selection Process: Multidiscipline Advisory Panel

Please read carefully!
Do not contact any listed organization unless you fulfill all eligibility requirements.

Notification Process: Letter
Formal Report of Grant Required: Yes

➤ SCHOLARSHIP PROGRAM
CONTACT: JULIE BAILEY, DIRECTOR OF PARTNERSHIP PROGRAM
Phone: 515-281-4018
Purpose: To encourage the development of high school seniors and college students who excel in the arts and have enrolled in educational programs leading to careers in the arts
Eligibility:
Citizenship: U.S.
Residency: Iowa
Special Requirements: Recent high school graduate or full-time undergraduate student
Art Forms: All disciplines
Type of Support: $1,000 scholarship
Scope of Program: 5 awards annually
Application/Selection Process:
Deadline: April 1, annually
Preferred Initial Contact: Call or write for application/guidelines
Application Procedure: Submit application form, references; 10 finalists interviewed
Selection Process: Individuals outside organization
Notification Process: Letter 4 months after deadline
Formal Report of Grant Required: No

TECHNICAL ASSISTANCE PROGRAMS AND SERVICES

Programs of Special Interest: IAC offers residency and performance opportunities through its Artist-in-Schools/Communities program and Arts To Go touring program (contact Kay A. Swan, Director, Arts Education, 515-281-4100 or Julie Bailey, 515-281-4018). Artists may apply for inclusion in the IAC's Artist Resource Book; accepted artists are eligible for Art in State Buildings Projects (contact Bruce Williams, 515-281-6787).

THE JAPAN FOUNDATION

152 West 57th Street, 39th floor
New York, NY 10019
212-489-0299
FAX: 212-489-0409

PROFILE OF FINANCIAL SUPPORT TO ARTISTS
Total Funding/Value of In-Kind Support: n/a

Please read carefully!
Do not contact any listed organization unless you fulfill all eligibility requirements.

Competition for Funding: Total applications, 32; total individuals funded/provided with in-kind support, 4 (figures reflect Artist Fellowship and Cultural Properties Specialists Fellowship)

Grant Range: n/a

DIRECT SUPPORT PROGRAMS
➤ ### ARTIST FELLOWSHIP PROGRAMS

Purpose: The Artist Fellowship provides artists and specialists in the arts the opportunity to pursue creative projects in Japan and to meet and consult with their Japanese counterparts. The Cultural Properties Specialists Fellowship provides specialists in the conservation and restoration of cultural properties—such as remains, artistic objects, handicrafts, old documents, films and records—with the opportunity to conduct joint research with Japanese specialists and/or to develop their professional skills

Eligibility:
    Citizenship: U.S., or permanent resident
    Residency: U.S. or temporarily living abroad
    Age: Open
    Special Requirements: Students are not eligible; must be an established artist or cultural administrator; previous recipients ineligible for three years
    Art Forms: All disciplines in the arts, cultural administrators (i.e., curators), and specialists in the conservation and restoration of cultural properties

Type of Support: Support for projects ranging from 1 to 6 months (amount of award depends on duration of project and the grantee's professional status); monthly stipend and other allowances, travel expenses paid to and from Japan, traveler's insurance provided

Scope of Program: 4 awards given for FY 1993-94

Application/Selection Process:
    Deadline: December 1, annually
    Preferred Initial Contact: Call or write for application/guidelines after August
    Application Procedure: Submit application form and supporting documents
    Selection Process: Japan Foundation Headquarters (Tokyo) staff
    Notification Process: Letter by late March
    Formal Report of Grant Required: Yes

Please read carefully!
Do not contact any listed organization unless you fulfill all eligibility requirements.

JEROME FOUNDATION

West 1050 First National Bank Building
332 Minnesota Street
St. Paul, MN 55101-1312
612-224-9431
FAX: 612-224-3439
CONTACT: CYNTHIA A. GEHRIG, PRESIDENT

PROFILE OF FINANCIAL SUPPORT TO ARTISTS
Total Funding/Value of In-Kind Support: n/a
Competition for Funding: Total applications, n/a; total individuals funded/provided with in-kind support, 36 in FY 1991-92
Grant Range: n/a

DIRECT SUPPORT PROGRAMS
➤ **NEW YORK CITY FILM AND VIDEO PROGRAM**
Purpose: To support emerging film and video artists who make creative use of their media and who have not had the support needed to fully display their work
Eligibility:
  Citizenship: U.S. (permanent residents also eligible)
  Residency: New York City (Bronx, Brooklyn, Manhattan, Queens, Staten Island)
  Special Requirements: Must have completed formal education; preference to projects in their early stages and to personal, low budget work in which the artist exercises complete creative control over production; requests considered for projects with total budgets of $75,000 or less (strong preference to projects with budgets under $50,000); previous applicants ineligible for 1 year
  Art Forms: Film, video
Type of Support: $8,000-$20,000 grants
Scope of Program: 15 grants in 1991-92
Application/Selection Process:
  Deadline: Open; applications may be submitted throughout the year, but are reviewed 3 times per year; contact for exact dates
  Preferred Initial Contact: Call or write for application/guidelines
  Application Procedure: Submit project description, project budget, resumé for applicant and other principals involved in project, statement specifying applicant's role in production, excerpt of script (for works with major narrative element), list of other sources (or potential sources) of project support; work samples are submitted later for panel review, not with initial application

Please read carefully!
Do not contact any listed organization unless you fulfill all eligibility requirements.

    Selection Process: Panel of artists and arts professionals, board of
directors
Notification Process: Letter 3-5 months after application
Formal Report of Grant Required: Yes

➤ **TRAVEL AND STUDY GRANTS**

Purpose: To allow artists significant time for professional
development through artist-to-artist communication on aesthetic
issues, the experience of seeing artistic work outside of Minnesota,
time for reflection and individualized study, a chance to develop
future work and collaborations, and opportunities for the presentation or development of their work in other locations

Eligibility:
    Citizenship: U.S.
    Residency: Twin Cities 7-county metropolitan area of Minnesota,
1 year
    Age: Open
    Special Requirements: Professional artists or administrators only
    Art Forms: All disciplines

Type of Support: $1,000-$5,000 for travel

Scope of Program: $92,000 available for FY 1992-93
    Deadline: May 1 and October 1, annually
    Preferred Initial Contact: Call or write for application/guidelines
    Application Procedure: Submit application form, travel proposal,
resumé, samples of work
    Selection Process: Panel of arts professionals, board of directors
    Notification Process: Within 6 weeks of deadline
    Formal Report of Grant Required: Yes

JUNEAU ARTS AND HUMANITIES COUNCIL

P.O. Box 20562
Juneau, AK 99802-0562
907-586-2787
FAX: 907-586-2148
CONTACT: NATALEE ROTHAUS, EXECUTIVE DIRECTOR

PROFILE OF FINANCIAL SUPPORT TO ARTISTS

Total Funding/Value of In-Kind Support: $7,610 for FY 1992

Competition for Funding: Total applications, 25; total individuals
funded/provided with in-kind support, 13

Grant Range: $150-$1,000

Please read carefully!
Do not contact any listed organization unless you fulfill all eligibility requirements.

DIRECT SUPPORT PROGRAMS

➤ **INDIVIDUAL ARTISTS ASSISTANCE PROGRAM**

Purpose: To enable experienced artists of exceptional talent to produce works of art or advance their careers

Eligibility:
    Citizenship: U.S.
    Residency: Juneau, 1 year
    Special Requirements: Previous grantees ineligible for 2 years
    Art Forms: All disciplines

Type of Support: Up to $1,000 for a specific activity

Scope of Program: 13 awards in 1992

Application/Selection Process:
    Deadline: 2 deadlines per year; contact for exact dates
    Preferred Initial Contact: Call or write for application/guidelines
    Application Procedure: Submit application form, samples of work, resumé, financial statement, project budget, copies of other grant applications related to project
    Selection Process: Organization staff, board of directors, individuals outside of organization, peer panel of artists
    Notification Process: Phone and letter
    Formal Report of Grant Required: Yes

TECHNICAL ASSISTANCE PROGRAMS AND SERVICES

Programs of Special Interest: JAHC posts solicitation requests from Alaska's Percent for Arts Program, sponsors artists in schools and an annual Very Special Arts Festival for children with special needs, maintains a resource library, and works with other arts organizations to closely monitor legislation regarding the arts.

KANSAS ARTS COMMISSION (KAC)

Jayhawk Tower
700 SW Jackson, Suite 1004
Topeka, KS 66603-3758
913-296-3335
TDD: 800-766-3777 (via Kansas Relay Center)
FAX: 913-296-4989

CONTACT: CONCHITA REYES, ARTS PROGRAM COORDINATOR

PROFILE OF FINANCIAL SUPPORT TO ARTISTS

Total Funding/Value of In-Kind Support: $43,000 for FY 1993 (figures include folk arts grants)

Please read carefully!
Do not contact any listed organization unless you fulfill all eligibility requirements.

Competition for Funding: Total applications, 116; total individuals funded/provided with in-kind support, 33

Grant Range: $344-$5,000

DIRECT SUPPORT PROGRAMS

➤ **ARTIST FELLOWSHIPS**

Purpose: To recognize outstanding Kansas artists and to assist them in furthering their careers

Eligibility:
> **Residency:** Kansas
> **Special Requirements:** No full-time students pursuing degrees; no previous recipients
> **Art Forms:** Awards rotate yearly among the following disciplines: Visual arts (includes 2D, 3D, crafts, photography), performing arts (includes film/video, interdisciplinary, performance art), literature

Type of Support: $5,000 awards

Scope of Program: 3 annual awards

Application/Selection Process:
> **Deadline:** October, annually; contact for exact date
> **Preferred Initial Contact:** Call or write for application/guidelines
> **Application Procedure:** Submit application form, samples of work, resumé, artist's statement
> **Selection Process:** Panels of arts professionals chaired by a KAC member
> **Notification Process:** 4-5 months after deadline
> **Formal Report of Grant Required:** Yes

➤ **PROFESSIONAL DEVELOPMENT GRANT**

Purpose: To encourage artists in the next step of their development while creating original works of art in any discipline

Eligibility:
> **Residency:** Kansas
> **Special Requirements:** Originating artists only; artists must match grant in cash or combination of cash and in-kind services; no students; no previous recipients
> **Art Forms:** All disciplines

Type of Support: $100-$500 matching grant for specific project

Scope of Program: $6,000 available for FY 1993

Application/Selection Process:
> **Deadline:** Varies; contact for date information
> **Preferred Initial Contact:** Call or write for application/guidelines
> **Application Procedure:** Submit application form, resumé, project description and budget, financial statement, samples of work, support materials

Please read carefully!
Do not contact any listed organization unless you fulfill all eligibility requirements.

Selection Process: Panels of arts professionals chaired by a KAC member
Notification Process: Letter
Formal Report of Grant Required: Yes

TECHNICAL ASSISTANCE PROGRAMS AND SERVICES
Programs of Special Interest: KAC administers an Arts in Education Artist in Residency Program; film and video artist residencies last 2 weeks to 9 months. A monthly bulletin and a quarterly newsletter supply information about arts events and opportunities.

KENTUCKY ARTS COUNCIL (KAC)

31 Fountain Place
Frankfort, KY 40601
502-564-3757
FAX: 502-564-2839
CONTACT: IRWIN PICKETT, DIRECTOR OF VISUAL ARTS

PROFILE OF FINANCIAL SUPPORT TO ARTISTS
Total Funding/Value of In-Kind Support: $130,000 for FY 1992 (Al Smith Fellowships only)
Competition for Funding: Total applications, 285 (Fellowships)/20 (Artists Projects); total individuals funded/provided with in-kind support, 38 (Fellowships)/10 (Artists Projects)
Grant Range: $300-$5,000

DIRECT SUPPORT PROGRAMS
➤ **AL SMITH FELLOWSHIPS**
Purpose: To support individual Kentucky artists in developing their art forms
Eligibility:
Citizenship: U.S.
Residency: Kentucky
Age: 18 or older
Special Requirements: Previous grantees ineligible for 4 years; students ineligible
Art Forms: Disciplines alternate yearly: Visual arts (includes photography and crafts)/media arts/new genres (includes installation and conceptual art) in odd-numbered years; writers/composers/choreographers/interdisciplinary arts (includes performance art) in even-numbered years

Please read carefully!
Do not contact any listed organization unless you fulfill all eligibility requirements.

Type of Support: $5,000 fellowships, $1,000 assistance awards

Scope of Program: Up to 22 fellowships, 20 assistance awards

Application/Selection Process:
Deadline: September 15, annually
Preferred Initial Contact: Write for application and guidelines
Application Procedure: Submit application form, samples of work, resumé
Selection Process: Board of directors, peer panel of artists
Notification Process: Letter
Formal Report of Grant Required: No

➤ **ARTISTS PROJECTS**

Purpose: To support Kentucky artists and advocate public, artist-initiated projects

Eligibility:
Citizenship: U.S.
Residency: Kentucky
Age: 21 and older
Special Requirements: Project must terminate or take place with public benefit and involve a wide and diverse population of the community. Grant must be matched 50% and application requires a nonprofit sponsor with 501(c)3 status; students ineligible; previous recipients ineligible for four years
Art Forms: All disciplines

Type of Support: Up to $3,000 (must be matched by applying organization)

Scope of Program: 10 awards given to individuals in 1992

Application/Selection Process:
Deadline: March 15, annually
Preferred Initial Contact: Write or call for information
Application Procedure: Submit project description, a project application form, resumé, documentation of art work
Selection Process: Peer panel
Notification Process: Letter within 60 days of deadline
Formal Report of Grant Required: Yes

TECHNICAL ASSISTANCE PROGRAMS AND SERVICES

Programs of Special Interest: KAC coordinates a major annual exhibition of works by Kentucky artists. The Visual Arts Marketing Program (VAMP) holds workshops to assist artists with business-related concerns and operates the Visual Arts Resource Service (VARS), which maintains a slide registry, an annotated list of art spaces and commercial outlets, and a quarterly listing of art competitions, fellowships, and other opportunities for artists.

Please read carefully!
Do not contact any listed organization unless you fulfill all eligibility requirements.

KENTUCKY FOUNDATION FOR WOMEN

1215 Heyburn Building
332 West Broadway
Louisville, KY 40202
502-562-0045

PROFILE OF FINANCIAL SUPPORT TO ARTISTS

Total Funding/Value of In-Kind Support: $150,000 in 1993

Competition for Funding: Total applications, n/a; total individuals funded/provided with in-kind support, 37

Grant Range: $500-$10,000

DIRECT SUPPORT PROGRAM

➤ **KENTUCKY FOUNDATION FOR WOMEN GRANTS PROGRAM**

Purpose: To support women who use the arts for social change

Eligibility:

Citizenship: n/a

Residency: Must be living in Kentucky or area immediately adjacent to Kentucky in Indiana, Ohio, West Virginia, Tennessee

Age: Open

Special Requirements: No grants for tuition or stipends for work undertaken to complete an academic degree; recipients of a grant are ineligible in that discipline for a 4-year period

Art Forms: Visual arts (painting, sculpture, puppetry, crafts, photography, exhibits, multi-media, etc.) and performance arts (dance, theater, music and performance art) apply in odd-numbered years; film, writing, and feminist scholarship apply in even-numbered years

Type of Support: $500-$10,000 grants; average grant of $4,000

Scope of Program: $150,000 total in 1993

Application/Selection Process:

Deadline: October 1, annually

Preferred Initial Contact: Write or call for application/guidelines

Application Procedure: Submit application form, work sample, resumé, budget, 2 letters of recommendation

Selection Process: Board of directors

Notification Process: By letter before January 15

Formal Report of Grant Required: Yes

KING COUNTY ARTS COMMISSION (KCAC)

1115 Smith Tower
506 Second Avenue
Seattle, WA 98104
206-296-7580 (Voice/TDD)
FAX: 206-296-8629
CONTACT: LEONARD GARFIELD, MANAGER, CULTURAL RESOURCES DIVISION

PROFILE OF FINANCIAL SUPPORT TO ARTISTS
Total Funding/Value of In-Kind Support: n/a
Competition for Funding: n/a
Grant Range: $1,000-$5,000

DIRECT SUPPORT PROGRAMS
➤ **NEW WORKS PROJECTS**
CONTACT: KRISTINA GONZALEZ-OLSON, ASSOCIATE DIRECTOR
Purpose: To encourage experimentation and to support the creation of new works
Eligibility:
    Residency: Western Washington State
    Special Requirements: Professional, originating artists only; previous recipients ineligible for 2 years
    Art Forms: Literature, media arts, performing arts, interdisciplinary
Type of Support: $1,000-$5,000
Scope of Program: 8-10 awards per year
Application/Selection Process:
    Deadline: December, annually; contact for exact date
    Preferred Initial Contact: Consult with staff before applying
    Application Procedure: Submit application form, samples of work, project narrative
    Selection Process: Peer panel of artists, commission members
    Formal Report of Grant Required: Yes

TECHNICAL ASSISTANCE PROGRAMS AND SERVICES
Programs of Special Interest: African-American, Latino, Asian-American/Pacific Islander, and Native American artists may apply for arts-in-education residencies through the Ethnic Artists-in-Residence program; the Disabled Artists-in-Residence places blind and visually-impaired, deaf and hearing-impaired, deaf-blind, or physically disabled artists in arts-in-education residencies (contact Kristina Gonzalez-Olson, Associate Director).

Please read carefully!
Do not contact any listed organization unless you fulfill all eligibility requirements.

LAKE REGION ARTS COUNCIL, INC. (LRAC)

112 West Washington Avenue
P.O. Box 661
Fergus Falls, MN 56538-0661
218-739-5780
CONTACT: SONJA PETERSON, DIRECTOR

PROFILE OF FINANCIAL SUPPORT TO ARTISTS

Total Funding/Value of In-Kind Support: $6,350 for FY 1992

Competition for Funding: Total applications, 13; total individuals funded/provided with in-kind support, 7

Grant Range: Up to $1,000

DIRECT SUPPORT PROGRAMS

➤ **LRAC/MCKNIGHT INDIVIDUAL ARTISTS GRANT PROGRAM**

Purpose: To provide small but critical grants to artists for specific projects that contribute directly to their growth and development as professionals

Eligibility:
   Citizenship: U.S.
   Residency: Minnesota (Becker, Clay, Douglas, Grant, Otter Tail, Pope, Stevens, Traverse, and Wilkin counties)
   Special Requirements: No students
   Art Forms: All disciplines

Type of Support: Up to $1,000 for expenses such as production and presentation of work, training, supplies, or services

Scope of Program: $7,000 budget in FY 1993

Application/Selection Process:
   Deadline: October, annually; contact for specific date
   Preferred Initial Contact: Call or write for application/guidelines
   Application Procedure: Submit application form, samples of work, references, resumé, project budget
   Selection Process: LRAC board of directors
   Notification Process: Letter in November
   Formal Report of Grant Required: Yes

TECHNICAL ASSISTANCE PROGRAMS AND SERVICES

Programs of Special Interest: LRAC maintains an unjuried registry of artists, publishes a monthly newsletter, and holds grantwriting workshops.

THE LATINO COLLABORATIVE

280 Broadway
Suite 412
New York, NY 10007
212-732-1121
FAX: 212-732-1297

TECHNICAL ASSISTANCE PROGRAMS AND SERVICES

Programs of Special Interest: The Latino Collaborative, a nonprofit film and video organization, publishes a bimonthly newsletter, *LC News*, which includes profiles on emerging Latino film and video artists as well as information pertinent to Latinos working in film and video. Members are provided with opportunities to show and discuss their work among fellow artists at bimonthly Membership Screenings. The organization also maintains a Skills Bank which refers members to appropriate job opportunities. Depending on availability of funds, a regrant program provides seed grants for Latino film and videomakers in the Northeast. The Latino Collaborative holds workshops, publishes a title directory of members' works, and initiates various film series to showcase emerging Latino film and video artists. Membership is $25 for individuals, $50 for organizations.

LONG BEACH MUSEUM OF ART/LBMA—VIDEO

5373 East Second Street
Long Beach, CA 90803
310-439-0751
FAX: 310-438-1508
CONTACT: JOE LEONARDI, GENERAL MANAGER, VIDEO ANNEX

PROFILE OF FINANCIAL SUPPORT TO ARTISTS

Total Funding/Value of In-Kind Support: $18,000 in 1992

Competition for Funding: Total applications, 100; total number of individuals/nonprofit organizations funded/provided with in-kind support, 8

Grant Range: $2,000 cash grants; up to $5,000 in-kind support

DIRECT SUPPORT PROGRAMS

➤ **OPEN CHANNELS: VIDEO PRODUCTION GRANT PROGRAM**

Purpose: To support new video art pieces less than 15 minutes in length

Please read carefully!
Do not contact any listed organization unless you fulfill all eligibility requirements.

Eligibility:
Residency: California
Special Requirements: No full-time students; preference to works not already in progress and to applicants who have not received this grant before
Art Forms: Video

Type of Support: $2,000, supply of tape stock, 8 days access to production and post-production facilities at a local cable studio (participating facilities typically provide an ENG production package or a 3-camera studio, and access to 3/4" editing)

Scope of Program: 2 grants per year

Application/Selection Process:
Deadline: May or June, annually; contact for exact date
Preferred Initial Contact: Call or write for application/guidelines
Application Procedure: Submit application form, resumé, samples of work
Selection Process: Panel of independent jurors and staff
Notification Process: Letter
Formal Report of Grant Required: No

➤ **VIDEO ACCESS PROGRAM (VAP)**

Purpose: To provide production and post-production facility access grants to artists, noncommercial independent producers, and non-profit organizations for the creation or completion of new works

Eligibility:
Citizenship: Open internationally
Residency: Open
Art Forms: Video

Type of Support: 5 days of production and post-production from LBMA Video Annex; grantees must provide 3/4" copy of completed project for LBMA Video Collection and must provide LBMA Video with nonexclusive exhibition, cable, and broadcast rights

Scope of Program: 6 awards per year

Application/Selection Process:
Deadline: Ongoing
Preferred Initial Contact: Call or write for application/guidelines
Application Procedure: Submit application form, project description, resumé, samples of work
Selection Process: Jury
Notification Process: Letter within 6 weeks
Formal Report of Grant Required: No

EQUIPMENT ACCESS

Video: Production for S-VHS, 3/4", 1", Betacam; post-production for VHS, S-VHS, 3/4", 1", Betacam

Please read carefully!
Do not contact any listed organization unless you fulfill all eligibility requirements.

Comments: LBMA's facilities include production studios. Artists receive access to facilities and equipment at subsidized rates.

TECHNICAL ASSISTANCE PROGRAMS AND SERVICES

Programs of Special Interest: The LMBA exhibits single-channel video and video installations. The cable television series "Viewpoints on Video" showcases video art.

LOS ANGELES CONTEMPORARY EXHIBITIONS (LACE)

1804 Industrial Street
Los Angeles, CA 90021
213-624-5650
FAX: 213-624-6679
Note: As of January 1994, contact LACE at its new address:
6522 Hollywood Boulevard
Hollywood, CA 90028
213-957-1777

EQUIPMENT ACCESS

CONTACT: VIDEO COORDINATOR

Comments: Artists working on noncommercial video and audio projects may apply to the On-line program, which offers access to professional post-production and recording facilities and technicians at reduced rates (membership fee and administrative fee required). LACE also guides artists to sources of production equipment rentals and inexpensive off-line editing.

TECHNICAL ASSISTANCE PROGRAMS AND SERVICES

Programs of Special Interest: LACE, in conjunction with New Langton Arts (1246 Folsom, San Francisco, CA 94103; 415-626-5416) administers the National Endowment for the Arts' Artists Projects Regional Initiative in California and Hawaii; this program seeks to encourage innovative projects that push the boundaries of contemporary art and challenge traditional formats; contact for further details. LACE maintains a listing of grants for video and audio artists and a bulletin board of festival and other announcements. LACE screens work by emerging and established artists from Los Angeles and elsewhere. Workshops and consultations on technical subjects are also available. (Membership and administrative fees apply to some services.)

Please read carefully!
Do not contact any listed organization unless you fulfill all eligibility requirements.

LOS ANGELES CULTURAL AFFAIRS DEPARTMENT

433 South Spring Street
10th Floor
Los Angeles, CA 90013
213-620-8635
FAX: 213-485-6835

PROFILE OF FINANCIAL SUPPORT TO ARTISTS

Total Funding/Value of In-Kind Support: $614,000 for FY 1991-92

Competition for Funding: Total applications, 326; total individuals funded/provided with in-kind support, 72

Grant Range: $4,000-$7,000 average

DIRECT SUPPORT PROGRAMS

➤ **ARTISTS IN THE COMMUNITY—CULTURAL GRANTS**

Purpose: To offer arts experiences within a community setting to nonprofessional artists and to bring professional artists in direct contact with the public

Eligibility:
  Citizenship: U.S.
  Residency: City or County of Los Angeles
  Special Requirements: Artist must submit a letter of agreement with proposed host venue to produce the project if funded; project must take place in the City of Los Angeles in a site with public access
  Art Forms: Dance, interdisciplinary, multi-disciplinary, literature, media arts, music, theater, urban and design arts, traditional and folk arts, visual arts

Type of Support: $1,500-$15,000 for project

Scope of Program: n/a

Application/Selection Process:
  Deadline: Fall, annually; contact for exact date
  Preferred Initial Contact: Call or write for application/guidelines
  Application Procedure: Submit application form, materials as outlined in guidelines
  Selection Process: Peer panel of artists
  Notification Process: Letter 5-6 months after deadline
  Formal Report of Grant Required: Yes

LOUISIANA DIVISION OF THE ARTS (DOA)

1051 North Third Street
Baton Rouge, LA 70804
504-342-8180
FAX: 504-342-8173
CONTACT: ANN RUSSO, VISUAL ARTS PROGRAM DIRECTOR

PROFILE OF FINANCIAL SUPPORT TO ARTISTS

Total Funding/Value of In-Kind Support: $74,000 for 1992

Competition for Funding: Total applications, 188; total individuals funded/provided with in-kind support, 19

Grant Range: $3,400-$5,000

DIRECT SUPPORT PROGRAMS

➤ **ARTIST FELLOWSHIPS**

Purpose: To enable artists of exceptional talent to pursue their artistic goals

Eligibility:
  Residency: Louisiana, 2 years
  Special Requirements: Professional artists only; no students; previous grantees ineligible
  Art Forms: Crafts, dance, design arts, folk arts, literature, media arts, music, theater, visual arts

Type of Support: $5,000 fellowships

Scope of Program: 9 awards in 1992

Application/Selection Process:
  Deadline: March 1, annually
  Preferred Initial Contact: Write for application/guidelines
  Application Procedure: Submit application form, samples of work, resumé; application workshops held in January
  Selection Process: Individuals outside of organization
  Notification Process: Letter 5 months after deadline
  Formal Report of Grant Required: Yes

➤ **INDIVIDUAL ARTIST PROJECTS: FISCAL AGENTS**

Purpose: To support projects of exceptional merit initiated by individual artists

Eligibility:
  Residency: Louisiana
  Special Requirements: Must apply through a Louisiana-based non-profit organization, but project must clearly be an individual artist's project rather than an extension of the organization's programming
  Art Forms: All disciplines

Please read carefully!
Do not contact any listed organization unless you fulfill all eligibility requirements.

Type of Support: $3,000-$5,000 grant
Scope of Program: 3-5 grants annually
Application/Selection Process:
   Deadline: March 1, annually
   Preferred Initial Contact: Write for application/guidelines
   Application Procedure: Organization submits project assistance
   form (includes project description and budget)
   Selection Process: Panel review in appropriate discipline
   Notification Process: Letter by July
   Formal Report of Grant Required: Yes

TECHNICAL ASSISTANCE PROGRAMS AND SERVICES
Programs of Special Interest: The Louisiana Artist Roster lists
artists approved for Arts in Education residencies and projects.

LOWER MANHATTAN CULTURAL COUNCIL (LMCC)

1 World Trade Center, Suite 1717
New York, NY 10048-0202
212-432-0900
FAX: 212-432-3646

PROFILE OF FINANCIAL SUPPORT TO ARTISTS
Total Funding/Value of In-Kind Support: $100,000 in FY 1992
Competition for Funding: n/a
Grant Range: n/a

DIRECT SUPPORT PROGRAMS
➤ MANHATTAN COMMUNITY ARTS FUND
Purpose: To develop projects of artistic interest and excellence that
are of relevance to local Manhattan communities; to increase
support to community-based and emerging organizations and artists
by providing them with government funds to which they normally
do not have access
Eligibility:
   Residency: Artist must live and work in Manhattan; applicant and
   sponsoring organization must also be located in Manhattan
   Special Requirements: Individual artists must apply under the
   aegis of a qualifying organization which must have nonprofit
   status or be sponsored by a nonprofit organization; applicant

artists and organizations cannot have received funding from New York State Council on the Arts (NYSCA) or the National Endowment for the Arts (NEA) or New York City Department of Cultural Affairs (DCA) for 2 years prior to application; sponsoring organizations can be recipients of funding from NYSCA, NEA or DCA

Art Forms: All disciplines

Type of Support: Up to $3,000 for a specific project; grant range in FY 1992 was $500-$1,500

Scope of Program: $52,000 available in FY 1993

Application/Selection Process:
  Deadline: January, annually; contact for exact date
  Preferred Initial Contact: Write for information/guidelines
  Application Procedure: Applicant submits application consisting of project description, project and organization budget, resumé of artist(s), organization's or sponsor's proof of nonprofit status, list of staff members and board members, and current brochure or fact sheet
  Selection Process: Staff reviews application for completeness; panel of artists and arts professionals makes decision
  Notification Process: Letter within 12 weeks; please do not call as notification will not be provided by phone

TECHNICAL ASSISTANCE PROGRAMS AND SERVICES

Programs of Special Interest: LMCC administers the Artists Projects Regional Initiative for New York City artists for the NEA. The program, however, is by nomination only; individuals cannot apply. The Performing Arts Program hires artists for mid-day public performance events in downtown Manhattan. These performances are scheduled primarily during the summer months. LMCC's Petrosino Park program, where artists create temporary installations in a small traffic triangle in Soho, is not currently being funded; artists who can self-fund an installation are invited to submit proposals for review.

JOHN D. AND CATHERINE T. MACARTHUR FOUNDATION

140 South Dearborn Street
Chicago, IL 60603

PROFILE OF FINANCIAL SUPPORT TO ARTISTS
Total Funding/Value of In-Kind Support: n/a

Please read carefully!
Do not contact any listed organization unless you fulfill all eligibility requirements.

Competition for Funding: n/a
Grant Range: n/a

DIRECT SUPPORT PROGRAMS

➤ **GENERAL PROGRAM**

Purpose: To support media projects that increase the diversity of voices in television and radio and improve public access to media production facilities and new technologies; some documentaries by individual media artists are considered for support

Eligibility:
Citizenship: Open
Residency: Open
Special Requirements: Individuals must be sponsored by a non-profit organization; the great majority of projects funded are community-based media centers, national public radio and public television series such as "P.O.V." and "American Playhouse"; narrative films are ineligible
Art Forms: Broad range of arts and humanities activities including documentary film and video

Type of Support: One-year to three-year grants to institutions; up to $25,000 to community-based media centers; varying amounts for individuals

Scope of Program: n/a

Application/Selection Process:
Deadline: Open; proposals reviewed monthly
Preferred Initial Contact: Individuals, see application process; media centers, request guidelines and application form
Application Procedure: Submit a 2- to 3-page letter of inquiry describing project and type of funding desired; staff review letters and request more information if project is of interest to the foundation; media artists with projects related to the foundation's programmatic interests in world environment and resources, peace and international cooperation, education, and world population should address letters of inquiry to the Office of Grants Management, Research and Information at the address listed above
Selection Process: Staff review
Notification Process: Letter
Formal Report of Grant Required: Yes

THE MACDOWELL COLONY

100 High Street
Peterborough, NH 03458
603-924-3886, 212-966-4860
FAX: 603-924-9142
CONTACT: PAT DODGE, ADMISSIONS COORDINATOR

PROFILE OF FINANCIAL SUPPORT TO ARTISTS

Total Funding/Value of In-Kind Support: $780,000 for FY 1992

Competition for Funding: Total applications, 1,275; total individuals funded/provided with in-kind support, 230

Grant Range: n/a

DIRECT SUPPORT PROGRAMS

➤ **ARTIST RESIDENCY PROGRAM**

Purpose: To provide a place where creative artists can find freedom to concentrate on their work

Eligibility:
  Special Requirements: Professional artists and emerging artists of recognized ability; previous applicants ineligible for 1 year
  Art Forms: Music composition, literature, visual arts, architecture, film/video, mixed media, interdisciplinary

Type of Support: Residency including room, board, and studio for up to 2 months; funds available to defray travel costs to and from colony; artists who have financial resources pay on a voluntary basis

Scope of Program: 200+ residencies averaging 6 weeks

Application/Selection Process:
  Deadline: January 15 (Summer), April 15 (Fall-Winter), September 15 (Winter-Spring)
  Preferred Initial Contact: Call or write for application/guidelines
  Application Procedure: Submit application form, samples of work, references, resumé, $20 fee
  Selection Process: Peer panel of artists
  Notification Process: Letter 2 months after deadline
  Formal Report of Grant Required: No

MAINE ARTS COMMISSION (MAC)

55 Capitol Street
Station 25
Augusta, ME 04333-0025
207-287-2724
TDD: 207-287-5613
FAX: 207-287-2335
CONTACT: KATHY ANN JONES, MUSEUM/VISUAL ARTS ASSOCIATE

PROFILE OF FINANCIAL SUPPORT TO ARTISTS
Total Funding/Value of In-Kind Support: $18,000 for FY 1992
(fellowships only)
Competition for Funding: Total applications, 150; total individuals
funded/provided with in-kind support, 6
Grant Range: $3,000

DIRECT SUPPORT PROGRAMS
➤ **INDIVIDUAL ARTIST FELLOWSHIPS**
Purpose: To provide financial support for artists to advance their
careers, to acknowledge artistic excellence, and to promote public
awareness of Maine artists
Eligibility:
    Residency: Maine, minimum 183 days the year prior to application
    Age: 18 or older
    Special Requirements: No students
    Art Forms: Awards rotate yearly among visual arts, writing/design
    arts, performing/traditional/media arts
Type of Support: $3,000
Scope of Program: 6 awards in 1992
Application/Selection Process:
    Deadline: First week of September, annually; call for exact date
    Preferred Initial Contact: Call or write for application/guidelines
    Application Procedure: Submit application form, samples of
    work, resumé, statement of intent (optional)
    Selection Process: Individuals from outside of organization
    Notification Process: Phone call and follow-up letter to recipients;
    letter to nonrecipients
    Formal Report of Grant Required: Yes

TECHNICAL ASSISTANCE PROGRAMS AND SERVICES
Programs of Special Interest: The commission maintains a registry
of slides, video/audio tapes, and portfolios of the work of hundreds

Please read carefully!
Do not contact any listed organization unless you fulfill all eligibility requirements.

of artists for use by galleries, curators, the commission's staff and the general public. The registry is also linked to an active Percent for Art program. Contact the commission for detailed information on how and when to apply. The Artist in Residence Program offers ten-day to year-long residencies in schools and other nonprofit institutions. The Maine Touring Artists Program provides organizations with a list of artists who will travel throughout the state to present performances, workshops, residencies, and educational services.

MANITOBA ARTS COUNCIL (MAC)

525-93 Lombard Avenue
Winnipeg, Manitoba
Canada R3B 3B1
204-945-4537
FAX: 204-945-5925
CONTACT: DEBRA MOSHER, ASSOCIATE VISUAL ARTS OFFICER

PROFILE OF FINANCIAL SUPPORT TO ARTISTS
Total Funding/Value of In-Kind Support: $1,282,333 for FY 1992-93
Competition for Funding: n/a
Grant Range: Up to $20,000

DIRECT SUPPORT PROGRAMS
➤ **FILM PROJECT GRANTS/VIDEO PROJECT GRANTS**
Purpose: To assist independent Manitoba filmmakers in the creation and production of high quality, innovative films
Eligibility:
    Citizenship: Canada (landed immigrants also eligible)
    Residency: Manitoba, 1 year
    Special Requirements: Professional artists only; must have completed basic training; no students; principal creator/director of film/video must apply; applicant must retain artistic control and rights; commissioned, instructional, promotional, and industrial projects ineligible; pilots for commercial or educational television ineligible
    Art Forms: Film, video
Type of Support: Up to $6,000
Scope of Program: 6 grants, totalling $34,060, in FY 1992-93
Application/Selection Process:
    Deadline: April 1 and October 1, annually
    Preferred Initial Contact: Consult with Associate Visual Arts Officer before applying

Please read carefully!
Do not contact any listed organization unless you fulfill all eligibility requirements.

Application Procedure: Submit application form, project proposal and budget, resumé, filmography/videography, synopsis and draft script (dramatic works), outline (documentaries), storyboard (animated works), film/video treatment, shooting script, samples of work
Selection Process: Jury of independent professionals in the visual arts
Notification Process: 2 months after deadline
Formal Report of Grant Required: Yes

➤ **FILM PRODUCTION GRANTS/VIDEO PRODUCTION GRANTS**

Purpose: To assist independent Manitoba film and video artists in the creation and production of high quality, innovative work
Eligibility:
    Citizenship: Canada (landed immigrants also eligible)
    Residency: Manitoba, 1 year
    Special Requirements: Professional artists only; must have completed basic training; no students; principal creator/director of film/video must apply; applicant must retain artistic control and rights; commissioned, instructional, promotional, and industrial projects ineligible; pilots for commercial or educational television ineligible
    Art Forms: Film, video
Type of Support: Up to $20,000
Scope of Program: 7 grants, totalling $67,440, in FY 1992-93
Application/Selection Process:
    Deadline: April 1 and October 1, annually
    Preferred Initial Contact: Consult with Associate Visual Arts Officer before applying
    Application Procedure: Submit application form, project proposal and budget, resumé, filmography/videography, synopsis and draft script (dramatic works), outline (documentaries), storyboard (animated works), film/video treatment, shooting script, samples of work
    Selection Process: Jury of independent professionals in the visual arts
    Notification Process: 2 months after deadline
    Formal Report of Grant Required: Yes

➤ **FILM SCRIPT DEVELOPMENT GRANTS/VIDEO SCRIPT DEVELOPMENT GRANTS**

Purpose: To assist independent Manitoba film and video artists or writers in the creation of scripts for film or video
Eligibility:
    Citizenship: Canada (landed immigrants also eligible)
    Residency: Manitoba, 1 year

Please read carefully!
Do not contact any listed organization unless you fulfill all eligibility requirements.

Special Requirements: Professional artists only; must have completed basic training; no students; applicant must retain artistic control over script; scripts for commissioned, instructional, promotional, and industrial projects ineligible
Art Forms: Film scripts, video scripts
Type of Support: Up to $6,000
Scope of Program: 5 grants, totalling $26,500, in 1992-93
Application/Selection Process:
   Deadline: April 1 and October 1, annually
   Preferred Initial Contact: Consult with Associate Visual Arts Officer before applying
   Application Procedure: Submit application form, project proposal and budget, resumé, filmography/videography, outline of script, samples of work
   Selection Process: Jury of independent professionals in the visual arts
   Notification Process: 2 months after deadline
   Formal Report of Grant Required: Yes

➤ **ARTVENTURES "A" GRANTS**

Purpose: To support developmental and innovative programs in the arts
Eligibility:
   Citizenship: Canada
   Residency: Manitoba, 1 year
   Art Forms: All disciplines
Type of Support: Up to $5,000
Scope of Program: 30 grants, totalling $149,000, to individuals and organizations in various disciplines in FY 1992-93
Application/Selection Process:
   Deadline: May 1 and October 1, annually
   Preferred Initial Contact: Call or write for application/guidelines
   Application Procedure: Submit application form, additional materials as requested
   Selection Process: Peer review panel, jury decision
   Notification Process: Letter
   Formal Report of Grant Required: Yes

➤ **SHORT-TERM PROJECT GRANTS FOR VISUAL ARTS/CRAFTS/FILM & VIDEO**

Purpose: To assist professional Manitoba visual artists, media artists or craftspeople with short-term projects and professional development programs by defraying expenses of short-term study or master classes, workshops or seminars, exhibition, travel
Eligibility:
   Citizenship: Canada

Please read carefully!
Do not contact any listed organization unless you fulfill all eligibility requirements.

Residency: Manitoba, 1 year
Special Requirements: Professional artists only; must have been practicing art for 3 years including duration of study; no students; limit 1 award per fiscal year
Art Forms: Visual arts, crafts, media arts
Type of Support: Up to $1,000
Scope of Program: $21,675 to visual artists, $4,750 to craftspeople, $6,746 to film/video artists in FY 1992-93
Application/Selection Process:
Deadline: 1 month before project
Preferred Initial Contact: Consult with Associate Visual Arts Officer before applying
Application Procedure: Submit application form, statement of artistic activities, project budget, resumé, written confirmation of event or registration (if applicable), samples of work
Selection Process: Staff review
Notification Process: 1 month after application
Formal Report of Grant Required: Yes

TECHNICAL ASSISTANCE PROGRAMS AND SERVICES

Programs of Special Interest: The Artists in the Schools Program maintains a roster of professional artists eligible for short-term and long-term residencies in Manitoba schools (contact Ann Atkey, Arts Education Officer, 204-945-2978).

MARIN ARTS COUNCIL

251 North San Pedro Road
San Rafael, CA 94903
415-499-8350

PROFILE OF FINANCIAL SUPPORT TO ARTISTS

Total Funding/Value of In-Kind Support: $155,000 in 1992
Competition for Funding: Total applications, 372; total individuals funded/provided with in-kind support, 46
Grant Range: Up to $10,000

DIRECT SUPPORT PROGRAMS
➤ **INDIVIDUAL ARTISTS GRANTS PROGRAM**
Purpose: To support Marin's working artists by providing unrestricted fellowships

Please read carefully!
Do not contact any listed organization unless you fulfill all eligibility requirements.

Eligibility:

Residency: Marin County, 1 year

Age: 18 or older

Special Requirements: Original artwork only; no undergraduate students; no graduate students enrolled in programs related to discipline of application; professional artists only; previous grantees ineligible for 3 years

Art Forms: Playwriting, screenwriting, literature, poetry, crafts, sculpture/3D, painting/2D, photography, music composition, choreography, film/video, interdisciplinary media (including performance art, conceptual art, artists' books and nontraditional media), and art for youth

Type of Support: $2,000-$10,000 fellowships

Scope of Program: $105,000 available in 1993

Application/Selection Process:

Deadline: January 30 (playwriting, poetry, fiction, creative prose), May 15 (all other disciplines), annually

Preferred Initial Contact: Send SASE for application

Application Procedure: Submit application form, samples of work; finalists asked to submit additional materials

Selection Process: Jury of artists and arts professionals

Notification Process: 3 months after deadline

Formal Report of Grant Required: No

➤ **COMMUNITY ARTS GRANTS PROGRAM**

Purpose: To encourage artistic activities that provide excellent or unusual opportunities for the public to actively practice the arts with arts professionals in community settings

Eligibility:

Special Requirements: Arts organizations, groups, and individuals are eligible; projects must take place in Marin County and actively involve the public in artistic activity; previous grantees ineligible for 1 year

Art Forms: All disciplines

Type of Support: Up to $5,000

Scope of Program: $100,000 available in 1993-94

Application/Selection Process:

Deadline: July and December, annually; contact for exact dates

Application Procedure: Submit application form, project budget, letter of support

Selection Process: Panel of arts professionals and community members, board of trustees

Notification Process: 2-3 months after deadline

Formal Report of Grant Required: Yes

Please read carefully!

Do not contact any listed organization unless you fulfill all eligibility requirements.

TECHNICAL ASSISTANCE PROGRAMS AND SERVICES

Programs of Special Interest: The council provides management assistance in areas such as finance, long-range planning and marketing. The annual *Arts Resource Directory* profiles Marin-based arts organizations, businesses, arts educators, and individual artists. *Artists Dialogue* is a bimonthly publication produced by and for members. The council also offers group health insurance to members (membership fees: $25 individual; $35 family or nonprofit organization).

MARYLAND STATE ARTS COUNCIL (MSAC)

601 North Howard Street
Baltimore, MD 21201
410-333-8232
TDD: 410-333-6926
FAX: 410-333-1062

PROFILE OF FINANCIAL SUPPORT TO ARTISTS

Total Funding/Value of In-Kind Support: $175,000 for FY 1992

Competition for Funding: Total applications, 1,200; total individuals funded/provided with in-kind support, 94

Grant Range: $1,000 to $6,000

DIRECT SUPPORT PROGRAMS

➤ **INDIVIDUAL ARTIST AWARDS**

Purpose: To identify, develop, and sustain artistic excellence in Maryland

Eligibility:

    Citizenship: U.S., or permanent resident

    Residency: Maryland, 6 months prior to application date

    Age: 18 or older

    Special Requirements: No students; previous grantees ineligible for 1 year

    Art Forms: Apply for visual arts 2-D and 3-D (painting, sculpture, works-on-paper, etc.), crafts, photography, media arts, new genre visual arts (collaborations, installations, interdisciplinary, multi-media) in even-numbered years; apply for choreography, fiction, music composition, new genre performing arts, playwriting, poetry in odd-numbered years

Type of Support: $1,000-$6,000

Scope of Program: 94 awards in 1992

Please read carefully!
Do not contact any listed organization unless you fulfill all eligibility requirements.

Application/Selection Process:
    Deadline: Contact by mid-September for deadline details
    Preferred Initial Contact: Call or write for application/guidelines
    Application Procedure: Submit application form, samples of work
    Selection Process: Peer panel of artists, MSAC board
    Notification Process: Letter in May or June
    Formal Report of Grant Required: Yes

TECHNICAL ASSISTANCE PROGRAMS AND SERVICES

Programs of Special Interest: The MSAC Visual Arts Resource Center and Slide Registry are located at Maryland Art Place, 218 West Saratoga Street, Baltimore, MD 21201; 410-962-8565. MSAC sponsors an Arts-in-Education program. Contact Linda Vlasik, Program Director.

MASSACHUSETTS CULTURAL COUNCIL (MCC)

80 Boylston Street
Suite 1000
Boston, MA 02116
617-727-3668
TDD: 617-338-9153
FAX: 617-727-0044

PROFILE OF FINANCIAL SUPPORT TO ARTISTS

Total Funding/Value of In-Kind Support: $239,000 in 1992

Competition for Funding: Total applications, 220; total individuals funded/provided with in-kind support, 154

Grant Range: n/a

DIRECT SUPPORT PROGRAMS
➤ **EVENT AND RESIDENCY GRANTS**
CONTACT: CAROL GUIDICE, EDUCATION PROGRAM AND SERVICES COORDINATOR

Purpose: Event and Residency Grants allow schools to bring artists into the classroom for short-term events and long-term residencies

Eligibility:
    Citizenship: U.S. or legal resident
    Residency: Applicants must be legal residents of Massachusetts
    Age: 18 years of age or older
    Special Requirements: Professional artists only; individuals enrolled in degree or certificate granting programs are ineligible
    Art Forms: All disciplines

Please read carefully!
Do not contact any listed organization unless you fulfill all eligibility requirements.

Type of Support: Depends on specifics and length of event or residency; artists apply to be listed in MCC's *Cultural Resources Directory* from which schools may select individual artists; an average fee is $150 per day

Scope of Program: 52 residencies, 78 events funded in 1993

Application/Selection Process:

Deadline: Schools apply by April 15 (for fall) and November 15 (for spring)

Preferred Initial Contact: Write or call for application/guidelines

Application Procedure: Schools submit forms for Events and Residencies; artists required to fill out portion of Residency applications only

Selection Process: Review by professional artists and arts educators

Notification Process: Letter

Formal Report of Grant Required: Yes

TECHNICAL ASSISTANCE PROGRAMS AND SERVICES

Programs of Special Interest: The council funds local cultural councils across the state to give grants to artists and organizations. October 15 is the annual deadline; contact MCC for details. MCC's Individual Project Support Program has been suspended, but the council is currently developing a fellowship program for individual artists. There is also a file of job openings, competitions and fellowships available to artists. Council staff provide technical assistance workshops on a variety of topics throughout the year.

MAYOR'S OFFICE OF ART, CULTURE AND FILM (MOACF), CITY AND COUNTY OF DENVER

280 14th Street
Denver, CO 80202
303-640-2678
FAX: 303-640-2737
CONTACT: JOYCE OBERFELD, DIRECTOR

TECHNICAL ASSISTANCE PROGRAMS AND SERVICES

Programs of Special Interest: The staff of the Mayor's Office of Art, Culture and Film are available on a regular basis to provide technical assistance to nonprofit arts organizations and individual artists on grantsmanship. Call for times and for additional information. Opportunities for commissioned work may become available to film and video artists; contact the organization for information.

Please read carefully!
Do not contact any listed organization unless you fulfill all eligibility requirements.

MEDIA ALLIANCE

c/o Thirteen/WNET
356 West 58th Street
New York, NY 10019
212-560-2919
FAX: 212-560-6866

PROFILE OF FINANCIAL SUPPORT TO ARTISTS
Total Funding/Value of In-Kind Support: n/a
Competition for Funding: Total applications, 125; total individuals funded/provided with in-kind support, 3 in 1992
Grant Range: $5,000

DIRECT SUPPORT PROGRAM
➤ **MEDIA ARTS FELLOWSHIP PROGRAM**
Purpose: To support media artists who are not financially privileged and who have achieved a significant level of skill/expertise and commitment to media arts, but who have not yet made a transition into a professional career
Eligibility:
Citizenship: n/a
Residency: New York State
Age: 30 years old or under
Special Requirements: Post-college/post-formal training required; college degree not required; applicants must be economically disadvantaged; artists of color are especially encouraged to apply; students are ineligible; copy required of grantees finished work
Art Forms: Media arts
Type of Support: $5,000 grant
Scope of Program: 3 in 1992
Application/Selection Process:
Deadline: October 1, annually
Preferred Initial Contact: Call or write for application/guidelines
Application Procedure: Submit application form, letters of reference, resumé, work sample; materials will be returned if proper container/postage is included with application
Selection Process: Panel review
Notification Process: Letter in December
Formal Report of Grant Required: Yes

Please read carefully!
Do not contact any listed organization unless you fulfill all eligibility requirements.

EQUIPMENT ACCESS

Comments: The ON-LINE Program gives professional producers creating noncommercial artistic projects and documentaries access to state-of-the-art production and post-production services at commercial facilities in New York State at rates 50%-80% lower than commercial rates. ($30 membership fee and $35 per project administrative fee required.)

TECHNICAL ASSISTANCE PROGRAMS AND SERVICES

Programs of Special Interest: Media Alliance maintains a mailing list of independent producers, publishes a bimonthly newsletter, and conducts workshops on managing and marketing the media arts. (Some services for members only; individual membership fees $20-$30; additional fees required for workshops.)

MEDIA ARTS CENTER/ARTS COUNCIL OF GREATER NEW HAVEN

70 Audubon Street, 2nd Floor
New Haven, CT 06510
203-772-2788

EQUIPMENT ACCESS

Video: Production for 3/4", Hi-8, VHS; post-production interformat 3/4", Hi-8, S-VHS

Comments: The Media Arts Center offers affordable equipment rental rates to members working on noncommercial projects. A $50 Access Membership provides access to in-house post-production equipment and some production equipment during regular business hours; a $150 Full Access Membership provides access to all production and post-production equipment on a 24-hour basis. Production services for not-for-profit organizations are also available.

TECHNICAL ASSISTANCE PROGRAMS AND SERVICES

Programs of Special Interest: The Media Arts Center offers courses and workshops on media-related topics, and provides networking opportunities for local as well as national media artists. Membership services include discounts on all equipment, facilities and courses as well as information about jobs, festivals and grants. Insurance is available to individuals through the Arts Council of Greater New Haven; contact for details.

Please read carefully!
Do not contact any listed organization unless you fulfill all eligibility requirements.

MEDIA NETWORK/ALTERNATIVE MEDIA INFORMATION CENTER

39 West 14th Street
Suite 403
New York, NY 10011
212-929-2663
FAX: 212-929-2732

TECHNICAL ASSISTANCE PROGRAMS AND SERVICES

Programs of Special Interest: Media Network acts as a fiscal agent
for independent film and video artists whose work addresses social,
political, or cultural issues; publishes guides of social issue media;
organizes conferences and community-based media literacy workshops that teach people successful strategies for using videotapes in
their work as educators and counsellors; publishes a quarterly newsletter, *ImMEDIAte Impact*, which explores the relationship between
media and social change. Annual membership for individuals is $25.

MEMORIAL FOUNDATION FOR JEWISH CULTURE

15 East 26th Street, Room 1903
New York, NY 10010
CONTACT: DR. JERRY HOCHBAUM, EXECUTIVE VICE PRESIDENT

PROFILE OF FINANCIAL SUPPORT TO ARTISTS

Total Funding/Value of In-Kind Support: n/a
Competition for Funding: n/a
Grant Range: $1,000-$4,000

DIRECT SUPPORT PROGRAM

➤ **INTERNATIONAL FELLOWSHIPS IN JEWISH STUDIES**

Purpose: To assist well-qualified individuals in carrying out an inde-
pendent scholarly, literary or art project, in a field of Jewish speciali-
zation, which makes a significant contribution to the understanding,
preservation, enhancement or transmission of Jewish culture
Eligibility:
  Citizenship: Open
  Residency: Open
  Age: Open

Please read carefully!
Do not contact any listed organization unless you fulfill all eligibility requirements.

Special Requirements: Any qualified scholar, researcher or artist who possesses the knowledge and experience to formulate and implement a project in a field of Jewish specialization can apply; recipients can apply for a second year, but must request renewal in writing and submit a new application; usually, no more than two grants will be made to an individual

Art Forms: All disciplines

Type of Support: $1,000 to $4,000; amount varies in accordance with the cost of living in the country in which the fellowship recipient resides

Scope of Program: n/a

Application/Selection Process:

   Deadline: October 31, annually

   Preferred Initial Contact: Write only for application/guidelines

   Application Procedure: Submit application form, references, slides of work (Note: materials, including slides, will not be returned)

   Selection Process: Experts outside the foundation; foundation committee

   Notification Process: Notification by August of following year

   Formal Report of Grant Required: Yes

METROPOLITAN REGIONAL ARTS COUNCIL (MRAC)

345 St. Peter Street
Suite 700
St. Paul, MN 55102
612-292-8010
FAX: 612-292-0025

PROFILE OF FINANCIAL SUPPORT TO ARTISTS

Total Funding/Value of In-Kind Support: n/a

Competition for Funding: Total applications, 126; total individuals funded/provided with in-kind support, 52

Grant Range: n/a

DIRECT SUPPORT PROGRAMS

➤ ARTS ACTIVITIES SUPPORT GRANTS

Purpose: One- and two-year grants to support nonprofit organizations or informal groups of three or more artists to undertake time-specific arts activities that produce art

Eligibility:

   Residency: Artists must be residents of the seven-county Minneapolis/St. Paul metropolitan area

Please read carefully!
Do not contact any listed organization unless you fulfill all eligibility requirements.

Special Requirements: Individual artists must apply in groups of 3 or more; project must take place in the seven-county Minneapolis/St. Paul metropolitan area; applicants must have matching funds or in-kind support; projects must not be exclusively for or by student organizations or schools
Art Forms: All disciplines
Type of Support: Maximum $7,500 for up to 50% of project or program (match may include in-kind support)
Scope of Program: $350,000 budget for 1993
Application/Selection Process:
  Deadline: Spring and fall, annually; contact for exact dates
  Preferred Initial Contact: Call or write for information
  Selection Process: Panel of artists and arts professionals
  Notification Process: Letter 3 months after deadline
  Formal Report of Grant Required: Yes

TECHNICAL ASSISTANCE PROGRAMS AND SERVICES

Programs of Special Interest: Groups in the seven-county Minneapolis/St. Paul metro area may also apply for Small Grants which fund first-time initiatives in community arts and help support them in their early years of development. Community arts activities are collaborative efforts between artist, arts organizations and community groups. Grants range from $500 to $2,000.

MICHIANA ARTS AND SCIENCES COUNCIL, INC.

P.O. Box 1543
South Bend, IN 46634
219-235-9160
CONTACT: LESLIE J. CHOITZ, ARTS PROGRAM DIRECTOR

TECHNICAL ASSISTANCE PROGRAMS AND SERVICES

Programs of Special Interest: MASC maintains a resource library for the arts, a job bank, and a computerized file of performing and visual artists. Fellowship opportunities may be available for artists of all disciplines who are residents of St. Joseph, Elkhart, LaPorte, Kosciusko counties for at least one year. In 1993, the deadline is October 15; contact the council for further details.

Please read carefully!
Do not contact any listed organization unless you fulfill all eligibility requirements.

MICHIGAN COUNCIL FOR ARTS AND CULTURAL AFFAIRS

1200 Sixth Street, Suite 1180
State Plaza Building
Detroit, MI 48226-2461
313-256-3731
TDD: 313-256-3734
FAX: 313-256-3781

TECHNICAL ASSISTANCE PROGRAMS AND SERVICES

Programs of Special Interest: The council funds a visual arts touring program which features minority artists throughout the state and pays them a stipend, but which is administered by New Initiatives for the Arts, P.O. Box 3382, Grand Rapids, MI 49506; contact Cedric Ward, Program Officer, at 616-771-4163. The Creative Artist Grant program is being administered by the Arts Foundation of Michigan (see separate listing). The council maintains a listing of Michigan artists and operates an Artists-in-Schools program. The Touring Arts Program provides support to organizations and nonprofit groups that present performances or exhibitions by juried Michigan artists. For more information contact the Touring Arts Agency, Midland Center for the Arts, 1801 West St. Andrews, Midland, MI 48640-2695; 517-631-5930.

MID ATLANTIC ARTS FOUNDATION

11 East Chase Street
Suite 2A
Baltimore, MD 21202-2524
410-539-6656
TDD: 410-539-4241
FAX: 410-837-5517
CONTACT: KATE CHANG, DIRECTOR OF VISUAL ARTS

PROFILE OF FINANCIAL SUPPORT TO ARTISTS

Total Funding/Value of In-Kind Support: $269,000 for FY 1993

Competition for Funding: Total applications, 1,500; total individuals funded/provided with in-kind support, 60

Grant Range: $1,200-$6,000

Please read carefully!
Do not contact any listed organization unless you fulfill all eligibility requirements.

DIRECT SUPPORT PROGRAMS

➤ **VISUAL ARTS RESIDENCY PROGRAM**

Purpose: To provide opportunities for artists, especially those based in rural and/or culturally diverse communities, to pursue special projects and create new work in new environments; to provide opportunities for direct dialogue between professional art critics and working artists; to promote the sharing of arts resources and expertise and the exchange of ideas in communities throughout the mid-Atlantic region

Eligibility:

Citizenship: U.S. or permanent resident

Residency: Delaware, District of Columbia, Maryland, New Jersey, New York, Pennsylvania, Virginia, West Virginia, U.S. Virgin Islands; host organization and artist must both be from this region; artist cannot apply to a host within her/his own state

Special Requirements: While individual artists may not apply directly, they are encouraged to initiate residency projects in collaboration with organizations eligible to apply; the foundation publishes a directory of host organizations to facilitate this (see Technical Assistance below)

Art Forms: Visual arts (includes media arts and new genres)

Type of Support: Artists and critics receive residency fees ranging from $1,200-$6,000 depending on length of residency

Scope of Program: 22 nonprofit organizations awarded grants in support of projects involving 29 artists and critics

Application/Selection Process:

Deadline: July, annually; contact for exact date; application available in March

Preferred Initial Contact: Write or call for application/guidelines

Application Procedure: Sponsoring organization submits application

Selection Process: Panel of artists and arts professionals

Notification Process: Host organization notified by November 1

Formal Report of Grant Required: Yes

TECHNICAL ASSISTANCE PROGRAMS AND SERVICES

Programs of Special Interest: Mid Atlantic Arts Foundation develops periodic technical assistance projects and schedules focus groups and networking sessions in conjunction with regional conferences, showcases, festivals, and exhibitions. The Arts Information Exchange (AIEX) is a regional database containing information on approximately 40,000 artists and arts organizations. The information is used to compile directories and mailing lists intended for not-for-profit use. The *Visual Arts Residencies: Sponsor Organization* directory

Please read carefully!
Do not contact any listed organization unless you fulfill all eligibility requirements.

profiles organizations that host residencies and is useful to artists seeking residencies in the mid-Atlantic region.

MILLENNIUM FILM WORKSHOP

66 East 4th Street
New York, NY 10003
212-673-0090

EQUIPMENT ACCESS

Film: Production and post-production for 16mm, Super 8

Video: Production and post-production equipment available beginning in Fall of 1993; contact for details

Comments: Equipment and facilities, including a production studio, are available at low cost to independent filmmakers, artists, and students. ($15, 6-month, or $20, 1-year, membership fee, and $20 monthly equipment access fee required.)

TECHNICAL ASSISTANCE PROGRAMS AND SERVICES

Programs of Special Interest: Millennium Film Workshop offers an extensive equipment loan program as well as in-house rental (fees vary). The Personal Cinema Series screens new works of avant-garde film and video with guest artists to present/discuss their work. *Millennium Film Journal*, published twice per year beginning in 1994, serves as a forum for debate and discussion of issues relating to avant-garde film and video. Millennium also offers film and video workshop classes throughout the year.

MILWAUKEE ARTS BOARD (MAB)

809 North Broadway
Milwaukee, WI 53202
414-286-5700
FAX: 414-286-5904

PROFILE OF FINANCIAL SUPPORT TO ARTISTS

Total Funding/Value of In-Kind Support: n/a

Competition for Funding: n/a

Grant Range: n/a

Please read carefully!
Do not contact any listed organization unless you fulfill all eligibility requirements.

Direct Support Programs
➤ **NEIGHBORHOOD ARTS PROGRAM**

Purpose: To assist nonprofit, neighborhood-based organizations in Milwaukee to strengthen their capacity to work with local artists and to provide local arts programming

Eligibility:
   Residency: Preference given to Milwaukee artists
   Special Requirements: Artists must apply with nonprofit sponsor organization that serves a particular Milwaukee neighborhood and whose governing board is composed primarily of community residents; project must serve a Milwaukee neighborhood; grant must be matched 1:1 (in-kind matches acceptable for first-time applicants)
   Art Forms: All disciplines

Type of Support: Up to $7,000 matching grant

Scope of Program: n/a

Application/Selection Process:
   Deadline: April 1, annually
   Preferred Initial Contact: Call or write for application/guidelines
   Application Procedure: Sponsor submits application form, project budget, financial statement, artist's resumé
   Selection Process: Peer panel of artists, individuals outside of organization, board of directors
   Notification Process: Letter
   Formal Report of Grant Required: Yes

Technical Assistance Programs and Services
Programs of Special Interest: MAB is developing a technical assistance workshop series.

Minnesota State Arts Board

432 Summit Avenue
St. Paul, MN 55102
612-297-2603
TDD: 612-297-5353
FAX: 612-297-4304
CONTACT: KAREN MUELLER, ARTIST ASSISTANCE PROGRAM ASSOCIATE

Profile of Financial Support to Artists
Total Funding/Value of In-Kind Support: $222,000 for FY 1993 (fellowships and career opportunity grants)

Please read carefully!
Do not contact any listed organization unless you fulfill all eligibility requirements.

Competition for Funding: Total applications, 700; total individuals funded/provided with in-kind support, 54

Grant Range: $100-$6,000

DIRECT SUPPORT PROGRAMS

➤ **FELLOWSHIPS**

Purpose: To support artists by providing time, materials, or living expenses

Eligibility:
    Citizenship: U.S.
    Residency: Minnesota, 6 months
    Age: 18 or older
    Special Requirements: Professional artists only; previous recipients ineligible for 2 years
    Art Forms: All disciplines

Type of Support: $6,000 fellowships

Scope of Program: 34 fellowships in FY 1993

Application/Selection Process:
    Deadline: Visual arts: July, annually; contact for exact date
    Preferred Initial Contact: Call or write for application/guidelines
    Application Procedure: Submit application form, samples of work, resumé
    Selection Process: Peer panel of artists and arts professionals, board of directors
    Notification Process: Letter
    Formal Report of Funding Required: Yes

➤ **CAREER OPPORTUNITY GRANTS**

Purpose: To help artists take advantage of opportunities that will significantly advance their work or careers

Eligibility:
    Citizenship: U.S.
    Residency: Minnesota, 6 months
    Age: 18 or older
    Special Requirements: Professional artists only; previous recipients ineligible for 1 year
    Art Forms: All disciplines

Type of Support: $100-$1,000 for specific project

Scope of Program: $20,000 available annually

Application/Selection Process:
    Deadline: 3 times per year; contact for exact dates
    Preferred Initial Contact: Call or write for application/guidelines
    Application Procedure: Submit application form, samples of work, resumé

Please read carefully!
Do not contact any listed organization unless you fulfill all eligibility requirements.

Selection Process: Organization staff, board of directors
Notification Process: Letter
Formal Report of Grant Required: Yes

➤ CULTURAL COLLABORATIONS

Purpose: To encourage collaborations between artists of color and nonprofit arts organizations or community groups in Minnesota

Eligibility:
Citizenship: U.S.
Residency: Minnesota
Age: Over 18
Special Requirements: Artists must be Asian/Pacific Islander, African American, Latino/a, or Native American/Alaskan Native; priority given to artists working within their communities; artists must work with a nonprofit organization
Art Forms: All disciplines

Type of Support: $500-$10,000 matching grants

Scope of Program: $100,000 available in 1993

Application/Selection Process:
Deadline: April 1, 1994; after Spring of 1994, contact directly for deadline information
Preferred Initial Contact: Write or call for guidelines
Application Procedure: As described in guidelines
Selection Process: Committee review
Notification Process: By letter, 2-3 months after deadline
Formal Report of Grant Required: Yes

TECHNICAL ASSISTANCE PROGRAMS AND SERVICES

Programs of Special Interest: Minnesota artists may apply through the arts board for residencies at the Headlands Center for the Arts in Sausalito, California. Artists with school residency experience may apply for inclusion in the Artists in Education Roster of Artists. The Percent for Art in Public Places Program purchases and commissions work from artists nationwide; the arts board distributes prospectuses for specific projects and maintains a slide registry used in artist selection.

Please read carefully!
Do not contact any listed organization unless you fulfill all eligibility requirements.

MISSISSIPPI ARTS COMMISSION

239 North Lamar Street
Suite 207
Jackson, MS 39201
601-359-6030
CONTACT: CINDY JETTER, PROGRAM ADMINISTRATOR, VISUAL ARTS; DEBORAH BOYKIN, FOLK ARTS DIRECTOR

PROFILE OF FINANCIAL SUPPORT TO ARTISTS
Total Funding/Value of In-Kind Support: $25,000 for FY 1992
Competition for Funding: Total applications, 30; total individuals funded/provided with in-kind support, 5
Grant Range: $5,000

DIRECT SUPPORT PROGRAMS
➤ **ARTIST FELLOWSHIPS**
Purpose: To encourage and support the creation of new art and to recognize the contributions of artists of exceptional talent
Eligibility:
   Citizenship: U.S. or permanent residents
   Residency: Mississippi
   Age: 18 or older
   Special Requirements: No students; professional artists and folk artists only; previous grantees ineligible for 5 years
   Art Forms: Disciplines rotate on 2-year cycle: Visual arts (painting, sculpture, works on paper, photography) and crafts (clay, fiber, glass, leather, metal, paper, wood, mixed media), literary arts, folk arts (visual and craft) in odd numbered years; visual arts and design (architectural, fashion, graphic, landscape architecture), performing arts (includes performance art), folk arts (performing) in even numbered years
Type of Support: $5,000 grants
Scope of Program: 5 awards in 1992
Application/Selection Process:
   Deadline: March 1, annually
   Preferred Initial Contact: Call or write for application/guidelines
   Application Procedure: Submit application form, samples of work, resumé
   Selection Process: Peer panel of artists, board of directors
   Notification Process: Letter in early July
   Formal Report of Grant Required: Yes

Please read carefully!
Do not contact any listed organization unless you fulfill all eligibility requirements.

➤ **ARTS IN EDUCATION: ARTS DEMONSTRATORS**
CONTACT: KATHLEEN STEPT, ARTS EDUCATION DIRECTOR

Purpose: To allow artists and arts educators to participate as arts demonstrators in the Arts Demonstration Program

Eligibility:
  Citizenship: U.S. or permanent resident
  Residency: Open
  Age: 18 or older
  Special Requirements: All approved applicants must attend the commission's training program
  Art Forms: All disciplines

Type of Support: An opportunity to work with teachers in the Mississippi public school system through teacher workshops and residencies; status as Arts Demonstrator good for three years; approval to be an Arts Demonstrator does not guarantee work, but helps publicize an individual artist's qualifications and availability

Scope of Program: About 25 artists currently working in the program

Application/Selection Process:
  Deadline: March 1, annually
  Preferred Initial Contact: Write or call for information
  Application Procedure: Application form, resumé, letters of reference, slides of work (visual, craft, design artists), videotape of work (film, video artists)
  Selection Process: Panel review, commission decision
  Notification Process: Letter in early July

TECHNICAL ASSISTANCE PROGRAMS AND SERVICES

Programs of Special Interest: The commission's Arts Management Library holds books and periodicals covering a broad range of subjects relating to the arts and arts management and is open to the public.

MISSOURI ARTS COUNCIL

Wainwright Office Complex
111 North 7th Street
Suite 105
St. Louis, MO 63101-2188
314-340-6845
TDD: 800-735-2966 (via Relay Missouri)
FAX: 314-340-7215

TECHNICAL ASSISTANCE PROGRAMS AND SERVICES

Programs of Special Interest: Applications for film and video productions may be accepted from Missouri-based nonprofit

Please read carefully!
Do not contact any listed organization unless you fulfill all eligibility requirements.

organizations sponsoring/collaborating with individual media artists. Artists selected for the Missouri Touring Program roster are eligible to tour Missouri communities to present arts-related activities, including exhibitions, lecture-demonstrations, and residencies. The arts council administers an Artists-in-Education program that provides residencies (2-week minimum) and hosts the annual Missouri Arts Conference, which includes a variety of technical assistance workshops for artists and arts organizations.

MONEY FOR WOMEN/BARBARA DEMING MEMORIAL FUND, INC.

P.O. Box 40-1043
Brooklyn, NY 11240-1043
CONTACT: PAM MCALLISTER, ADMINISTRATOR

PROFILE OF FINANCIAL SUPPORT TO ARTISTS
Total Funding/Value of In-Kind Support: n/a
Competition for Funding: n/a
Grant Range: Up to $1,000

DIRECT SUPPORT PROGRAM
➤ **GRANTS PROGRAM**
Purpose: To give small grants to individual feminists in the arts whose work speaks for peace and justice
Eligibility:
    Citizenship: U.S. or Canada
    Age: n/a
    Special Requirements: The fund does not give educational assistance, monies for personal study or loans, monies for dissertation or research projects, grants for group projects or business ventures
    Art Forms: Visual arts (including photography), film, music, dance, literature (writers, poets, playwrights)
Type of Support: Up to $1,000
Scope of Program: n/a
Application/Selection Process:
    Deadline: December 31 and June 30, annually
    Preferred Initial Contact: Write only
    Application Procedure: Send SASE for application; $5 processing fee
    Selection Process: n/a
    Notification Process: n/a
    Formal Report of Grant Required: n/a

MONTANA ARTS COUNCIL (MAC)

316 North Park Avenue, Room 252
Helena, MT 59620
406-444-6430
TDD: 800-253-4091 (via Montana Relay Service)
FAX: 406-444-6548
CONTACT: MARTHA SPRAGUS, DIRECTOR OF ARTISTS SERVICES PROGRAMS

PROFILE OF FINANCIAL SUPPORT TO ARTISTS

Total Funding/Value of In-Kind Support: $14,000 for FY 1993
(fellowships only)
Competition for Funding: Total applications, n/a; total individuals
funded/provided with in-kind support, 7
Grant Range: $2,000

DIRECT SUPPORT PROGRAMS

➤ **INDIVIDUAL ARTIST FELLOWSHIP PROGRAM**

Purpose: To recognize, reward, and encourage outstanding
professional artists in Montana
Eligibility:
   Citizenship: U.S.
   Residency: Montana
   Age: 18 or older
   Special Requirements: No students; previous grantees ineligible
   Art Forms: Dance, music, opera/musical theater, theater, visual
   arts, crafts, photography, media arts, literature (alternate years only)
Type of Support: $2,000 grants
Scope of Program: 7 awards in 1993
Application/Selection Process:
   Deadline: April 30, annually
   Preferred Initial Contact: Call or write for application/guidelines
   Application Procedure: Submit application form, samples of
   work, resumé, support materials (optional)
   Selection Process: Peer panel of artists, board of directors
   Notification Process: Phone call to recipients in early July; letter
   to nonrecipients
   Formal Report of Grant Required: Yes

TECHNICAL ASSISTANCE PROGRAMS AND SERVICES

Programs of Special Interest: MAC provides technical assistance
through telephone consultation and office visits, maintains a database of individual artists, and publishes *ArtistSearch*, a monthly bulletin

---

Please read carefully!
Do not contact any listed organization unless you fulfill all eligibility requirements.

describing competitions, job openings, and workshops. The council administers Percent for Art project competitions, a visual arts competition for high school students, and an Artists in Schools/Communities program that offers 1-week to 10-month residencies.

NATIONAL ENDOWMENT FOR THE ARTS, INTERNATIONAL PROGRAM

Nancy Hanks Center
1100 Pennsylvania Avenue, NW, Room 618
Washington, DC 20506
202-682-5422
TDD: 202-682-5496
CONTACT: PROGRAM OFFICER

PROFILE OF FINANCIAL SUPPORT TO ARTISTS

Total Funding/Value of In-Kind Support: $200,000 for FY 1993

Competition for Funding: Total applications, n/a; total individuals funded/provided with in-kind support, 15

Grant Range: n/a

DIRECT SUPPORT PROGRAMS

➤ **UNITED STATES/JAPAN ARTISTS' EXCHANGE FELLOWSHIP PROGRAM**

Purpose: To enable American artists to enrich their art by living and working in Japan, to observe Japanese artistic developments in their fields of interest, and to meet with their professional counterparts and pursue opportunities for artistic growth

Eligibility:
    Citizenship: U.S. (permanent residents also eligible)
    Special Requirement: No students; artists who have previously spent more than a total of 3 months in Japan ineligible; artists may not earn additional income in Japan for lectures or demonstrations of their work
    Art Forms: All disciplines

Type of Support: 6-month residency in Japan; the five artists selected will receive a monthly stipend sufficient to cover housing, living expenses, and modest professional support services and/or materials. In addition, each artist will receive round-trip transportation and a baggage/storage allowance. If the artist is accompanied by a spouse and/or unmarried children up to the age of 18, round-trip transportation will be provided for them also

Scope of Program: 5 residencies per year

Please read carefully!
Do not contact any listed organization unless you fulfill all eligibility requirements.

Application/Selection Process:
    Deadline: December 10, 1993 (design artists); March 11, 1994 (all other artists); after that, contact directly for deadline information
    Preferred Initial Contact: Call for information
    Application Procedure: Submit application form, samples of work, references, resumé, financial statement, project budget
    Selection Process: Discipline panels, American Selection Committee of artists and arts managers, Japanese Agency for Cultural Affairs
    Notification Process: Letter
    Formal Report of Grant Required: Yes

➤ **UNITED STATES-MEXICO CREATIVE ARTISTS' RESIDENCIES**

Purpose: To enable artists to work on specific projects and to enrich their art through interaction with professional counterparts and interested publics in Mexico. Artists will also be able to observe artistic developments in their field, deepen their understanding of an art form and/or create new work that draws inspiration from the experience in Mexico

Eligibility:
    Citizenship: U.S. or permanent residents
    Residency: Open
    Special Requirements: Participants must be able to spend two consecutive months in Mexico; students, scholars, curators, administrators or critics of the arts are not eligible
    Art Forms: Candidates must be creative (rather than interpretive) artists working in either traditional or contemporary forms

Type of Support: Participants are placed by program administrators at a site which is appropriate for their discipline; U.S. artists are provided with room (hotel, university residence, or artist's home), board, studio space, basic materials, local transportation, health insurance, round-trip transportation, miscellaneous costs

Scope of Program: 10 U.S. artists chosen for residencies in Mexico; 10 Mexican artists chosen for residencies in U.S.

Application/Selection Process:
    Deadline: December 10, 1993 (design artists); March 11, 1994 (all other artists); after that, contact the program directly for deadline information
    Preferred Initial Contact: Call or write for information
    Application Procedure: Submit form with approximately 3 pages of narrative responses to questions, work samples, and 3 letters of recommendation
    Selection Process: Panel review initially, bi-national panel makes final selections
    Notification Process: Letter by late October
    Formal Report of Grant Required: Yes

Please read carefully!
Do not contact any listed organization unless you fulfill all eligibility requirements.

NATIONAL ENDOWMENT FOR THE ARTS, MEDIA ARTS PROGRAM

Nancy Hanks Center
1100 Pennsylvania Avenue, NW
Room 720
Washington, DC 20506
202-682-5452
TDD: 202-682-5496
FAX: 202-682-5744

PROFILE OF FINANCIAL SUPPORT TO ARTISTS

Total Funding/Value of In-Kind Support: $714,000 in 1992 (Film/Video Production grants only)

Competition for Funding: Total applications, 497; total individuals and organizations funded/provided with in-kind support, 20

Grant Range: $10,000-$35,000 for individuals

DIRECT SUPPORT PROGRAMS

➤ **FILM/VIDEO PRODUCTION GRANTS**

CONTACT: MARY SMITH, PROGRAM SPECIALIST

Purpose: To support the creation or completion of film or video artworks of the highest quality

Eligibility:
   Citizenship: U.S. (permanent residents also eligible)
   Special Requirements: Must have substantial professional experience; instructional, promotional, and student projects ineligible; documentation or simple recordings of performances or events for archival purposes are ineligible
   Art Forms: Film, video

Type of Support: $10,000-$35,000 grants for individual producers

Scope of Program: $714,000 granted to individuals and organizations in 1992

Application/Selection Process:
   Deadline: October or November, annually; contact for exact date
   Preferred Initial Contact: Call or write for application/guidelines
   Application Procedure: Submit application form, samples of work, project description and budget, screenplay or treatment (if available), reviews (optional)
   Selection Process: Peer panel, National Council on the Arts, NEA chair
   Notification Process: Letter in June
   Formal Report of Grant Required: Yes

Please read carefully!
Do not contact any listed organization unless you fulfill all eligibility requirements.

NATIONAL ENDOWMENT FOR THE ARTS, PRESENTING AND COMMISSIONING

Nancy Hanks Center
1100 Pennsylvania Avenue, NW
Room 726
Washington, DC 20506
202-682-5444
TDD: 202-682-5496

PROFILE OF FINANCIAL SUPPORT TO ARTISTS

Total Funding/Value of In-Kind Support: $1,100,000 for FY 1991

Competition for Funding: Total applications, 1,989; total groups funded/provided with in-kind support, 163

Grant Range: $1,000-$6,000

DIRECT SUPPORT PROGRAMS

➤ **ARTISTS PROJECTS REGIONAL INITIATIVE**

Purpose: To support independent artists whose work challenges or extends traditional artistic forms

Eligibility:

Residency: CT, ME, MA, NH, RI, VT contact New England Foundation for the Arts, 678 Massachusetts Avenue, Cambridge, MA 02139; 617-492-2914

DE, MD, NJ, PA, VA, WV, DC contact Painted Bride Art Center, 230 Vine Street, Philadelphia, PA 19106; 215-925-9914

GA, KY, NC, SC, TN contact Alternate Roots, Little Five Points Community Center, 1083 Austin Avenue, NE, Atlanta, GA 30307; 404-577-1079

AL, AR, LA, MS contact Contemporary Arts Center, P.O. Box 30498, New Orleans, LA 70190; 504-523-1216

FL contact Florida Dance Association, Miami Dade Community College, Wolfson Campus, 300 NE Second Avenue, Suite 1412, Miami, FL 33132; 305-237-3413

PR contact Puerto Rico Community Foundation, Royal Bank Center, Suite 1417, Ponce de Leon Avenue, Hato Rey, PR 00917; 809-751-3885

AZ, NM, OK, TX contact Mexic-Arte, P.O. Box 2632, Austin, TX 78768; 512-480-9373

IL, IN, MI, MO, OH contact Randolph Street Gallery, 756 North Milwaukee, Chicago, IL 60622; 312-666-7737

IA, MN, KS, NE, ND, SD, WI contact Intermedia Arts Minnesota, 425 Ontario Street SE, Minneapolis, MN 55414; 612-627-4444

CO, ID, MT, NV, WY, UT contact Helena Presents, 15 North Ewing,

---

Please read carefully!
Do not contact any listed organization unless you fulfill all eligibility requirements.

Helena, MT 59601; 406-443-0287

AK, OR, WA contact On the Boards, 153 14th Avenue, Seattle, WA 98122; 206-325-7901

CA, HI contact Los Angeles Contemporary Exhibitions after January 1, 6522 Hollywood Boulevard, Hollywood, CA 90028; 213-957-1777 or New Langton Arts, 1246 Folsom, San Francisco, CA 94103; 415-626-5416

Special Note: New York State and New York City artists cannot directly apply for project funding because the two organizations which administer this program in the state (Pyramid Arts Center, Rochester; Lower Manhattan Cultural Council, Manhattan) have designated nominators which select artists

Art Forms: Interdisciplinary, multi-disciplinary

Type of Support: $1,000-$6,000 project support

Scope of Program: $440,000 granted through 15 organizations

Application/Selection Process: Contact appropriate arts organization from list above

NATIONAL ENDOWMENT FOR THE ARTS, VISUAL ARTS PROGRAM

Nancy Hanks Center
1100 Pennsylvania Avenue, NW
Room 729
Washington, DC 20506
202-682-5448
TDD: 202-682-5496

PROFILE OF FINANCIAL SUPPORT TO ARTISTS

Total Funding/Value of In-Kind Support: $1,420,000 for FY 1992

Competition for Funding: Total applications, 3,372; total individuals funded/provided with in-kind support, 71

Grant Range: $15,000-$20,000

DIRECT SUPPORT PROGRAMS

➤ VISUAL ARTIST FELLOWSHIPS

Purpose: To encourage the creative development of professionally practicing artists, enabling them to pursue their work

Eligibility:

Citizenship: U.S. (permanent residents also eligible)

Please read carefully!
Do not contact any listed organization unless you fulfill all eligibility requirements.

Special Requirements: Professional artists only; no students pursuing undergraduate or graduate degrees; previous recipients who received $15,000 or more ineligible for 2 cycles; artists may apply in only 1 fellowship area per cycle

Art Forms: Eligible media rotate on 2-year cycle: painting, works on paper (includes printmaking, drawing, artists' books), other genres (includes installation, computer, conceptual, performance, video) eligible in odd-numbered years; photography, sculpture, crafts eligible in even-numbered years

Type of Support: $15,000-$20,000 fellowships

Scope of Program: $1,420,000 awarded to 71 artists in FY 1992

Application/Selection Process:

Deadline: Photography (January 25, 1994); sculpture (February 15, 1994); crafts (March 15, 1994); other genres, painting, works on paper will have deadlines in the first quarter of 1995

Preferred Initial Contact: Call or write for application/guidelines

Application Procedure: Submit application form, samples of work, resumé

Selection Process: Peer panel of artists, National Council on the Arts, NEA chair

Notification Process: Letter in September

Formal Report of Grant Required: Yes

NATIONAL ENDOWMENT FOR THE HUMANITIES, MEDIA PROGRAM

1100 Pennsylvania Avenue, NW
Washington, DC 20506
202-606-8278
TDD: 202-606-8338
FAX: 202-606-8557

PROFILE OF FINANCIAL SUPPORT TO ARTISTS

Total Funding/Value of In-Kind Support: $11,400,000 for FY 1992 (includes grants to organizations)

Competition for Funding: Total applications, 195; total individuals funded/provided with in-kind support, 45

Grant Range: n/a

DIRECT SUPPORT PROGRAMS

➤ HUMANITIES PROJECTS IN MEDIA

Purpose: To provide support for the planning, scripting, or production of film, television, and radio programs on humanities subjects

Please read carefully!
Do not contact any listed organization unless you fulfill all eligibility requirements.

Eligibility:
    Citizenship: U.S. (permanent residents also eligible)
    Residency: Open
    Special Requirements: Projects must involve humanities subjects and be suited for a national audience; projects must involve collaborations among humanities scholars and experienced producers, directors, and writers; individual recipients who do not have tax-exempt status must have a nonprofit organization serve as fiscal sponsor
    Art Forms: Film, video, radio

Type of Support: Planning grants, up to $20,000; scripting grants, $20,000-$90,000; production grants, $150,000-$900,000 (ranges of funding approximate)

Scope of Program: $11,400,000 awarded in 1992

Application/Selection Process:
    Deadline: March and September, annually; contact for exact dates
    Preferred Initial Contact: Call or write for guidelines and application form; the NEH encourages applicants to call for a preliminary discussion of their project to ensure a smoother application process
    Application Procedure: Submit application form, samples of work
    Selection Process: Review by panels, staff, the National Council on the Humanities and the chairman
    Notification Process: Letter approximately 4 months after deadline
    Formal Report of Grant Required: Yes

NATIONAL FOUNDATION FOR ADVANCEMENT IN THE ARTS (NFAA)

3915 Biscayne Boulevard
4th Floor
Miami, FL 33137
305-573-0490
FAX: 305-573-4870
CONTACT: PROGRAMS DEPARTMENT

PROFILE OF FINANCIAL SUPPORT TO ARTISTS

Total Funding/Value of In-Kind Support: $200,000 for FY 1992

Competition for Funding: Total applications, 7,000; total individuals funded/provided with in-kind support, 300

Grant Range: $100-$5,000

DIRECT SUPPORT PROGRAMS
➤ **CAREER ADVANCEMENT OF VISUAL ARTISTS (CAVA)**

Purpose: To provide unencumbered work time, an opportunity to work in a different environment, and professional exposure for young artists who have completed their formal education

Eligibility:
 Citizenship: U.S. or permanent resident
 Age: 19-39
 Special Requirements: Must have completed formal education at least 1 year ago
 Art Forms: Visual arts, photography, media arts

Type of Support: 4-month residencies in Miami including transportation, living and studio facilities, supplies, and $1,000 monthly stipend; residents' work exhibited at a Miami gallery or museum; residencies renewable annually for up to 3 years

Scope of Program: 3 new residencies per year

Application/Selection Process:
 Deadline: October 1, annually
 Preferred Initial Contact: Call or write for application/guidelines
 Application Procedure: Submit application form, samples of work
 Selection Process: Individuals outside of organization
 Notification Process: Letter in December

TECHNICAL ASSISTANCE PROGRAMS AND SERVICES

Programs of Special Interest: The NFAA also administers the Arts Recognition and Talent Search (ARTS) program which awards cash grants to high school seniors in all arts disciplines to assist them in their educational and chosen professional careers; the Charles Cinnamon Award provides project grants to members of the ARTS program four to five years after their initial recognition.

NATIVE AMERICAN
PUBLIC BROADCASTING CONSORTIUM, INC.

P.O. Box 83111
Lincoln, NE 68501
402-472-3522
FAX: 402-472-8675
CONTACT: FRANK BLYTHE, EXECUTIVE DIRECTOR

PROFILE OF FINANCIAL SUPPORT TO ARTISTS
Total Funding/Value of In-Kind Support: n/a

Please read carefully!
Do not contact any listed organization unless you fulfill all eligibility requirements.

Competition for Funding: Total applications, 100; total individuals funded/provided with in-kind support, 12 (figures represent an annual average)

Grant Range: $3,000-$30,000

DIRECT SUPPORT PROGRAMS

➤ **NATIVE AMERICAN PROGRAM GRANTS**

Purpose: To support public television film and video programs that address Native American subjects

Eligibility:
    Citizenship: U.S. or permanent resident
    Residency: Open
    Age: 21 or older
    Special Requirements: Work should originate from and address the Native American experience
    Art Forms: Film and video television programs

Type of Support: $3,000-$30,000

Scope of Program: 10-12 awards annually

Application/Selection Process:
    Preferred Initial Contact: Write or call for application/guidelines
    Deadline: Spring, annually; contact for exact date
    Application Procedure: Submit application form, additional materials as requested
    Selection Process: Panel review; final approval by board of directors
    Notification Process: Notice of receipt of application; letter approximately 3 months after deadline
    Formal Report of Grant Required: Yes

TECHNICAL ASSISTANCE PROGRAMS AND SERVICES

Programs of Special Interest: Matching travel support grants are available to Native American producers for attendance at national public radio and television conferences.

NEBRASKA ARTS COUNCIL (NAC)

3838 Davenport
Omaha, NE 68131-2329
402-595-2122 (Voice and TDD)
FAX: 402-595-2334

TECHNICAL ASSISTANCE PROGRAMS AND SERVICES

Programs of Special Interest: NAC offers grants workshops and operates the Arts Information Referral Service, an unpublished,

Please read carefully!
Do not contact any listed organization unless you fulfill all eligibility requirements.

unjuried directory of Nebraska artists. NAC publicizes 1% for Art competitions and approves artists for 1-week to 12-month Artists-in-Schools/Communities residencies and for participation in the Nebraska Touring Program.

NEVADA STATE COUNCIL ON THE ARTS (NSCA)

329 Flint Street
Reno, NV 89501
702-688-1225
FAX: 702-688-1110
CONTACT: SHARON ROSSE, DIRECTOR OF SERVICES

PROFILE OF FINANCIAL SUPPORT TO ARTISTS
Total Funding/Value of In-Kind Support: $34,488 for FY 1993
Competition for Funding: Total applications, 37; total individuals funded/provided with in-kind support, 5 (fellowships only)
Grant Range: $250-$10,000

DIRECT SUPPORT PROGRAMS
➤ **FELLOWSHIPS**
Purpose: To assist artists' efforts to advance their careers by supporting the creation of new works
Eligibility:
  Citizenship: U.S. (resident aliens also eligible)
  Residency: Nevada, 1 year
  Special Requirements: Professional artists only
  Art Forms: Visual arts (includes film and video) and literature, apply in even-numbered years; performing arts, apply in odd-numbered years
Type of Support: $2,000-$10,000
Scope of Program: $18,000 in FY 1993
Application/Selection Process:
  Deadline: June 1, annually
  Preferred Initial Contact: Call or write for application/guidelines
  Application Procedure: Submit application form, samples of work, resumé
  Selection Process: Peer panel of artists, state arts council
  Notification Process: Letter
  Formal Report of Grant Required: Yes

Please read carefully!
Do not contact any listed organization unless you fulfill all eligibility requirements.

➤ **MINI-GRANTS**

Purpose: To provide short-term project support to meet immediate needs

Eligibility:
   Citizenship: U.S. (resident aliens also eligible)
   Residency: Nevada, 1 year
   Special Requirements: Professional artists only
   Art Forms: All disciplines

Type of Support: Up to $1,000

Scope of Program: $10,000 in FY 1993 awarded to individuals and organizations; amount of funding expected to increase in FY 1994

Application/Selection Process:
   Deadline: Ongoing
   Preferred Initial Contact: Call or write for application/guidelines
   Application Procedure: Submit application form, samples of work, resumé, project budget
   Selection Process: Executive director, chairman
   Notification Process: Letter
   Formal Report of Grant Required: Yes

TECHNICAL ASSISTANCE PROGRAMS AND SERVICES

Programs of Special Interest: The Artist-in-Residence program provides residencies for practicing, professional artists in a variety of settings.

NEW BRUNSWICK DEPARTMENT OF MUNICIPALITIES, CULTURE AND HOUSING— ARTS BRANCH

P.O. Box 6000
Fredericton, New Brunswick
Canada E3B 5H1
506-453-2555
CONTACT: ARTS BRANCH STAFF

PROFILE OF FINANCIAL SUPPORT TO ARTISTS

Total Funding/Value of In-Kind Support: $363,700 for 1991
Competition for Funding: n/a
Grant Range: Up to $10,000

Please read carefully!
Do not contact any listed organization unless you fulfill all eligibility requirements.

DIRECT SUPPORT PROGRAMS

➤ **TRAVEL PROGRAM**

Purpose: To increase participation in regional, national, and international festivals, fairs, and competitions, and to increase exposure of New Brunswick arts products

Eligibility:
> **Citizenship:** Canada (landed immigrants also eligible)
> **Residency:** New Brunswick, 2 of past 4 years
> **Age:** 18 or older
> **Special Requirements:** Must have received recognized honor at the provincial level or provide a letter of invitation
> **Art Forms:** All disciplines

Type of Support: Maximum $5,000 for up to 30% of costs

Scope of Program: $25,000 annual budget

Application/Selection Process:
> **Deadline:** January 15, March 15, July 15, September 15
> **Application Procedure:** Submit application form, supporting materials as specified
> **Selection Procedure:** Multi-disciplinary jury of professional artists
> **Notification Process:** Letter 2 months after deadline
> **Formal Report of Grant Required:** Yes

➤ **PRODUCTION AND CREATION GRANTS**

Purpose: To support research and development or approved projects by artists or curators

Eligibility:
> **Citizenship:** Canada (landed immigrants also eligible)
> **Residency:** New Brunswick, 2 of past 4 years
> **Art Forms:** All disciplines

Type of Support: $1,000-$6,000 grants

Scope of Program: $182,000 annual budget

Application/Selection Process:
> **Deadline:** January 15 and July 15, annually
> **Application Procedure:** Submit application form, supporting materials as specified
> **Selection Process:** Multi-disciplinary jury of professional artists
> **Notification Process:** Letter 2 months after deadline
> **Formal Report of Grant Required:** Yes

➤ **EXCELLENCE AWARDS**

Purpose: To reward and honor excellence in the arts

Eligibility:
> **Citizenship:** Canada (landed immigrants also eligible)
> **Residency:** New Brunswick, 2 of past 4 years

Please read carefully!
Do not contact any listed organization unless you fulfill all eligibility requirements.

Special Requirements: Must be nominated by an individual or group
Art Forms: Visual arts, literature, crafts, performing arts, cinematic arts
Type of Support: Cash prize
Scope of Program: $35,000 distributed according to jury's discretion
Application/Selection Process:
Deadline: September 15 for nominations
Application Procedure: Nominator submits nomination form, supporting materials as specified
Selection Process: Multi-disciplinary jury of professional artists
Notification Process: Letter 2 months after deadline
Formal Report of Grant Required: No

NEW ENGLAND FOUNDATION FOR THE ARTS (NEFA)

678 Massachusetts Avenue
Suite 801
Cambridge, MA 02139
617-492-2914
FAX: 617-876-0702
CONTACT: BJ LARSON, PROGRAM COORDINATOR

PROFILE OF FINANCIAL SUPPORT TO ARTISTS
Total Funding/Value of In-Kind Support: $175,000 for FY 1992
Competition for Funding: Total applications, 1,240; total individuals funded/provided with in-kind support, 40
Grant Range: $2,000-$5,000

DIRECT SUPPORT PROGRAMS
➤ **ARTISTS PROJECTS REGIONAL INITIATIVE**
Purpose: To support projects by lesser-known artists whose work explores new definitions of cultures, artistic disciplines, or traditions and is not easily defined by historical Western-European fine arts traditions
Eligibility:
Citizenship: U.S. (permanent residents also eligible)
Residency: Connecticut, Maine, Massachusetts, New Hampshire, Rhode Island, Vermont
Special Requirements: No students

Please read carefully!
Do not contact any listed organization unless you fulfill all eligibility requirements.

Art Forms: Experimental work that is innovative in form or content, collaborative or traditional work that explores new forms or contexts (eligible projects include performance art, multi-media, installations, dance, environmental work, textiles, theater work)

Type of Support: $2,000-$5,000 for project support

Scope of Program: 20 awards given in 1992

Application/Selection Process:
  Deadline: Deadline varies; contact for details
  Preferred Initial Contact: Call or write for application/guidelines
  Application Procedure: Submit application form, samples of work, resumé, project budget and description; informational workshops are planned at sites throughout New England to answer questions and provide details about the program
  Selection Process: Peer panel of artists and arts professionals
  Notification Process: Letter
  Formal Report of Grant Required: Yes

➤ **MIXED SIGNALS CABLE TELEVISION SERIES**

Purpose: To bring the work of outstanding film and video artists to New England audiences

Eligibility:
  Citizenship: Open internationally; students eligible
  Special Requirements: None
  Art Forms: Film, video

Type of Support: Work broadcast on Mixed Signals, a New England cable television series; artists paid $30 per running minute

Scope of Program: 16-20 recipients per year

Application/Selection Process:
  Deadline: Call or write for details
  Preferred Initial Contact: Call for application/guidelines
  Application Procedure: Submit film or video
  Selection Process: Curator
  Notification Process: Letter

TECHNICAL ASSISTANCE PROGRAMS AND SERVICES

Programs of Special Interest: New England Foundation for the Arts offers workshops to individuals on a variety of topics. Contact the foundation directly for details. The foundation has initiated the formation of the New England Artists Trust, a new organization which will be artist-directed and will seek to serve artists throughout New England by creating an information network, providing funding and services, and offering benefits to its members.

Please read carefully!
Do not contact any listed organization unless you fulfill all eligibility requirements.

NEW HAMPSHIRE STATE COUNCIL ON THE ARTS

40 North Main Street
Concord, NH 03301-4974
603-271-2789
TDD: 800-735-2964
CONTACT: AUDREY SYLVESTER, ARTIST SERVICES COORDINATOR

PROFILE OF FINANCIAL SUPPORT TO ARTISTS

Total Funding/Value of In-Kind Support: $35,500 for FY 1993
Competition for Funding: Total applications, 133; total individuals
funded/provided with in-kind support, 22
Grant Range: $500-$3,000

DIRECT SUPPORT PROGRAMS

➤ INDIVIDUAL ARTIST FELLOWSHIPS

Purpose: To recognize artistic excellence and professional commitment
Eligibility:
    Residency: New Hampshire, 1 year
    Age: 18 or older
    Special Requirements: Must demonstrate professional commit-
    ment; no full-time students; previous recipients ineligible for 1 year
    Art Forms: All disciplines
Type of Support: $3,000 Fellowships; finalists eligible to apply for
up to $500 matching cash Artist Opportunity Grant for professional
development project; Fellowship winners asked to make public
presentation of their work
Scope of Program: 11 Fellowships, 11 Artist Opportunity Grants in
FY 1993
Application/Selection Process:
    Deadline: July 1, annually
    Preferred Initial Contact: Call or write for application/guidelines
    Application Procedure: Submit application form, samples of
    work, resumé
    Selection Process: Peer panel of artists
    Notification Process: Letter or phone call in October
    Formal Report of Grant Required: Yes

TECHNICAL ASSISTANCE PROGRAMS AND SERVICES

Programs of Special Interest: NHSCA maintains a roster of
professional New Hampshire artists eligible for Arts in Education
residencies (contact Arts in Education coordinator). The Percent for
Art Program coordinates the commission and purchase of artwork

Please read carefully!
Do not contact any listed organization unless you fulfill all eligibility requirements.

for state buildings and facilities; New Hampshire visual artists wishing to have work considered for purchase should register with the NHSCA artist slide registry. Other council programs of interest to individual artists include the Community Arts and New Hampshire Touring programs. The council publishes a quarterly listing of artist opportunities in *New Hampshire Arts* and maintains information on legal, health and business issues affecting artists.

NEW JERSEY STATE COUNCIL ON THE ARTS (NJSCA)

CN 306
Trenton, NJ 08625
609-292-6130
TDD: 609-633-1186
FAX: 609-989-1440
CONTACT: STEVEN R. RUNK, GRANTS COORDINATOR

PROFILE OF FINANCIAL SUPPORT TO ARTISTS

Total Funding/Value of In-Kind Support: $429,000 for FY 1993

Competition for Funding: Total applications, 992; total individuals funded/provided with in-kind support, 73

Grant Range: $5,000-$12,000

DIRECT SUPPORT PROGRAMS

➤ **FELLOWSHIP AWARDS**

Purpose: To enable experienced, professional artists to set aside time and purchase materials to create original works of art

Eligibility:
   Residency: New Jersey
   Special Requirements: No students; previous grantees ineligible for 3 years
   Art Forms: Choreography, crafts, design arts, experimental art, graphics, interdisciplinary, music composition, painting, photography, playwriting, prose, poetry, sculpture, and media

Type of Support: $5,000–$12,000

Scope of Program: 73 awards, averaging $6,000, in 1993

Application/Selection Process:
   Deadline: February, annually; contact for exact date
   Preferred Initial Contact: Call or write for application/guidelines
   Application Procedure: Submit application form, samples of work, resumé
   Selection Process: Peer panel of artists

Please read carefully!
Do not contact any listed organization unless you fulfill all eligibility requirements.

Notification Process: Letter 7 months after deadline
Formal Report of Grant Required: Yes

TECHNICAL ASSISTANCE PROGRAMS AND SERVICES
Programs of Special Interest: NJSCA maintains a slide registry open to all artists. Through the Arts Inclusion program, artists selected from the registry are invited to submit proposals for percent for art projects. The Artists-in-Education (AIE) program determines artists' eligibility for 4-day to 4-month residencies in schools and communities.

NEW LANGTON ARTS

1246 Folsom
San Francisco, CA 94103
415-626-5416
FAX: 415-255-1453

TECHNICAL ASSISTANCE PROGRAMS AND SERVICES
Programs of Special Interest: New Langton Arts, in conjunction with Los Angeles Contemporary Exhibitions (see separate listing) administers the National Endowment for the Arts' Artists Projects Regional Initiative in California and Hawaii; this program seeks to encourage innovative projects that push the boundaries of contemporary art and challenge traditional formats; contact for further details. New Langton Arts maintains a video screening room for exhibitions.

NEW LIBERTY PRODUCTIONS (NLP)

3500 Lancaster Avenue
Philadelphia, PA 19104
215-387-2296

EQUIPMENT ACCESS
Film: Post-production for 16mm
Video: Post-production for VHS, Hi-8; video toaster, Amiga graphics
Comments: NLP provides artists with low-cost access to equipment.

TECHNICAL ASSISTANCE PROGRAMS AND SERVICES
Programs of Special Interest: NLP assists young artists in grant preparation and offers fiscal project management services for

experienced and novice producers. NLP offers workshops as well as individual instruction, and maintains a small library of technical, professional and independent oriented film and video journals. Local artists are recruited to work in technical capacities on New Liberty productions.

NEW MEXICO ARTS DIVISION

228 East Palace Avenue
Santa Fe, NM 87501
505-827-6490 (Voice & TDD)
FAX: 505-827-7308

PROFILE OF FINANCIAL SUPPORT TO ARTISTS
Total Funding/Value of In-Kind Support: $128,000 in FY 1992-93
Competition for Funding: Total applications, 96; total individuals funded/provided with in-kind support, 41
Grant Range: Up to $5,000

DIRECT SUPPORT PROGRAMS
➤ ARTS PROJECTS—FOLK ARTS PROJECTS/CULTURALLY DIVERSE ARTS PROJECTS/OTHER ARTS PROJECTS
CONTACT: GRANTS AND SERVICES OFFICE STAFF

Purpose: Folk Arts Projects recognize the wide variety of distinctive folk arts in New Mexico by purchasing short-term arts services from folk artists; Culturally Diverse Arts Projects recognize culturally specific and multicultural arts in New Mexico by procuring short-term arts services from those who practice such arts; Other Arts Projects support projects in all disciplines that do not meet eligibility requirements for Folk Arts or Culturally Diverse Arts
Eligibility:
 Residency: Projects involving New Mexico artists encouraged
 Special Requirements: Artists must apply with a nonprofit organization that agrees to act as a fiscal agent; project must be publicly presented in New Mexico; Other Arts Project applicants must provide 1:1 cash match of grant; Folk Arts Projects and Culturally Diverse Arts Projects applicants must provide cash matches after 2 years of funding; Folk Arts Projects artists must be members of same cultural group to which art form belongs; Culturally Diverse Arts Projects must be by and for culturally specific groups (Hispanic, American Indian, African-American, Asian-American artists encouraged to apply)
 Art Forms: All disciplines

Please read carefully!
Do not contact any listed organization unless you fulfill all eligibility requirements.

Type of Support: Up to $5,000

Scope of Program: 31 projects funded in FY 1992-93

Application/Selection Process:

    Deadline: February, annually; contact for exact date

    Preferred Initial Contact: Consult with Grants and Services Office staff

    Application Procedure: Fiscal agent submits application forms, samples of artist's work, artist's resumé, project budget

    Selection Process: Peer panel of artists, commission

    Notification Process: July

    Formal Report of Grant Required: Yes

TECHNICAL ASSISTANCE PROGRAMS AND SERVICES

Programs of Special Interest: Artists selected for the Arts in Education (AIE) program's *Directory of Artists 1993-1995* are eligible for residencies in community, rural, and institutional settings (contact AIE staff, 505-827-6490). Artists interested in public art commissions should submit a resumé and 5-10 slides of work to the New Mexico Artists/Slide Registry. The Special Funding to Present New Mexico Artists program provides fee support to organizations presenting artists listed in the *Directory of Artists.* The Southwest Arts Conference, which takes place in Scottsdale, AZ, each March, offers workshops for artists.

NEW ORLEANS VIDEO ACCESS CENTER (NOVAC)

2010 Magazine Street
New Orleans, LA 70130-5018
504-524-8626

PROFILE OF FINANCIAL SUPPORT TO ARTISTS

Total Funding/Value of In-Kind Support: $2,500 in 1992

Competition for Funding: Total applications, 15; total individuals funded/provided with in-kind support, 5

Grant Range: n/a

DIRECT SUPPORT PROGRAM

➤ **NOVAC EQUIPMENT ACCESS GRANTS**

Purpose: To provide production/post-production equipment access to television producers and/or not-for-profit organizations for the creation or completion of new non-commercial video works

Eligibility:

    Citizenship: n/a

Please read carefully!
Do not contact any listed organization unless you fulfill all eligibility requirements.

Residency: Louisiana
Special Requirements: Students and previous recipients eligible; grantees must provide a copy of the completed project for the NOVAC library
Art Forms: Video
Type of Support: $2,500 worth of equipment access at NOVAC; premiere of grant-sponsored work
Scope of Program: 3 projects (5 artists) funded in 1992
Application/Selection Process:
    Deadline: September, annually; contact for exact date
    Preferred Initial Contact: Write or call for information
    Application Procedure: Submit application form, project description, resumé(s) of applicant(s), project budget, detailed production and post-production schedule, work sample, SASE for return of material
    Selection Process: Panel review; panel composed of video artists and media professionals
    Notification Process: Letter in October
    Formal Report of Grant Required: Yes

EQUIPMENT ACCESS

Video: Production and post-production for 3/4", S-VHS, Hi-8, 3/4" SP

Comments: NOVAC equipment and facilities are available at low rates to independent producers working on original projects that evidence innovation or experimentation, or that deal with subject matter not traditionally supported by commercial financing. ($25 annual membership required.)

TECHNICAL ASSISTANCE PROGRAMS AND SERVICES

Programs of Special Interest: NOVAC is a membership organization that offers basic and advanced video workshops, fiscal sponsorship, internships, information on resources and opportunities, and a bi-monthly newsletter that includes job listings for video professionals. NOVAC exhibits the works of local and international artists, holds an annual video shorts festival, and makes production services (equipment and staff) available to outside projects for a fee.

NEW YORK CITY DEPARTMENT OF CULTURAL AFFAIRS (DCA)

2 Columbus Circle
New York, NY 10019
212-841-4100
FAX: 212-247-4216

PROFILE OF FINANCIAL SUPPORT TO ARTISTS
Total Funding/Value of In-Kind Support: n/a
Competition for Funding: n/a
Grant Range: n/a

DIRECT SUPPORT PROGRAMS
➤ **MATERIALS FOR THE ARTS (MFA)**
410 West 16th Street, 4th Floor
New York, NY 10011
212-255-5924
FAX: 212-924-1925
CONTACT: SUSAN GLASS, DIRECTOR

Purpose: To link materials donations from both private and governmental sources to nonprofit cultural organizations and individual artists involved in public projects
Eligibility:
   Special Requirements: Must be working with a registered, nonprofit cultural organization on a specific project in a public setting in New York City; materials not available for day-to-day studio use
   Art Forms: All disciplines
Type of Support: Donated equipment, furniture, and supplies
Scope of Program: Over $1,430,000 in goods distributed to 1,048 organizations in FY 1992
Application/Selection Process:
   Application Procedure: Submit resumé, proposal, letter from 1 sponsoring organization

TECHNICAL ASSISTANCE PROGRAMS AND SERVICES
Programs of Special Interest: The Percent for Art Program maintains a slide registry that is a primary resource for agencies, arts groups, and consultants seeking artists for independent as well as city-sponsored projects. Call for an application form 212-841-4177, fax number 212-307-6490. The Arts Partners arts-in-education program identifies and works with arts organizations to enhance the curriculum of New York City public schools by providing access to professional

artists; programming includes classroom workshops, artist residencies, and performances. The Community Arts Development Program provides grants to nonprofit arts groups and organizations that provide cultural services in low- or moderate-income areas of the city; eligible activities include the purchase of professional arts equipment, minor space renovation, and a limited number of large scale works of public art. For additional information call 212-841-4230, fax number 212-489-9594. The Department of Cultural Affairs offers free career counseling services to students, post graduates and professionals interested in focusing career goals in the arts administrative field. Counseling services include assistance in preparing resumés and advice in finding entry-level positions and resources for the job search. The service is available on Thursday afternoons between 1:30 and 3:30 p.m. DCA also offers some housing assistance to artists through their Artist Certification Program. This legally enables artists to live as residents in lofts located in Soho and Noho that would normally be zoned for manufacturing only.

NEW YORK FOUNDATION FOR THE ARTS (NYFA)

155 Avenue of the Americas, 14th floor
New York, NY 10013
212-366-6900
FAX: 212-366-1778
CONTACT: DAVID GREEN, DIRECTOR, COMMUNICATIONS

PROFILE OF FINANCIAL SUPPORT TO ARTISTS

Total Funding/Value of In-Kind Support: $791,000 in fellowships for FY 1993

Competition for Funding: Total applications, 5,213; total individuals funded/provided with in-kind support, 113

Grant Range: $7,000

DIRECT SUPPORT PROGRAMS

➤ ARTISTS' FELLOWSHIPS

Purpose: To support individual, originating artists from diverse cultures and at all stages of professional development

Eligibility:

Citizenship: Open

Residency: New York State, 2 years

Age: 18 or older

Please read carefully!

Do not contact any listed organization unless you fulfill all eligibility requirements.

Special Requirements: Originating artists only; no students; previous grantees ineligible for 3 years
Art Forms: Disciplines rotate on a 2-year cycle: painting, photography, video, architecture, fiction, playwriting, screenwriting, choreography, music composition in odd-numbered years; sculpture, drawing, printmaking, crafts, artists' books, film, performance art, emergent forms, nonfiction literature, poetry in even-numbered years
Type of Support: $7,000
Scope of Program: 113 awards in FY 1993
Application/Selection Process:
   Deadline: September or October, annually; call for exact dates
   Preferred Initial Contact: Call or write for application/guidelines
   Application Procedure: Submit application form, samples of work, SASE
   Selection Process: Peer panel of artists
   Notification Process: Letter in May
   Formal Report of Grant Required: Yes

TECHNICAL ASSISTANCE PROGRAMS AND SERVICES

Programs of Special Interest: New York Foundation for the Arts holds workshops for individual artists who want to apply for the NYFA fellowship in the months immediately preceding its application deadline. The Artists' New Works Program helps individual artists—especially in film and video—find funding for projects (contact Lynda Hansen, Director). An important project in the New Works Program is American Independents and Features Abroad (AIFA), which represents independently-made American film and video at the Berlin Film Festival and other international festivals and markets. The Artists in Residence Program awards matching grants to organizations to support school and community residencies. Grants range from $500 to $10,000 and must be matched by the school/organization. The suggested fee for artists is $250 per day. Interested artists should request the Sponsor Guidelines and are encouraged to seek and build upon relationships they may have had with schools and other organizations to develop programs. The annual Common Ground conference addresses the concerns of arts councils, individual artists, and educators. The free quarterly newsletter *FYI* contains information on NYFA activities, trends and issues in the arts (including advocacy, health insurance, and arts in education) and has a section on grant deadlines and resources for individual artists. Management Services assists organizations with financial and administrative professional services.

Please read carefully!
Do not contact any listed organization unless you fulfill all eligibility requirements.

NEW YORK STATE COUNCIL ON THE ARTS (NYSCA)

915 Broadway
New York, NY 10010
212-387-7000 (or 800-438-2787 within New York State)
FAX: 212-387-7164
CONTACT: LINDA EARLE, DIRECTOR OR GARY SCHIRO, ASSOCIATE, INDIVIDUAL
ARTISTS PROGRAM

PROFILE OF FINANCIAL SUPPORT TO ARTISTS
Total Funding/Value of In-Kind Support: $350,000 for FY 1993

Competition for Funding: Total applications, 330; total
individuals funded/provided with in-kind support, 42

Grant Range: $2,500-$25,000

DIRECT SUPPORT PROGRAMS
➤ **INDIVIDUAL ARTISTS PROGRAM**

Purpose: To provide financial support that allows artists to create,
develop, and present new work

Eligibility:
  Residency: New York State
  Age: 18 or older
  Special Requirements: Artists must find a sponsoring nonprofit
organization based in New York State to submit an application on
their behalf; previous recipients may re-apply for subsequent
phase of production; films that are primarily educational or that
are for documentation of performances, exhibitions or events are
not eligible; films commissioned by an organization are ineligible;
student films or projects undertaken toward fulfillment of a
degree or certificate program are ineligible

  Art Forms: Film (includes animation, narrative, experimental,
documentary, new forms), composers commissions (includes
scoring for film, video, theater) in odd-numbered years; media
production (video, audio) and theater commissions in even-
numbered years

Type of Support: Up to $25,000 for production (for any phase of
production); average grant range is $10,000-$20,000 (average amount
for theater and composer commissions is less)

Scope of Program: 42 awards in FY 1993 (26 in media production)

Application/Selection Process:
  Deadline: March 1, annually (sponsor's application); supplemental
application deadline varies annually
  Preferred Initial Contact: Call or write for guidelines (if calling,
use above phone numbers to request guidelines); more detailed

Please read carefully!
Do not contact any listed organization unless you fulfill all eligibility requirements.

questions can be referred to Individual Artists Program at
212-387-7061

Application Procedure: Sponsor submits application form (artist
provides project description for application); artist later submits
supplemental application form, expanded project description,
resumé, itemized budget, samples of work, artist's statement
(optional)

Selection Process: Peer panel of artists, council committee, and
board of directors

Notification Process: Letter in 6-8 months after deadline

Formal Report of Grant Required: Yes

NEWFOUNDLAND AND LABRADOR ARTS COUNCIL

P.O. Box 98
St. John's, Newfoundland
Canada A1C 5H5
709-726-2212
FAX: 709-726-0619

CONTACT: RANDY FOLLETT, EXECUTIVE DIRECTOR
OR REG WINSOR, ASSISTANT DIRECTOR

PROFILE OF FINANCIAL SUPPORT TO ARTISTS

Total Funding/Value of In-Kind Support: $200,000 in 1992

Competition for Funding: Total applications, 216; total individuals
funded/provided with in-kind support, 154

Grant Range: $500-$2,000

DIRECT SUPPORT PROGRAM

➤ PROJECT GRANTS

Purpose: To support production, operating, travel and study costs
relating to a specific project to be undertaken by an artist, arts group
or organization

Eligibility:

Citizenship: Canada or landed immigrant
Residency: Newfoundland and Labrador, 1 year prior to application
Age: 18 or older, unless a post-secondary standing is held at the
time of application
Special Requirements: Grants must be applied for in advance of the
start date of the project; retroactive applications not considered
Art Forms: Visual arts, film, writing, theatre, music, dance

Type of Support: $500-$2,000 grants

Please read carefully!
Do not contact any listed organization unless you fulfill all eligibility requirements.

Scope of Program: $200,000 in 1992

Application/Selection Process:
   Deadline: Postmarked by January 15 (projects starting after March 1), April 15 (projects starting after June 1), September 15 (projects starting after November 1)
   Preferred Initial Contact: Write or call for application/guidelines
   Application Procedure: Submit application form
   Selection Process: Evaluation committee; final decision by full council
   Notification Process: Letter, approximately 6 weeks after deadline
   Formal Report of Grant Required: Yes

TECHNICAL ASSISTANCE PROGRAMS AND SERVICES

Programs of Special Interest: The Newfoundland & Labrador Arts Council, in conjunction with the Department of Education and the Newfoundland Teachers Association, supports a Visiting Artist Program. Contact the council office for further details.

911 MEDIA ARTS CENTER

117 Yale Avenue North
Seattle, WA 98109
206-682-6552
FAX: 206-682-7422
CONTACT: ROBIN REIDY, EXECUTIVE DIRECTOR

EQUIPMENT ACCESS

CONTACT: ALAN PRUZAN, PROGRAM DIRECTOR

Film: Production and post-production for Super-8, 16 mm
Video: Production for Hi-8; post-production for Hi-8, VHS, 3/4"
Comments: 911 provides equipment access at low rates to independent producers ($35 membership fee required).

TECHNICAL ASSISTANCE PROGRAMS AND SERVICES

Programs of Special Interest: 911 offers regular film and video screenings (many with the artist present), rents out a screening room for media arts events, maintains a video art library, offers fiscal sponsorship services, and conducts regular workshops in media production, aesthetics, grantwriting and media literacy (contact Heather Palmer, Workshop Director).

Please read carefully!
Do not contact any listed organization unless you fulfill all eligibility requirements.

NORTH CAROLINA ARTS COUNCIL

Department of Cultural Resources
Raleigh, NC 27601-2807
919-733-2111
TDD: 800-735-2962 (via Dual Party Relay Service)
FAX: 919-733-4834
CONTACT: JEFFREY PETTUS, VISUAL ARTS PROGRAM COORDINATOR

PROFILE OF FINANCIAL SUPPORT TO ARTISTS

Total Funding/Value of In-Kind Support: $78,000 to visual and
media artists in FY 1992-93 (fellowships and project grants)
Competition for Funding: Total applications, 325; total individuals
funded/provided with in-kind support, 12
Grant Range: $5,000-$8,000

DIRECT SUPPORT PROGRAMS

➤ **VISUAL ARTISTS FELLOWSHIPS**

Purpose: To encourage the continued achievement of North Carolina's
finest creative artists and recognize the central contribution visual
artists make to the creative environment of the state
Eligibility:
  Residency: North Carolina, 1 year prior to application
  Special Requirements: No students in degree-granting programs;
  previous grantees ineligible for 3 years
  Art Forms: Visual arts (includes film and video)
Type of Support: $8,000 fellowships in FY 1992-93
Scope of Program: 6 artists (visual and media) in FY 1992-93
Application/Selection Process:
  Deadline: February 1, annually
  Preferred Initial Contact: Call or write for application
  Application Procedure: Submit application form, samples of
  work, resumé, SASE for return of materials
  Selection Process: Individuals from outside of organization
  Notification Process: Letter within 5 months of deadline
  Formal Report of Funding Required: Yes

➤ **VISUAL ARTISTS PROJECT GRANTS**

Purpose: To encourage significant development in the work of
individual artists and in the medium in which they work, and to
support the realization of specific artistic ideas
Eligibility:
  Citizenship: n/a
  Residency: North Carolina, one year prior to application

Please read carefully!
Do not contact any listed organization unless you fulfill all eligibility requirements.

Special Requirements: No students in degree-granting programs; previous grantees ineligible for 3 years
Art Forms: Visual arts (includes film and video)
Type of Support: Up to $5,000
Scope of Program: 7 artists (visual and media) in FY 1992-93
Application/Selection Process:
Deadline: February 1, annually
Preferred Initial Contact: Call or write for application/guidelines
Application Procedure: Submit application form, samples of work, resumé, project budget, SASE for return of materials
Selection Process: Panel of visual arts peer professionals
Notification Process: Letter by summer
Formal Report of Grant Required: Yes

➤ **LA NAPOULE FOUNDATION RESIDENCY**

Purpose: To provide an international experience and time to work for North Carolina artists
Eligibility:
Residency: North Carolina, one year prior to application
Special Requirements: No students may apply while enrolled in degree granting programs; artists cannot receive a fellowship and a La Napoule residency in the same fiscal year; recipients ineligible for 3 years
Art Forms: Visual arts (includes film and video)
Type of Support: 2- to 3-month residency at the La Napoule Foundation in Southern France, including studio space, housing, meals, travel to and from La Napoule, $1,000 stipend
Scope of Program: 1 residency in visual arts, annually (includes film and video)
Application/Selection Process:
Deadline: February 1, annually
Preferred Initial Contact: Call or write for information
Application Procedure: Submit application form, samples of work, resumé, SASE for return of materials
Selection Process: Fellowship review panel composed of out-of-state professionals
Notification Process: Letter by summer
Formal Report of Grant Required: Yes

TECHNICAL ASSISTANCE PROGRAMS AND SERVICES

Programs of Special Interest: The Visual Arts Section administers the Artworks for State Buildings Program; contact the council for more details. Residencies are available through the Community Development Section Artists-in-Schools and Visiting Artist programs. North Carolina artists may apply for 8- to 12-week residencies at the Headlands Center for the Arts in California; for applications, contact the council or write directly to the Headlands Center for the Arts, 944 Fort Barry, Sausalito, CA 94965. The council's Folklife Section may fund projects that utilize the expertise of documentary film/videomakers and photographers in preserving the state's traditional culture. Information on competitions, galleries and museums in North Carolina is also available from the council.

NORTH DAKOTA COUNCIL ON THE ARTS (NDCA)

Black Building
Suite 606
Fargo, ND 58102
701-239-7150
FAX: 701-239-7153
CONTACT: MARK SCHULTZ, ARTISTS AND EDUCATION SERVICES COORDINATOR

PROFILE OF FINANCIAL SUPPORT TO ARTISTS
Total Funding/Value of In-Kind Support: $15,000 for FY 1992
Competition for Funding: Total applications, 12; total individuals funded/provided with in-kind support, 4
Grant Range: Up to $5,000

DIRECT SUPPORT PROGRAMS
➤ **ARTIST FELLOWSHIPS**
Purpose: To assist North Dakota artists in furthering their careers
Eligibility:
   Citizenship: U.S.
   Residency: North Dakota
   Age: 18 or older
   Special Requirements: No students pursuing college degrees
   Art Forms: Dance, music, opera/musical theater, theater, visual arts, crafts, photography, media arts, literature
Type of Support: Up to $5,000
Scope of Program: 4 awards in FY 1992
Application/Selection Process:
   Preferred Initial Contact: Call or write for application/guidelines
   Application Procedure: Submit application form, samples of work, resumé
   Selection Process: Panel of artists and arts professionals
   Notification Process: 6 weeks after deadline
   Formal Report of Grant Required: Yes

Please read carefully!
Do not contact any listed organization unless you fulfill all eligibility requirements.

TECHNICAL ASSISTANCE PROGRAMS AND SERVICES

Programs of Special Interest: The NDCA, in conjunction with the South Dakota Arts Council, sponsors the biennial Dakota Arts Congress for artists and arts professionals. The Artists-In-Residence Program maintains a roster of artists qualified to work in schools. The Touring Arts Program grants funding to nonprofit sponsors of touring events. The "Opportunities" section of the NDCA's bimonthly newsletter describes other available programs.

NORTHEAST HISTORIC FILM

P.O. Box 900
Bucksport, ME 04416
207-469-0924
FAX: 207-469-7875

EQUIPMENT ACCESS

Film: Post-production for 16mm, film-to-video transfer

Video: Post-production for VHS

Comments: Northeast Historic Film's main function is to serve as a regional archives for film and video, but post-production equipment is available at low rates to independent producers; members receive preference in equipment access. A newsletter, *Moving Image Reviews*, comes out twice per year for members and lists activities and opportunities. Membership is $25 annually for individuals.

NORTHWEST FILM CENTER/ PORTLAND ART MUSEUM (NWFC)

1219 SW Park Avenue
Portland, OR 97205
503-221-1156
FAX: 503-226-4842
CONTACT: BILL FOSTER, DIRECTOR

PROFILE OF FINANCIAL SUPPORT TO ARTISTS

Total Funding/Value of In-Kind Support: $100,000 annually

Competition for Funding: Total applications, 400 (average); total individuals funded/provided with in-kind support, 20-30

Grant Range: Up to $7,000

Please read carefully!
Do not contact any listed organization unless you fulfill all eligibility requirements.

DIRECT SUPPORT PROGRAMS

➤ **WESTERN STATES REGIONAL MEDIA ARTS FELLOWSHIPS (WSRMAF)**

CONTACT: COORDINATOR, WSRMAF

Purpose: To assist independent media artists whose work shows exceptional promise and demonstrates commitment

Eligibility:
  Citizenship: U.S.
  Residency: Alaska, Arizona, California, Colorado, Hawaii, Idaho, Montana, Nevada, New Mexico, Oregon, Utah, Washington State, Wyoming, Pacific territories
  Art Forms: Film, video

Type of Support: Up to $7,000

Scope of Program: 20-30 grants, totalling $100,000, per year

Application/Selection Process:
  Deadline: June 1, annually
  Preferred Initial Contact: Write for application/guidelines
  Application Procedure: Submit application form, supporting materials as requested
  Selection Process: Jury
  Notification Process: 5 months after deadline
  Formal Report of Grant Required: Yes

EQUIPMENT ACCESS

Film: Production and post-production for 16mm, Super 8

Video: Production and post-production (off-line) for VHS, 3/4"

Comments: NWFC offers equipment access at subsidized rates to independent media artists.

TECHNICAL ASSISTANCE PROGRAMS AND SERVICES

Programs of Special Interest: NWFC screens a wide variety of films and videos, and produces the regional Northwest Film and Video Festival in November and the Portland International Film Festival in February. NWFC offers classes on film and video production and editing; workshops are held on fundraising, grantwriting and distribution.

NORTHWEST TERRITORIES DEPARTMENT OF CULTURE AND COMMUNICATIONS

Government of the Northwest Territories
Box 1320
Yellowknife, Northwest Territories
Canada X1A 2L9
403-920-3103
FAX: 403-873-0107
CONTACT: PETER CULLEN, ARTS LIAISON COORDINATOR

PROFILE OF FINANCIAL SUPPORT TO ARTISTS

Total Funding/Value of In-Kind Support: $214,000 for FY 1992-93
Competition for Funding: Total applications, 55; total individuals funded/provided with in-kind support, 36
Grant Range: $100-$20,000

DIRECT SUPPORT PROGRAMS

➤ NWT ARTS COUNCIL PROGRAM

Purpose: To promote the arts in the Northwest Territories by approving funding for artistic work on a project-specific basis
Eligibility:
    Residency: Northwest Territories, 2 years
    Art Forms: Visual arts (includes film and video), performing arts, literature
Type of Support: Up to $20,000
Scope of Program: 36 awards in 1992-93
Application/Selection Process:
    Deadline: January 31 and April 30 (1 other deadline if funds available), annually
    Preferred Initial Contact: Call or write for application/guidelines
    Application Procedure: Submit application form, samples of work, 2 letters of support for project
    Selection Process: Members of NWT Arts Council
    Notification Process: Letter within 12 weeks of deadline
    Formal Report of Funding Required: Yes

Please read carefully!
Do not contact any listed organization unless you fulfill all eligibility requirements.

OHIO ARTS COUNCIL (OAC)

727 East Main Street
Columbus, OH 43205-1796
614-466-2613
TDD: 614-466-4541
CONTACT: KEN EMERICK, COORDINATOR, INDIVIDUAL ARTISTS PROGRAM

PROFILE OF FINANCIAL SUPPORT TO ARTISTS

Total Funding/Value of In-Kind Support: $490,000 for FY 1993
Competition for Funding: Total applications, 850; total individuals funded/provided with in-kind support, 103
Grant Range: Up to $10,000

DIRECT SUPPORT PROGRAMS

➤ **INDIVIDUAL ARTIST FELLOWSHIP PROGRAM**

Purpose: To recognize and support originating artists who have created excellent work
Eligibility:
　Residency: Ohio, 1 year
　Age: 18 or older
　Special Requirements: No students; practicing, professional, originating artists only; previous grantees ineligible for 1 year
　Art Forms: Visual arts, crafts, photography, design arts, media arts, interdisciplinary/performance art, choreography, creative writing, music composition
Type of Support: $5,000-$10,000 award and opportunity to apply for residency at the Headlands Center for the Arts in Sausalito, CA
Scope of Program: 102 awards in FY 1993
Application/Selection Process:
　Deadline: September 1, annually
　Preferred Initial Contact: Call or write for application/guidelines
　Application Procedure: Submit application form, samples of work
　Selection Process: Peer panel review; Ohio Arts Council Board makes final decisions
　Notification Process: Letter
　Formal Report of Grant Required: Yes

➤ **PROFESSIONAL DEVELOPMENT ASSISTANCE AWARDS (PDAA)**

Purpose: To provide assistance for artists to attend programs or events that will further their professional development
Eligibility:
　Residency: Ohio, 1 year

Please read carefully!
Do not contact any listed organization unless you fulfill all eligibility requirements.

Special Requirements: No students; professional, originating artists only; current Fellowship or Major Fellowship recipients ineligible; only one application allowed per budget year
Art Forms: Visual arts, crafts, photography, design arts, media arts, interdisciplinary/performance art, choreography, creative writing, music composition

Type of Support: Up to $1,000 to participate in such activities or programs as workshops, conferences, colonies, seminars, symposia, and rental of studio facilities

Scope of Program: n/a

Application/Selection Process:
Deadline: At least 60 days before event is to occur; awards given on first-come, first-served basis (fiscal year begins July 1)
Preferred Initial Contact: Consult with staff about availability of funds, suitability of project and application process
Application Procedure: Submit samples of work, resumé, artist's statement, project budget, information on the event
Selection Process: Organization staff
Notification Process: Letter within 2 to 4 weeks of application
Formal Report of Grant Required: Yes

TECHNICAL ASSISTANCE PROGRAMS AND SERVICES

Programs of Special Interest: The Arts in Education program publishes a directory of artists eligible for residencies in educational, arts, and community settings; deadline February 1, annually. Contact Vonnie Sanford, Arts in Education Coordinator. The council maintains the Ohio Artists Image Bank, an unjuried slide registry in which Ohio residents may participate at no cost; students are not eligible. A registration form must be completed and a SASE supplied if materials are to be returned. Artists interested in commissions through Ohio's 1% for Art Program may submit samples to the Percent for Art Slide Registry.

OKLAHOMA VISUAL ARTS COALITION (OVAC)

P.O. Box 54416
Oklahoma City, OK 73154
405-842-6991
CONTACT: JOHN MCNEESE, DIRECTOR

PROFILE OF FINANCIAL SUPPORT TO ARTISTS
Total Funding/Value of In-Kind Support: $10,000 for FY 1992

Please read carefully!
Do not contact any listed organization unless you fulfill all eligibility requirements.

Competition for Funding: Total applications, 175; total individuals funded/provided with in-kind support, 20

Grant Range: Up to $1,500

DIRECT SUPPORT PROGRAMS

➤ **AWARDS OF EXCELLENCE**

Purpose: To recognize and reward excellence in the visual arts

Eligibility:
  Citizenship: U.S. (permanent residents also eligible)
  Residency: Oklahoma, 1 year
  Age: 18 or older
  Special Requirements: No students; previous recipients ineligible 1-2 years
  Art Forms: Painting, sculpture, ceramics, photography, print-making, film, video, fiber, drawing, jewelry, performance art, art criticism

Type of Support: $1,000 or $1,500 grant

Scope of Program: 5-8 awards per year

Application/Selection Process:
  Deadline: Dates vary annually; contact for specific details
  Preferred Initial Contact: Call or write for application/guidelines
  Application Procedure: Submit application form, samples of work
  Selection Process: Independent juror
  Notification Process: Letter 1 month after deadline
  Formal Report of Grant Required: No

➤ **SUDDEN OPPORTUNITY FUND**

Purpose: To provide timely assistance to visual artists for career advancement opportunities

Eligibility:
  Citizenship: U.S. (permanent residents also eligible)
  Residency: Oklahoma only
  Age: 18 or older
  Art Forms: Painting, sculpture, ceramics, photography, printmaking, film, video, fiber, drawing, jewelry, performance art, art criticism

Type of Support: Up to $300 for career advancement opportunity

Scope of Program: 12-15 grants per year

Application/Selection Process:
  Deadline: Quarterly
  Preferred Initial Contact: Call or write for application/guidelines
  Application Procedure: Submit application form, samples of work
  Selection Process: Panel of artists and arts professionals
  Notification Process: Letter 2 weeks after deadline
  Formal Report of Funding Required: No

Please read carefully!
Do not contact any listed organization unless you fulfill all eligibility requirements.

TECHNICAL ASSISTANCE PROGRAMS AND SERVICES
Programs of Special Interest: OVAC maintains an unjuried slide registry open to Oklahoma visual artists, publishes a bimonthly journal on the visual arts in Oklahoma, and holds lectures and workshops.

ONTARIO ARTS COUNCIL (OAC)

151 Bloor Street West
Suite 500
Toronto, Ontario
Canada M5S 1T6
800-387-0058 (toll-free in Ontario) or 416-961-1660
CONTACT: DAVID CRAIG, FILM, PHOTOGRAPHY, VIDEO OFFICER

PROFILE OF FINANCIAL SUPPORT TO ARTISTS
Total Funding/Value of In-Kind Support: n/a

Competition for Funding: Total applications, n/a; total individuals funded/provided with in-kind support, n/a

Grant Range: Up to $40,000

DIRECT SUPPORT PROGRAMS
➤ **FILM GRANTS**

Purpose: To assist individual filmmakers who use the medium as a form of artistic expression

Eligibility:
   Citizenship: Canada (landed immigrants also eligible)
   Residency: Ontario
   Special Requirements: Students ineligible; previous applicants ineligible for 1 year; must have directed at least one film that can be provided as support material; commissioned, instructional, promotional, and industrial projects ineligible; pilots for commercial or educational television ineligible; filmmaker must have total artistic and creative control of production
   Art Forms: Film

Type of Support: Up to $40,000 grants

Scope of Program: $744,000 awarded to 49 recipients in FY 1991-92

Application/Selection Process:
   Deadline: April 1 and November 1, annually
   Preferred Initial Contact: Call or write for application/guidelines
   Application Procedure: Submit application form, at least one film directed by applicant, project description and budget, draft script

Please read carefully!
Do not contact any listed organization unless you fulfill all eligibility requirements.

(dramatic films), outline (documentaries), storyboards (animated films), filmography, resumé
Selection Process: Peer panel of artists
Notification Process: Letter 10-12 weeks after deadline
Formal Report of Grant Required: Yes

➤ **VIDEO GRANTS**

Purpose: To encourage the development of talented professional video artists through assistance with the production costs of their tapes
Eligibility:
   Citizenship: Canada (landed immigrants also eligible)
   Residency: Ontario
   Special Requirements: Must have directed at least one video that can be provided as support material; no students; previous applicants ineligible for 1 year; artist must have total editorial control over production; educational and promotional tapes ineligible; pilots for television series ineligible
   Art Forms: Video
Type of Support: Up to $40,000 grants
Scope of Program: 22 grants in FY 1991-92 totalling $244,000
Application/Selection Process:
   Deadline: February 1 and August 15, annually
   Preferred Initial Contact: Call or write for application/guidelines
   Application Procedure: Submit application form, at least one video directed by applicant, project description and budget, treatment or storyboard (dramatic productions), outline (documentaries), sketches and plans (installations), resumé
   Selection Process: Peer panel of artists
   Notification Process: Letter 10-12 weeks after deadline
   Formal Report of Grant Required: Yes

➤ **FIRST PROJECTS: FILM AND VIDEO**

Purpose: To encourage and support first time and emerging film and video artists undertaking an original project.
Eligibility:
   Citizenship: Canada, or landed immigrant
   Residency: Ontario
   Special Requirements: Applicants must have creative and editorial control over the proposed projects; projects must be independent and initiated by the applicant; collaborations between two or more individuals are recognized, but only one artist should complete the application; full-time students ineligible; projects commissioned by any government agency or private company, instructional or promotional projects, pilots for commercial or educational television series, industrial film/video projects and documentation of other art forms or performances are ineligible

Please read carefully!
Do not contact any listed organization unless you fulfill all eligibility requirements.

Art Forms: Film, video

Type of Support: Up to $5,000 towards cost of production

Scope of Program: 22 grants awarded in 1993 totalling $100,536

Application/Selection Process:

Deadline: March 1, 1994; after that contact directly for deadline information

Preferred Initial Contact: Call or write for application/guidelines

Application Procedure: Submit application form, project description, work samples or letters of support from mentors/technical advisors, support material (storyboard for dramatic material, outline for documentary productions, etc.), project budget, resumé

Selection Process: Jury of independent media artists/arts professionals

Notification Process: Approximately 12 weeks after application deadline

Formal Report of Grant Required: Yes

➤ **ELECTRONIC MEDIA GRANTS**

Purpose: To encourage the development of talented professional artists working in electronic media, through assistance with the costs of creating new works

Eligibility:

Citizenship: Canada (landed immigrants also eligible)

Residency: Ontario

Special Requirements: Professional artists only; previous applicants ineligible for 1 year; projects must use electronic media in ways that are unique to the potential of those media

Art Forms: Electronic media (computer, new technologies)

Type of Support: Up to $10,000 for project

Scope of Program: 6 grants in FY 1991-92

Application/Selection Procedure:

Deadline: May 1 and December 1, annually

Preferred Initial Contact: Call or write for application/guidelines; if project is collaborative, artists should consult with OAC officer before applying

Application Procedure: Submit application form, resumé, project budget, support material (e.g., videotape documentation)

Selection Process: Peer panel of artists, board of directors

Notification Process: Letter 10-12 weeks after deadline

Formal Report of Grant Required: Yes

Please read carefully!
Do not contact any listed organization unless you fulfill all eligibility requirements.

➤ **CREATIVE ARTISTS IN SCHOOLS (CAIS) PROJECTS**
CONTACT: STEVEN CAMPBELL, ARTS/EDUCATION OFFICER
416-969-7422
NOTE: This program will undergo administrative changes after January, 1994; contact the Arts/Education office directly for further details
Purpose: To enable students to explore and develop their individual artistic talents with the guidance of a professional artist in a school setting
Eligibility:
Citizenship: Canada (landed immigrants also eligible)
Residency: Ontario, 1 year
Special Requirements: Professional, originating artists only; project must be developed with school that will pay 35% of artist's fees; projects must fill at least 5 full school days
Art Forms: Visual arts, crafts, literature, theater, music, film, photography, video, dance
Type of Support: Up to $2,600 for 65% of artist's fees (recommended fee $200 per day), travel expenses up to $750 if artist must travel more than 50 km roundtrip, up to $250 for materials
Scope of Program: n/a
Application/Selection Process:
Deadline: October 1, 1993 (for projects after January 1); after that, contact directly for deadline information
Preferred Initial Contact: Call or write for application/guidelines
Application Procedure: Submit application form (signed by school), resumé, samples of work, project budget, letter of support from school (optional)
Selection Process: Jury of artists and educators
Notification Process: Letter 10 weeks after deadline
Formal Report of Grant Required: Yes

TECHNICAL ASSISTANCE PROGRAMS AND SERVICES
Programs of Special Interest: The juried Artists and the Workplace program assists professional artists in all fields to work in residence with the trade union movement on projects initiated by the trade union movement to make the arts more accessible to their membership (contact Naomi Lightbourn, Community Arts Development Officer).

OREGON ARTS COMMISSION (OAC)

550 Airport Road, SE
Salem, OR 97310
503-378-3625
TDD: 503-378-3772
FAX: 503-373-7789

TECHNICAL ASSISTANCE PROGRAMS AND SERVICES
Programs of Special Interest: The commission funds media artists
through the regional program administered by the Northwest Film
Center (see separate listing); Video/Filmmaker-in-Schools, funded
through the OAC's Arts In Education program, offers residencies in
filmmaking, animation, multi-image, film, and video production.
OAC cooperates with local arts agencies to present workshops and
seminars for artists.

ORGANIZATION OF INDEPENDENT ARTISTS (OIA)

19 Hudson Street, Room 402
New York, NY 10013
212-219-9213

TECHNICAL ASSISTANCE PROGRAMS AND SERVICES
Programs of Special Interest: OIA is a nonprofit organization which
sponsors artist-curated exhibitions in public spaces in New York City
and which offers support services to unaffiliated artists, including a
slide registry, an exhibition space for members, a resource center,
newsletter, bulletin board, slide nights, mailing list service, and a
place to meet other unaffiliated artists.

Please read carefully!
Do not contact any listed organization unless you fulfill all eligibility requirements.

PALENVILLE INTERARTS COLONY

2 Bond Street
New York, NY 10012
212-254-4614
Summer Address (June-Sept):
P.O. Box 59
Palenville, NY 12463
518-678-3332
CONTACT: JOANNA SHERMAN, COLONY DIRECTOR

PROFILE OF FINANCIAL SUPPORT TO ARTISTS

Total Funding/Value of In-Kind Support: $1,600 for FY 1992 (includes stipends only)

Competition for Funding: Total applications, 467; total individuals funded/provided with in-kind support, 10

Grant Range: n/a

DIRECT SUPPORT PROGRAMS

➤ **SUMMER ARTIST RESIDENCIES**

Purpose: To encourage new works and new insights by encouraging interdisciplinary and intercultural communication among recognized and emerging artists, collaborating artists, and groups of artists of the highest caliber

Eligibility:
   Special Requirements: Minimum 3 years' experience as professional artist
   Art Forms: All disciplines

Type of Support: 1- to 8-week residencies include housing, meals, and studio space as required; residents are asked to pay $175 per week but stipends and full or partial fee waivers available to artists in need

Scope of Program: 97 residencies in 1992; 19 received full fee waivers, 10 received $50-$125 weekly stipends

Application/Selection Process:
   Deadline: April, annually; contact for specific date
   Preferred Initial Contact: Call or write for application/guidelines
   Application Procedure: Submit application form, $10 fee, samples of work, references, resumé, supporting documentation (if available); accepted artists requesting financial aid submit financial statement
   Selection Process: Peer panel of artists, individuals outside of organization
   Notification Process: Phone and letter within 4 weeks of deadline
   Formal Report of Grant Required: No

Please read carefully!
Do not contact any listed organization unless you fulfill all eligibility requirements.

PENNSYLVANIA COUNCIL ON THE ARTS

216 Finance Building
Harrisburg, PA 17120
717-787-6883
FAX: 717-783-2538
CONTACT: PROGRAM DIRECTOR

PROFILE OF FINANCIAL SUPPORT TO ARTISTS
Total funding/value of in-kind support: n/a
Competition for Funding: n/a
Grant Range: Up to $5,000

DIRECT SUPPORT PROGRAMS
➤ **FELLOWSHIP PROGRAM**

Purpose: To support the development of Pennsylvania artists
Eligibility:
  Citizenship: U.S.
  Residency: Pennsylvania, 2 consecutive years prior to application
  Special Requirements: No students; professional artists only; previous grantees ineligible for 2 years
  Art Forms: Visual arts (includes photography), crafts, folk arts, interdisciplinary, media arts (includes audio/radio, screenwriting), dance, music, theater, literature
Type of Support: Up to $5,000
Scope of Program: Approximately 20 awards in 1992-93 to media artists
Application/Selection Process:
  Deadline: October 1, annually
  Preferred Initial Contact: Call or write to Program Director for application/guidelines
  Application Procedure: Submit application form, samples of work, resumé, project budget
  Selection Process: Out-of-state jurors from appropriate field
  Notification Process: Letter in December
  Formal Report of Grant Required: Yes

➤ **BROADCAST OF THE ARTS PROGRAM**

Purpose: To increase the quantity and quality of arts programming on radio and television in Pennsylvania
Eligibility:
  Citizenship: n/a
  Residency: Pennsylvania, 2 consecutive years prior to application

Please read carefully!
Do not contact any listed organization unless you fulfill all eligibility requirements.

Special Requirements: Nonprofit broadcasters, community access cable groups, and arts organizations eligible to apply; individual producers must apply through a nonprofit conduit, must have 1:1 matching funds (50% of match may be in-kind services); must have letter of intent to broadcast from a Pennsylvania broadcaster
Art Forms: Film, video (eligible content includes news, information, and documentaries about arts and artists; broadcasts of live or recorded performances, as well as music, drama, or works of performance art prepared specifically for broadcast are also eligible)

Type of Support: $1,000-$25,000 matching grant; up to $5,000 for individuals

Scope of Program: $200,000 granted in FY 1990-91

Application/Selection Process:
Deadline: April 1, annually
Preferred Initial Contact: Consult with Broadcast of Arts Program Director
Application Procedure: Submit application forms, resumé, samples of work, screenplay, project description and budget, financial statement for organization, letter of intent to broadcast
Selection Process: Peer panel of artists, board of directors
Notification Process: Letter
Formal Report of Grant Required: n/a

➤ **MEDIA ARTS PRODUCTION/NEW WORK PROGRAM**

Purpose: To support organizations and individuals in the production of film, video and audio/radio works

Eligibility:
Citizenship: n/a
Residency: Pennsylvania, 2 consecutive years prior to application
Special Requirements: Must apply through a nonprofit conduit organization; 1:1 matching funds required (up to 50% of match may be in-kind services); project must take place in Pennsylvania; projects for academic credit ineligible; individuals may receive only 1 fellowship or conduit grant per year; students ineligible
Art Forms: Film, video, audio/radio

Type of Support: Matching grant, $1,000-$5,000

Scope of Program: $100,000 granted in FY 1990-91

Application/Selection Process:
Deadline: April 1, annually
Preferred Initial Contact: Consult with Media Artist Program Director before applying and ask for guidelines
Application Procedure: Submit application form, resumé, samples of work, screenplay, project description and budget, financial statement for organization
Selection Process: Peer panel of artists, board of directors

Please read carefully!
Do not contact any listed organization unless you fulfill all eligibility requirements.

Notification Process: Letter
Formal Report of Grant Required: n/a

➤ **MEDIA ARTS FACILITIES ACCESS GRANTS**

Purpose: To encourage computer centers, public and cable television stations, radio stations, media centers, colleges and universities, art schools, museums, municipal and county authorities, and community arts organizations to allow artists access to equipment

Eligibility:
    Citizenship: n/a
    Residency: Pennsylvania, 2 consecutive years prior to application
    Special Requirements: Organizations and artists who initiate a proposal with the cooperation of the equipment center are eligible; applicant must supply matching funds
    Art Forms: Media arts

Type of Support: Matching grant for per hour charge for equipment use, artist's stipend, and administrative overhead

Scope of Program: n/a

Application/Selection Process:
    Deadline: April 1, annually
    Preferred Initial Contact: Consult with Media Arts Program Director
    Application Procedure: Submit application forms, artist's biography, list of available equipment, artist's resumé, samples of work, screenplay, project description and budget, financial statement for organization
    Selection Process: Peer panel of artists, board of directors
    Notification Process: Letter
    Formal Report of Grant Required: n/a

➤ **CONDUIT GRANTS**

Purpose: To support the creation/production of new work, which can include collaborative multidisciplinary projects

Eligibility:
    Citizenship: n/a
    Residency: Pennsylvania, 2 consecutive years prior to application
    Special Requirements: No students; professional artists only; artists must apply through a Pennsylvania nonprofit organization
    Art Forms: All disciplines

Type of Support: Matching grant for project funding

Scope of Program: n/a

Application/Selection Process:
    Deadline: April 1, annually
    Preferred Initial Contact: Call or write to Program Director for application/guidelines

Please read carefully!
Do not contact any listed organization unless you fulfill all eligibility requirements.

Application Procedure: Sponsor submits application form, project budget, financial statement, artist's resumé
Selection Process: Peer panel of artists, board of directors
Notification Process: Letter
Formal Report of Grant Required: Yes

➤ MINORITY ARTS PROGRAM—TECHNICAL ASSISTANCE TO INDIVIDUALS

Purpose: To provide partial funding for individual artists to attend conferences and other noncredit career advancement sessions, or for development of career marketing materials (slides, brochures, cassette tapes, videos, etc.)

Eligibility:
    Citizenship: n/a
    Residency: Pennsylvania
    Special Requirements: Must not be on staff of an organization; must be a member of an ethnic minority
    Art Forms: All disciplines

Type of Support: Up to $200

Scope of Program: n/a

Application/Selection Process:
    Deadline: 8 weeks before event
    Preferred Initial Contact: Call or write for application/guidelines
    Application Procedure: Submit application form, project budget, resumé, public relations material
    Selection Process: Minority Arts panel
    Notification Process: Letter
    Formal Report of Grant Required: Yes

TECHNICAL ASSISTANCE PROGRAMS AND SERVICES

Programs of Special Interest: The Media Arts Program provides exhibition and distribution assistance to organizations. The Arts in Education Program (deadline February 15, annually) places professional artists in school and community residencies lasting 10-180 days (priority to Pennsylvania artists). Resident artists spend 50% of the residency period working with the site population and the other 50% on their own creative projects.

PEW FELLOWSHIPS IN THE ARTS

The University of the Arts
250 South Broad Street, Suite 400
Philadelphia, PA 19102
215-875-2285
FAX: 215-875-2276
CONTACT: ELLA KING TORREY, DIRECTOR

DIRECT SUPPORT PROGRAM
➤ **PEW FELLOWSHIPS IN THE ARTS**

Purpose: To provide the day-to-day support that will free artists to pursue their long-term career and creative goals; Pew Fellowships are sponsored by The Pew Charitable Trusts and administered by The University of the Arts. They are for residents of the Philadelphia metropolitan area.

Eligibility:
   Citizenship: U.S. or permanent resident
   Residency: Philadelphia and the five-county region (Bucks, Chester, Delaware, Montgomery, Philadelphia counties), two years prior to application
   Age: At least 25 years of age
   Special Requirements: Full-time students are not eligible
   Art Forms: All disciplines; this has been a pilot program of which 2 rounds are already completed; the third year (1994) will offer fellowships in performance art, film and video, printmaking, photography, and writing; application deadline is in 1993; after that, contact the organization to determine whether the program will continue.

Type of Support: $50,000 fellowships

Scope of Program: Up to 16 fellowships awarded each year

Application/Selection Process:
   Deadline: Media arts: December 13, 1993; after that, contact the organization directly for deadline information
   Preferred Initial Contact: Call or write for application and guidelines (applications available in late August)
   Application Procedure: Submit application form and support material
   Selection Process: Panel review by artists and arts professionals; final selection of candidates will be based on the applicant's accomplishments and promise in his/her discipline, and the degree to which the fellowship will address a critical juncture in an artist's career and artistic development
   Notification Process: Letter
   Formal Report of Grant Required: Yes

Please read carefully!
Do not contact any listed organization unless you fulfill all eligibility requirements.

PINELLAS COUNTY ARTS COUNCIL (PCAC)

400 Pierce Boulevard
Clearwater, FL 34616
813-464-3327
CONTACT: JOYCE BARNETT, SUPPORT SERVICES DIRECTOR

PROFILE OF FINANCIAL SUPPORT TO ARTISTS

Total Funding/Value of In-Kind Support: $6,385 in FY 1992

Competition for Funding: Total applications, 18; total individuals
funded/provided with in-kind support, 7

Grant Range: $650-$1,000

DIRECT SUPPORT PROGRAMS

➤ **ARTISTS RESOURCE FUND (ARF)**

Purpose: To provide a source of nongovernmental financial
assistance to Pinellas County visual, literary and performing artists
for professional development

Eligibility:
  Residency: Pinellas County, 1 year
  Age: 18 or older
  Special Requirements: No students pursuing degrees; previous
  grantees ineligible for 3 years
  Art Forms: Visual arts (includes media arts, photography, crafts),
  dance, literature, music, theatre

Type of Support: Up to $1,000 for professional development project (e.g.,
attendance at workshops or seminars, presentation/ documentation of
work, materials/supplies for work pivotal to applicant's career)

Scope of Program: $8,000 available in FY 1993

Application/Selection Process:
  Deadline: February 1, annually
  Preferred Initial Contact: Call or write for application/guidelines
  Application Procedure: Submit application form, samples of
  work, resumé, project description and budget
  Selection Process: Peer panel of artists, board of directors
  Notification Process: Letter 6 weeks after deadline
  Formal Report of Grant Required: Yes

TECHNICAL ASSISTANCE PROGRAMS AND SERVICES

Programs of Special Interest: PCAC coordinates Arts-in-Education
projects for county schools, commissions local artists' work for
awards to community members, maintains a resource library and
mailing lists of artists, cosponsors a Very Special Arts Festival, and

publishes the *Arts Advocacy Handbook* and the annual *Florida Festival Directory*. The council offers workshops, seminars, and personal consultations on topics such as grantwriting and marketing.

THE PIONEER FUND

P.O. Box 33
Inverness, CA 94937

PROFILE OF FINANCIAL SUPPORT TO ARTISTS

Total Funding/Value of In-Kind Support: $70,000 per year

Competition for Funding: Total applications, 120; total individuals funded/provided with in-kind support, 20

Grant Range: $1,000-$5,000

DIRECT SUPPORT PROGRAMS

➤ **THE PIONEER FUND**

Purpose: To assist emerging documentary filmmakers and videomakers in advancing their careers

Eligibility:
Residency: California, Oregon, Washington State (artists must also work in these states)
Special Requirements: Must be sponsored by a nonprofit organization and have several years practical experience; student, instructional and performance documentaries ineligible
Art Forms: Documentary film or video

Type of Support: $1,000-$5,000

Scope of Program: 20 awards per year

Application/Selection Process:
Deadline: February 1, May 15, October 1, annually
Preferred Initial Contact: For basic information about the Pioneer Fund (including a profile and proposal summary sheet), write to The Pioneer Fund, c/o Film Arts Foundation, 346 Ninth Street, 2nd Floor, San Francisco, CA 94103 (include SASE); detailed questions can be sent to the main address in the heading
Application Procedure: Submit application form, project proposal and budget, resumé, letter of sponsorship
Selection Process: Panel review
Notification Process: Phone call to recipients, letter to nonrecipients approximately one month after deadline
Formal Report of Grant Required: Yes

Please read carefully!
Do not contact any listed organization unless you fulfill all eligibility requirements.

PITTSBURGH FILMMAKERS

3712 Forbes Avenue, 2nd Floor
Pittsburgh, PA 15213
412-681-5449
CONTACT: PATRICK SHEA, ARTIST SERVICES COORDINATOR

PROFILE OF FINANCIAL SUPPORT TO ARTISTS

Total Funding/Value of In-Kind Support: $104,125 in FY 1992-93

Competition for Funding: Total applications, 225; total individuals funded/provided with in-kind support, 31

Grant Range: $500-$15,000

DIRECT SUPPORT PROGRAMS

➤ **MID-ATLANTIC REGION MEDIA ARTS FELLOWSHIPS (MARMAF)**

Purpose: To assist independent film and video artists by providing funds for either works-in-progress or the creation of new works. The aim of the program is to aid established artists while also encouraging emerging artists of exceptional promise so as to encourage the expression of a diversity of cultures and points of view as a way of strengthening the fabric of American society.

Eligibility:
  Residency: Delaware, District of Columbia, Maryland, New Jersey, Pennsylvania, West Virginia, 1 year
  Art Forms: Film, video

Type of Support: $1,000-$15,000 (most grants $2,000-$5,000)

Scope of Program: 23 awards in 1993

Application/Selection Process:
  Deadline: March, annually; contact for exact date
  Preferred Initial Contact: Call or write for application/guidelines
  Application Procedure: Submit application form, samples of work, resumé, $5 for return shipping
  Selection Process: Peer panel review
  Notification Process: Letter by July 1
  Formal Report of Grant Required: Yes

➤ **EMERGING ARTIST GRANTS IN FILM AND VIDEO**

Purpose: To assist independent filmmakers and videomakers in Southwestern Pennsylvania to complete a first work that will make them competitive for other grants

Eligibility:
  Special Requirements: This is a one-time only grant; prior recipients ineligible
  Art Forms: Film, video

Please read carefully!
Do not contact any listed organization unless you fulfill all eligibility requirements.

Type of Support: Up to $1,000

Scope of Program: $10,000 awarded annually

Application/Selection Process:
    Deadline: February, annually; contact for exact date
    Preferred Initial Contact: Call or write for application/guidelines
    Application Procedure: Submit application form, work sample, resumé
    Selection Process: Peer panel review
    Notification Process: Letter 1 month after deadline
    Formal Report of Grant Required: Yes

EQUIPMENT ACCESS

Film: Production and post-production for 16mm, Super 8

Video: Production and post-production for VHS, S-VHS, 3/4"

Residency: Must be current resident of the Mid-Atlantic region (Delaware, District of Columbia, Maryland, New Jersey, Pennsylvania, West Virginia)

Comments: Artists may apply for membership in Pittsburgh Filmmakers; membership benefits include low-cost equipment access to produce non-commercial work over which artists exercise complete control of style and content.

TECHNICAL ASSISTANCE PROGRAMS AND SERVICES

Programs of Special Interest: Pittsburgh Filmmakers publishes a newsletter, conducts workshops, acts as a fiscal sponsor for independent artists, maintains a resource library for members and students, and exhibits film, video, and photography.

PRINCE EDWARD ISLAND COUNCIL OF THE ARTS

Box 2234
94 Great George Street
Charlottetown, Prince Edward Island
Canada C1A 8B9
902-368-4410
CONTACT: JUDY MACDONALD, EXECUTIVE DIRECTOR

PROFILE OF FINANCIAL SUPPORT TO ARTISTS

Total Funding/Value of In-Kind Support: $10,930 in 1992

Competition for Funding: Total applications, 9; total individuals funded/provided with in-kind support, 7

Grant Range: Up to $2,000

DIRECT SUPPORT PROGRAMS
➤ GRANTS PROGRAM—INDIVIDUAL GRANTS/
TRAVEL-STUDY GRANTS

Purpose: To assist individuals working in any of the arts disciplines
  Citizenship: Canada (landed immigrants also eligible)
  Residency: Prince Edward Island, 6 months
  Art Forms: Music, dance, theater, writing/publications, film/video,
  visual arts, crafts, environmental arts

Type of Support: $1,000-$2,000 individual grants; up to $800 travel-study grants

Scope of Program: 7 grants in 1992

Application/Selection Procedure:
  Deadline: April 30, September 15, December 15, annually
  Application Procedure: Submit application form, 2 letters
  of appraisal
  Selection Process: Committee review
  Notification Process: Letter 4 weeks after deadline
  Formal Report of Grant Required: Yes

TECHNICAL ASSISTANCE PROGRAMS AND SERVICES
Programs of Special Interest: The council offers workshops,
seminars, a referral service, a resource library, space for artists and
arts organizations, and office equipment for in-house use.

PUBLIC ART WORKS †

P.O. Box 150435
San Rafael, CA 94915-0435
415-457-9744
CONTACT: JUDY MORAN, EXECUTIVE DIRECTOR

PROFILE OF FINANCIAL SUPPORT TO ARTISTS
Total Funding/Value of In-Kind Support: n/a
Competition for Funding: Total applications, n/a; total individuals
funded/provided with in-kind support, 4
Grant Range: $5,500-$6,000

DIRECT SUPPORT PROGRAMS
➤ ON SITE EXHIBITION
Purpose: To commission an annual series of temporary installations
in public places, usually outdoors

Please read carefully!
Do not contact any listed organization unless you fulfill all eligibility requirements.

Eligibility:
  Art Forms: Disciplines vary according to location and project
Type of Support: $4,000-$4,500 commission and $1,500 honorarium
Scope of Program: 4 commissions per year
Application/Selection Process:
  Preferred Initial Contact: Call or write for information; artists on mailing list receive prospectus
  Application Procedure: Depends on project
  Selection Process: Jury
  Notification Process: Letter or phone call

QUAD CITY ARTS (QCA)

1715 Second Avenue
Rock Island, IL 61201
309-793-1213
CONTACT: ALISON ZEHR, EXECUTIVE DIRECTOR

PROFILE OF FINANCIAL SUPPORT TO ARTISTS
Total Funding/Value of In-Kind Support: $11,000 in 1993
Competition for Funding: Total applications, 38; total individuals funded/provided with in-kind support, 21
Grant Range: $250-$1,000

DIRECT SUPPORT PROGRAMS
➤ ARTS DOLLARS INDIVIDUAL GRANTS
Purpose: To support specific professional development projects for the creation, completion, presentation, or production of a new work
Eligibility:
  Residency: Illinois (Rock Island, Henry, Mercer counties), Iowa (Scott, Clinton, Muscatine counties); must be a resident for at least one year of one of these counties
  Age: 21 or older
  Art Forms: All disciplines
Type of Support: Up to $750 for specific project; one $1,000 award of merit
Scope of Program: 21 awards in 1993
Application/Selection Process:
  Deadline: November 30, annually
  Preferred Initial Contact: Call or write for information
  Application Procedure: Application forms available 60 days before deadline; submit application form and work samples

Please read carefully!
Do not contact any listed organization unless you fulfill all eligibility requirements.

Selection Process: Community review panel
Notification Process: Letter by end of January
Formal Report of Grant Required: Yes

TECHNICAL ASSISTANCE PROGRAMS AND SERVICES
Programs of Special Interest: QCA provides artist registry and information services. Quad City Arts Center features three gallery venues: the Quad City Arts Gallery features local and regional visual artists; ArtWorks features craft artists from around the nation; and Sales/Rental features visual artists from Iowa and Illinois.

QUÉBEC MINISTÈRE DE LA CULTURE/ QUÉBEC MINISTRY OF CULTURE

225 Grande-Allée est
Québec City, Québec
Canada G1R 5G5
418-644-7188
FAX: 418-644-0380

PROFILE OF FINANCIAL SUPPORT TO ARTISTS
Total Funding/Value of In-Kind Support: $5,097,214 in 1991-92
Competition for Funding: Total applications, 2,266; total individuals funded/provided with in-kind support, 762
Grant Range: $5,000-$25,000

DIRECT SUPPORT PROGRAM
➤ **SUPPORT PROGRAM FOR PROFESSIONAL ARTISTS**
Purpose: To develop artistic practice and make available to artists the resources necessary for creating works and for carrying out activities related to the cultural development of Québec
Eligibility:
  Citizenship: Canada or landed immigrant
  Residency: Province of Québec only
  Special Requirements: Professional artists only; "A" grants are intended for artists who have at least 7 years of artistic practice and whose works have been displayed in renowned places or at major events, nationally and internationally; "B" grants are intended for artists who have had at least two years of artistic practice in Québec or abroad, and some of whose works have been displayed in a professional context in Québec

Please read carefully!
Do not contact any listed organization unless you fulfill all eligibility requirements.

Art Forms: Visual arts, media arts, crafts, multi-disciplinary creation, performing arts, literary creation

Type of Support: Type "A" grants fund up to $25,000 for long-term projects and up to $7,000 for short-term projects; Type "B" grants fund up to $20,000 for long-term projects and up to $5,000 for short-term projects

Scope of Program: $5,097,214 in 1991-92

Application/Selection Process:

Deadline: Deadlines vary annually; contact for exact dates

Preferred Initial Contact: Call or write for application/guidelines

Application Procedure: Submit application form, resumé, project description, budget, work samples

Selection Process: Jury review

Notification Process: Letter approximately 3 months after deadline

Formal Report of Grant Required: Yes

RAGDALE FOUNDATION

1260 North Green Bay Road
Lake Forest, IL 60045
708-234-1063
CONTACT: MICHAEL WILKERSON, DIRECTOR

PROFILE OF FINANCIAL SUPPORT TO ARTISTS

Total Funding/Value of In-Kind Support: $200,000 in 1992

Competition for Funding: Total applications, 500; total individuals funded/provided with in-kind support, 150

Grant Range: n/a

DIRECT SUPPORT PROGRAMS

➤ **RESIDENCIES FOR ARTISTS**

Purpose: To provide a peaceful place and uninterrupted time for writers, artists and composers who are seriously committed to a specific project

Eligibility:

Art Forms: Music composition, visual arts, media arts, literature, interdisciplinary

Type of Support: 2-week to 2-month residencies include housing, work space, meals; residents asked to pay $10/day but financial assistance available

Scope of Program: 150 residencies in 1992

Please read carefully!
Do not contact any listed organization unless you fulfill all eligibility requirements.

Application/Selection Process:
Deadline: January 15 and August 15, annually
Preferred Initial Contact: Call or write for application/guidelines
Application Procedure: Submit application form, samples of work, references, resumé, financial statement (if seeking fee waiver)
Selection Process: Peer panel of artists
Notification Process: Letter or phone call 7 weeks after deadline

REAL ART WAYS (RAW)

56 Arbor Street
Hartford, CT 06106-1203
203-232-1006

EQUIPMENT ACCESS
Video: Post-production for 3/4"
Comments: Low-cost equipment access is provided to artists.

TECHNICAL ASSISTANCE PROGRAMS AND SERVICES
Programs of Special Interest: RAW is a presenter of new and experimental art, performance, video, spoken word and music.

RESOURCES AND COUNSELING FOR THE ARTS (RCA)

429 Landmark Center
75 West Fifth Street
St. Paul, MN 55102
612-292-3206
TDD: 612-292-3218
FAX: 612-292-4315
CONTACT: CHRIS OSGOOD, MANAGER OF ARTISTS SERVICES

TECHNICAL ASSISTANCE PROGRAMS AND SERVICES
Programs of Special Interest: RCA offers a variety of workshops for individual artists on topics such as fellowship and grant preparation, working with galleries and museums, legal issues, and marketing; fees for workshops average $15; RCA also offers legal referrals and individual consultations at no or low cost.

Please read carefully!
Do not contact any listed organization unless you fulfill all eligibility requirements.

RHODE ISLAND STATE COUNCIL ON THE ARTS (RISCA)

95 Cedar Street
Suite 103
Providence, RI 02903-1034
401-277-3880 (Voice/TDD)
FAX: 401-521-1351
CONTACT: COORDINATOR, INDIVIDUAL ARTIST PROGRAMS

PROFILE OF FINANCIAL SUPPORT TO ARTISTS

Total Funding/Value of In-Kind Support: $89,000 for FY 1993

Competition for Funding: Total applications, 208; total individuals funded/provided with in-kind support, 29

Grant Range: $1,000-$5,000

DIRECT SUPPORT PROGRAMS

➤ **FELLOWSHIPS**

Purpose: To encourage the creative development of originating artists by enabling them to set aside time to pursue their work and achieve specific career goals

Eligibility:
  Residency: Rhode Island, 1 year
  Age: 18 or older
  Special Requirements: Originating artists only; no students; previous recipients ineligible to apply in same category for 3 years; Artist Project awardees ineligible for 1 year
  Art Forms: Choreography, crafts, design, drawing and printmaking, film and video, folk arts, literature, music composition, new genres, painting, photography, 3-dimensional art

Type of Support: $1,000-$6,000 awards in 1992

Scope of Program: 9 awards in 1992

Application/Selection Process:
  Deadline: April 1, annually
  Preferred Initial Contact: Call or write for application/guidelines
  Application Procedure: Submit application form, samples of work, resumé
  Selection Process: Panels of artists and arts professionals
  Notification Process: Letter in mid-July
  Formal Report of Funding Required: Yes

➤ **ARTIST PROJECTS**

Purpose: Artist Projects awards enable an artist to create new work or complete works-in-progress

Please read carefully!
Do not contact any listed organization unless you fulfill all eligibility requirements.

Eligibility:
  Residency: Rhode Island, 1 year
  Age: 18 or older
  Special Requirements: No students; previous recipients ineligible for same grant for 1 year
  Art Forms: Choreography, crafts, design, drawing and printmaking, film and video, folk arts, interdisciplinary, literature, music composition, painting, photography, 3-dimensional art
Type of Support: Artist Projects, $1,500-$4,000 for specific project-related costs (completed work must be publicly presented in Rhode Island)
Scope of Program: 20 Artist Projects awards in 1992
Application/Selection Process:
  Deadline: October 1, annually
  Preferred Initial Contact: Call or write for application/guidelines
  Application Procedure: Submit application form, samples of work, project narrative and support letters for public presentation, resumé, project budget
  Selection Process: Panel of artists and arts administrators, board of directors
  Notification Process: Letter 8-10 weeks after deadline
  Formal Report of Grant Required: Yes

TECHNICAL ASSISTANCE PROGRAMS AND SERVICES
Programs of Special Interest: The council maintains a slide registry and the Arts in Education/Artist Roster, which lists artists eligible for school and community residencies.

ROCKEFELLER FOUNDATION

1133 Avenue of the Americas
New York, NY 10036
212-852-8431
FAX: 212-764-3468 (for information requests only)
CONTACT: SUSAN E. GARFIELD, MANAGER, BELLAGIO CENTER OFFICE

PROFILE OF FINANCIAL SUPPORT TO ARTISTS
Total Funding/Value of In-Kind Support: n/a
Competition for Funding: n/a
Grant Range: n/a

Please read carefully!
Do not contact any listed organization unless you fulfill all eligibility requirements.

Direct Support Programs

➤ **BELLAGIO STUDY AND CONFERENCE CENTER RESIDENCIES**

Purpose: To provide a site for artists and scholars who have significant publications, compositions, or shows to their credit to work on projects, particularly projects that will result in publications, exhibitions, or performances

Eligibility:
    Citizenship: Open internationally
    Residency: Open
    Age: n/a
    Special Requirements: Priority given to arts projects that increase artistic experimentation across cultures; artists/scholars must have a substantial body of work; previous recipients ineligible for 10 years
    Art Forms: All disciplines

Type of Support: 4- to 5-week residency at the Bellagio Center on Lake Como, Italy, including room and board

Scope of Program: 135 residencies per year; up to 9 for artists

Application/Selection Process:
    Deadline: Quarterly, 1 year before residency
    Preferred Initial Contact: Call or write for brochure; no SASE
    Application Procedure: Submit application form, project description, resumé, samples of work, reviews of work (if possible)
    Selection Process: Committee
    Notification Process: 3 months after deadline
    Formal Report of Grant Required: Yes

ROCKY MOUNTAIN FILM CENTER (RMFC)

Hunter 102
University of Colorado
Campus Box 316
Boulder, CO 80309-0316
303-492-1531

Equipment Access

Film: Production and post-production for Super 8, 16mm

Video: Production for VHS, S-VHS; post-production for VHS, S-VHS, 3/4", 3/4" SP

Comments: Film and video equipment available on a 24-hour basis to noncommercial users at very nominal rental rates; reservations must be made weekdays, between 10 a.m. and 1:45 p.m. for film and 1/2" video, 3:00 p.m. to 5 p.m. on Tuesdays and Thursdays for 3/4",

Please read carefully!
Do not contact any listed organization unless you fulfill all eligibility requirements.

3/4" SP and S-VHS video post-production suites. Reservations made at the RMFC office or by phone. Access to screening space is free.

TECHNICAL ASSISTANCE PROGRAMS AND SERVICES

Programs of Special Interest: Workshops are given on production and post-production in film and video formats available at the RMFC (including workshops for beginners); call 303-492-2070. The Film-makers Bulletin Board office allows filmmakers to contact one another, exchange services, and buy and sell equipment.

THE ROTUNDA GALLERY

33 Clinton Street
Brooklyn, NY 11201
718-875-4047
FAX: 718-488-0609
CONTACT: JANET RIKER, DIRECTOR

TECHNICAL ASSISTANCE PROGRAMS AND SERVICES

Programs of Special Interest: The Rotunda Gallery, a project of the Fund for the Borough of Brooklyn, Inc., presents Brooklyn-affiliated artists (those who live, work or have been born in Brooklyn), including at least one video exhibition annually. Brooklyn artists working in video installation may wish to apply to the gallery's Site-Specific Installation Program which awards up to two exhibition opportunities per year for individual artists or collaborative teams. Artists may also wish to come in to use the *Artist Opportunity Book,* which is simply a notebook of compiled opportunities for individuals, or to consult with the director about their work.

SALT LAKE CITY ARTS COUNCIL

54 Finch Lane
Salt Lake City, UT 84102
801-596-5000
CONTACT: KIM DUFFIN, ASSISTANT DIRECTOR

PROFILE OF FINANCIAL SUPPORT TO ARTISTS

Total Funding/Value of In-Kind Support: n/a

Competition for Funding: Total applications (individual artists), 12; total individuals funded/provided with in-kind support, 3

Grant Range: $500-$1,500

Please read carefully!
Do not contact any listed organization unless you fulfill all eligibility requirements.

DIRECT SUPPORT PROGRAMS
➤ **DEVELOPMENTAL SUPPORT GRANTS**

Purpose: To support professional development projects such as exhibitions, installations, and collaborative efforts

Eligibility:
  Residency: Preference to Salt Lake City artists
  Special Requirements: Cash match required; project must take place in Salt Lake City
  Art Forms: All disciplines

Type of Support: Matching grant for project

Scope of Program: 3 grants to individual artists in FY 1993-94

Application/Selection Process:
  Deadline: June, annually; contact for exact date
  Preferred Initial Contact: Call or write for application/guidelines
  Application Procedure: Submit application form; individual media, visual and literary artists must meet with staff prior to deadline
  Selection Process: Council grant review committee
  Notification Process: Letter to all applicants by mid-September
  Formal Report of Grant Required: Yes

TECHNICAL ASSISTANCE PROGRAMS AND SERVICES

Programs of Special Interest: Information and technical assistance is available to artists in all areas.

SAN ANTONIO DEPARTMENT OF ARTS AND CULTURAL AFFAIRS (DACA)

P.O. Box 839966
San Antonio, TX 78283-3966
210-222-2787
FAX: 210-228-0263
CONTACT: ERNESTO RUBIO, SENIOR ADMINISTRATOR

PROFILE OF FINANCIAL SUPPORT TO ARTISTS

Total Funding/Value of In-Kind Support: $27,000 in FY 1992

Competition for Funding: Total applications, 36; total individuals funded/provided with in-kind support, 9

Grant Range: $1,000-$3,000

Please read carefully!
Do not contact any listed organization unless you fulfill all eligibility requirements.

DIRECT SUPPORT PROGRAMS

➤ **INDIVIDUAL ARTISTS GRANTS PROGRAMS**

Purpose: To assist both emerging and established artists by supporting work of artistic merit, to encourage innovative projects (e.g., performance art, multi-disciplinary media, new genres), and to support projects by individuals who lack institutional support

Eligibility:
    Citizenship: U.S.
    Residency: Bexar County
    Special Requirements: Originating, professional artists only; no students; previous grantees ineligible for 1 year; project must take place in San Antonio; DACA encourages applications that represent cultural and geographic diversity of San Antonio and that represent women and the disabled; collaborations encouraged
    Art Forms: Dance, music, theater, visual arts, crafts, design arts, photography, media arts, literature, multi-disciplinary

Type of Support: Up to $3,000 for a project that takes place in San Antonio and leads to a public presentation

Scope of Program: 9 awards in FY 1992

Application/Selection Process:
    Deadline: Early spring, annually (usually March); contact for exact date
    Preferred Initial Contact: Call or write for application form
    Application Procedure: Arrange for pre-application interview with DACA staff before deadline; submit application form, samples of work, resumé, project budget, letter of support for public presentation
    Selection Process: Peer panel of artists
    Notification Process: Letter after panel meeting (July)
    Formal Report of Grant Required: Yes

TECHNICAL ASSISTANCE PROGRAMS AND SERVICES

Programs of Special Interest: DACA maintains a library and offers free workshops for artists on topics such as career development, working with galleries and museums, legal issues, marketing, and public relations.

Please read carefully!
Do not contact any listed organization unless you fulfill all eligibility requirements.

SAN FRANCISCO FOUNDATION

685 Market Street
Suite 910
San Francisco, CA 94105
415-495-3100

PROFILE OF FINANCIAL SUPPORT TO ARTISTS
Total Funding/Value of In-Kind Support: $15,000 in 1992
Competition for Funding: n/a
Grant Range: $2,500

DIRECT SUPPORT PROGRAMS
➤ **JAMES D. PHELAN ART AWARD**
Purpose: To encourage the work of California-born filmmakers, videographers, printmakers, and photographers
Eligibility:
   Special Requirements: Applicant must have been born in California; previous awardees ineligible
   Art Forms: Eligible disciplines alternate on 2-year cycle: film and video in even-numbered years; photography and printmaking in odd-numbered years
Type of Support: $2,500 cash awards
Scope of Program: 6 awards annually (3 in each eligible discipline)
Application/Selection Process: Call or write for information in February of appropriate year

SANTA BARBARA COUNTY ARTS COMMISSION

P.O. Box 2369
Santa Barbara, CA 93120
805-568-3432
FAX: 805-568-3431
CONTACT: EVE RAPPOPORT, DIRECTOR OF VISUAL ART

PROFILE OF FINANCIAL SUPPORT TO ARTISTS
Total Funding/Value of In-Kind Support: $17,000 for FY 1992-93
Competition for Funding: Total applications, 70; total individuals funded/provided with in-kind support, 10
Grant Range: $1,500 in 1992

Please read carefully!
Do not contact any listed organization unless you fulfill all eligibility requirements.

DIRECT SUPPORT PROGRAMS
➤ **INDIVIDUAL ARTISTS PROGRAM**

Purpose: To support the creative life of Santa Barbara County by assisting emerging artists in establishing and developing their professional careers in the arts

Eligibility:
  Citizenship: U.S.
  Residency: Santa Barbara County, 1 year
  Age: 18 or older
  Special Requirements: Originating artists only; no nonprofessionals or full-time students pursuing degrees; no previous recipients
  Art Forms: Visual art, dance, music, theatre, literature; film and video artists have not been funded in the past but may be in the future

Type of Support: $1,500 awards

Scope of Program: 10 awards in FY 1992-93

Application/Selection Process:
  Deadline: Fall, annually; call by August 31
  Preferred Initial Contact: Call or write for application/guidelines
  Application Procedure: Submit application form, samples of work, resumé, artist's statement, proof of residency
  Selection Process: Peer panel of artists, arts professionals, and community arts advocates
  Notification Process: Letter
  Formal Report of Grant Required: No

THE SCHOOL OF THE ART INSTITUTE OF CHICAGO

37 South Wabash Avenue
Chicago, IL 60603
312-899-5100

PROFILE OF FINANCIAL SUPPORT TO ARTISTS
Total Funding/Value of In-Kind Support: $1,500 in 1991

Competition for Funding: Total applications, 74; total individuals funded/provided with in-kind support, 2

Grant Range: $300-$1,500

Please read carefully!
Do not contact any listed organization unless you fulfill all eligibility requirements.

DIRECT SUPPORT PROGRAMS
➤ **BARBARA ARONOFSKY LATHAM MEMORIAL GRANTS**
CONTACT: OFFICE OF THE DEAN
Phone: 312-899-1236
Purpose: To further the work of emerging talent and to foster the excellence, diversity, vitality, and appreciation of experimental video and electronic visualization art
Eligibility:
    Citizenship: Open internationally
    Residency: Open
    Age: 18 or older
    Art Forms: Experimental video, electronic visualization art, writing on the history, theory, or criticism of video and electronic visualization art
Type of Support: $300-$1,500 for work-in-progress or new project
Scope of Program: 2 awards biennially
Application/Selection Process:
    Deadline: Varies; contact for exact date; grants are offered in odd-numbered years
    Preferred Initial Contact: Call or write for application/guidelines
    Application Procedure: Submit application form, samples of work, project description, resumé
    Selection Process: Professional jury
    Notification Process: 12 weeks after deadline
    Formal Report of Grant Required: No

SEATTLE ARTS COMMISSION (SAC)

312 First Avenue North
Seattle, WA 98109
206-684-7171
TDD: 206-587-5500
FAX: 206-684-7172

PROFILE OF FINANCIAL SUPPORT TO ARTISTS
Total Funding/Value of In-Kind Support: $825,000 in 1992 (includes commissions)
Competition for Funding: n/a
Grant Range: $2,000-$100,000

DIRECT SUPPORT PROGRAMS

➤ **PUBLIC ART PROGRAM**

Purpose: To commission and purchase artwork from visual artists internationally for City of Seattle Capital Improvement Projects and for locations throughout the city

Eligibility:
 Residency: Depends on project
 Art Forms: Painting, sculpture, printmaking, drawing, photography, video, audio, books, interdisciplinary

Type of Support: Commission or purchase award; commissions usually $7,500-$100,000 but can go up to $500,000

Scope of Program: Approximately $750,000 available annually

Application/Selection Procedure:
 Call or write for prospecti; project descriptions and deadlines also published in SAC's monthly newsletter

➤ **SEATTLE ARTISTS PROGRAM**

CONTACT: JOHN NAGUS, PROJECT MANAGER

Purpose: To fund the development of new work or works-in-progress in all disciplines; jointly administered by Public Art and Art Support programs

Eligibility:
 Residency: Seattle
 Special Requirements: Originating artists only
 Art Forms: All disciplines

Type of Support: $2,000 or $7,500 grant for project

Scope of Program: $150,000 available annually; 25 recipients in 1992

Application/Selection Process:
 Deadline: July, annually; contact for exact date
 Preferred Initial Contact: Call or write for information
 Application Procedure: Submit application form, work sample
 Selection Process: Peer panel review
 Notification Process: Letter
 Formal Report of Grant Required: Not for visual/media artists

TECHNICAL ASSISTANCE PROGRAMS AND SERVICES

Programs of Special Interest: The Arts in Education (AIE) program supports the use of professional artists and arts organizations in Seattle schools.

Please read carefully!
Do not contact any listed organization unless you fulfill all eligibility requirements.

SIERRA ARTS FOUNDATION (SAF)

200 Flint Street
Reno, NV 89501
702-329-1324
FAX: 702-329-1328

PROFILE OF FINANCIAL SUPPORT TO ARTISTS

Total Funding/Value of In-Kind Support: $16,000 for FY 1992; funding amount varies yearly depending on the foundation's resources

Competition for Funding: Total applications, 40; total individuals funded/provided with in-kind support, 20 (figures include organizations, groups and individuals)

Grant Range: $200-$2,000

DIRECT SUPPORT PROGRAMS

➤ **GRANTS PROGRAM**

Purpose: To provide grants-in-aid to individuals, groups, or nonprofit organizations to support projects of educational and community significance as well as imaginative, innovative, or experimental projects

Eligibility:
    Residency: Northern Nevada
    Special Requirements: Preference given to applicants who present evidence of matching funds or comparable in-kind support; previous grantees ineligible for 1 year
    Art Forms: All disciplines

Type of Support: Up to $2,000 for project

Scope of Program: n/a

Application/Selection Process:
    Deadline: Call for details
    Preferred Initial Contact: Call to check on availability of funds, discuss project with Grants Coordinator/Program Director
    Application Procedure: Submit application form, samples of work, project budget, resumé
    Selection Process: Organization staff, Grants Committee including board members
    Notification Process: Letter 1 month after deadline
    Formal Report of Grant Required: Yes

TECHNICAL ASSISTANCE PROGRAMS AND SERVICES

Programs of Special Interest: The Arts-in-Education program places local professional artists in month-long residencies in Washoe County elementary schools. The foundation maintains an artist registry and a community cultural events calendar. The Exhibition Program gives outstanding local artists an opportunity to exhibit their newest works in 6-week shows.

SOUTH CAROLINA ARTS COMMISSION (SCAC)

1800 Gervais Street
Columbia, SC 29201-3585
803-734-8696
TDD: 803-734-8983
FAX: 803-734-8526
CONTACT: JULIA JONES, DIRECTOR OF GRANTS AND CONTRACT SERVICES

PROFILE OF FINANCIAL SUPPORT TO ARTISTS
Total Funding/Value of In-Kind Support: $129,000 in 1992 (figures do not include arts-in-education fees or purchase awards)
Competition for Funding: n/a
Grant Range: Up to $7,500

DIRECT SUPPORT PROGRAMS
➤ PROJECT SUPPORT
Purpose: To help support specific, planned activities such as the production of new work, marketing, and professional development
Eligibility:
    Residency: South Carolina, 6 months prior to application and throughout grant period
    Special Requirements: No degree-seeking, full-time undergraduate students; professional artists only; matching funds required
    Art Forms: All disciplines
Type of Support: Up to 50% project cost (usually no more than $7,500)
Scope of Program: 19 grants in 1992 totalling approximately $50,000
Application/Selection Process:
    Deadline: December 15, annually
    Preferred Initial Contact: Call or write for application/guidelines
    Application Procedure: Submit application form, project narrative, samples of work, resumé, project budget
    Selection Process: Peer panel and board of directors
    Notification Process: Letter
    Formal Report of Grant Required: Yes

➤ MULTI-CULTURAL ARTS DEVELOPMENT PROGRAM

CONTACT: HENRY HARRISON, PROGRAM DIRECTOR

Purpose: To provide assistance to individual artists and arts organizations that primarily relate to an ethnic culture or to rural or tribal communities

Eligibility:

Citizenship: n/a

Residency: South Carolina, 6 months prior to application and throughout the grant period

Special Requirements: Degree-seeking, full-time undergraduate students are not eligible; recipients eligible to receive project support for two consecutive years only

Art Forms: All disciplines and indigenous art forms

Type of Support: Up to $500 grants to individuals (up to $2,500 to organizations); council provides 60% of funds, artist responsible for 40%

Scope of Program: 20 awards in 1992; $20,000 available for program

Application/Selection Process:

Deadline: Call or write for details

Preferred Initial Contact: Call or write for application/guidelines

Application Procedure: Submit application form, budget and support material (includes slides, resumé, etc.)

Selection Process: In-house staff panel review

Notification Process: Letter

Formal Report of Grant Required: n/a

➤ QUARTERLY GRANTS

Purpose: To provide assistance for specific arts activities, pilot projects, professional development, or career development for artistic staff or individual artists

Eligibility:

Residency: South Carolina, 6 months prior to application and throughout the grant period

Special Requirements: Degree-seeking, full-time undergraduate students are not eligible; applicants may apply each quarter, but may only receive 2 quarterly grants per fiscal year

Art Forms: All disciplines

Type of Support: Grants up to $1,000 (1:1 funding match)

Scope of Program: 20 awards in 1992; $14,000 available for program

Application/Selection Process:

Deadline: February 15, May 15, August 15, November 15, annually

Preferred Initial Contact: Call or write for application/guidelines

Application Procedure: Submit application form, samples of work, budget, resumé

Selection Process: In-house staff panel review

Please read carefully!
Do not contact any listed organization unless you fulfill all eligibility requirements.

Notification Process: By letter, within 3-4 weeks
Formal Report of Grant Required: Yes

EQUIPMENT ACCESS

CONTACT: CHARLES WEBB, EQUIPMENT ACCESS COORDINATOR
Film: Production and post-production for 16mm, Super 8
Video: Production and post-production for Betacam/Beta SP, S-VHS
Comments: SCAC's Media Arts Center offers low-cost equipment
access to media artists from around the country (preference to
Southeast artists); facilities include an audio room and Targa
Graphics system.

TECHNICAL ASSISTANCE PROGRAMS AND SERVICES

Programs of Special Interest: Through the Media Arts Center, SCAC
administers the Southern Circuit, a tour of national, independent
media artists throughout the Southeast, and hosts the annual Southeastern Media Institute, a series of intensive, professional media
workshops and seminars. The Media Arts Center sponsors New
View, a teleconference that broadcasts the available works of
independent distributors to buyers (such as schools, universities,
libraries) across the country. The center is coordinating a Media Arts
Education initiative in conjunction with the South Carolina State
Department of Education. For all programs through the Media Arts
Center, contact Susan Leonard, Acting Director, for further details.
Equipment access is also granted through the Southeast Media
Fellowship Program (see the entry on Appalshop, Inc., for information).
The *Independent Spirit* newsletter, published 3 times per year,
features criticism of southern independent media makers and lists
southeastern media events. Artists selected for SCAC's Approved
Artist Roster are eligible for the Arts-in-Education, Visiting Artist,
Rural Arts, and Mobile Arts programs.

SOUTH DAKOTA ARTS COUNCIL

230 South Phillips Avenue, Suite 204
Sioux Falls, SD 57102-0720
605-339-6646
TDD: 800-622-1770 (via Relay Service)
FAX: 605-332-7965
CONTACT: SHIRLEY SNEVE, ASSISTANT DIRECTOR

PROFILE OF FINANCIAL SUPPORT TO ARTISTS

Total Funding/Value of In-Kind Support: $40,000 for FY 1992

Please read carefully!
Do not contact any listed organization unless you fulfill all eligibility requirements.

Competition for Funding: Total applications, 79; total individuals funded/provided with in-kind support, 10

Grant Range: $1,000-$5,000

DIRECT SUPPORT PROGRAMS

➤ **ARTIST FELLOWSHIPS/ARTIST CAREER DEVELOPMENT GRANTS**

Purpose: Artist Fellowships recognize and encourage the creative achievement of South Dakota artists of exceptional talent in any arts discipline; Artist Career Development Grants assist artists who are committed to advancing their work and careers

Eligibility:
    Residency: South Dakota
    Special Requirements: No students; previous grantees ineligible for 2 years (Fellowships) or 3 years (Artist Career Development Grants)
    Art Forms: All disciplines

Type of Support: $5,000 (Fellowships), $1,000 (Artist Career Development Grants)

Scope of Program: 5 Fellowships, 5 Artist Career Development Grants in 1992

Application/Selection Process:
    Deadline: February 1, annually
    Preferred Initial Contact: Call or write for application/guidelines
    Application Procedure: Submit application form, resumé, samples of work, support documentation (optional)
    Selection Process: Arts disciplines panels, the council
    Notification Process: April
    Formal Report of Grant Required: Yes

TECHNICAL ASSISTANCE PROGRAMS AND SERVICES

Programs of Special Interest: The SDAC administers Artists-in-School and Touring Arts programs. Contact the council for further details on those programs. SDAC, in conjunction with North Dakota Council on the Arts, sponsors the biennial Dakota Arts Congress for artists and arts professionals.

Please read carefully!
Do not contact any listed organization unless you fulfill all eligibility requirements.

THE SOUTH FLORIDA CULTURAL CONSORTIUM

c/o Metro-Dade County Cultural Affairs Council
111 NW 1st Street
Suite 625
Miami, FL 33128
305-375-4634
FAX: 305-375-3068
CONTACT: GRANTS AND PROGRAMS ADMINISTRATOR

PROFILE OF FINANCIAL SUPPORT TO ARTISTS

Total Funding/Value of In-Kind Support: $90,000 for FY 1992-93

Competition for Funding: Total applications, 300; total individuals funded/provided with in-kind support, 6

Grant Range: $15,000

DIRECT SUPPORT PROGRAMS

➤ **INDIVIDUAL VISUAL AND MEDIA ARTISTS FELLOWSHIPS**

Purpose: To assist South Florida visual and media artists in improving their artistic skills and in furthering their careers

Eligibility:
    Residency: South Florida (Dade, Broward, Palm Beach, Martin, and Monroe counties), 1 year
    Age: 18 or older
    Special Requirements: No students pursuing degrees; professional artists only
    Art Forms: Painting, sculpture, drawing, photography, mixed media, printmaking/graphics, media arts (film, video)

Type of Support: $15,000 fellowship; exhibition of grantees' work in South Florida museums

Scope of Program: 6 awards in 1991-92

Application/Selection Process:
    Deadline: Fall, annually; contact for exact date
    Preferred Initial Contact: Call or write for application/guidelines
    Application Procedure: Submit application form, samples of work, resumé
    Selection Process: Nationally recognized artists and arts professionals
    Notification Process: Letter within 3 months of deadline
    Formal Report of Grant Required: No

Please read carefully!
Do not contact any listed organization unless you fulfill all eligibility requirements.

SOUTHWEST ALTERNATE MEDIA PROJECT (SWAMP)

1519 West Main
Houston, TX 77006
713-522-8592
FAX: 713-522-0953
CONTACT: TOM SIMS, MANAGING DIRECTOR

PROFILE OF FINANCIAL SUPPORT TO ARTISTS

Total Funding/Value of In-Kind Support: $50,000 for 1993

Competition for Funding: Total applications, 100; total individuals funded/provided with in-kind support, 12

Grant Range: Up to $5,000

DIRECT SUPPORT PROGRAMS

➤ **INDEPENDENT PRODUCTION FUND (IPF)**

Purpose: To provide production grants for independent filmmakers and videomakers

Eligibility:
    Residency: Texas, Arkansas, Oklahoma, Kansas, Nebraska, Missouri, Puerto Rico, U.S. Virgin Islands, 1 year
    Age: 18 or older
    Special Requirements: No full-time students or projects associated with degree programs; applicant must have primary control over project
    Art Forms: Film, video

Type of Support: Up to $5,000; past IPF grantees not receiving the maximum $5,000 award per project may reapply for additional funds up to a maximum of $2,500 or the difference between the original award and project maximum

Scope of Program: $50,000 available in 1993

Application/Selection Process:
    Deadline: May 1, annually
    Preferred Initial Contact: Call or write for application/guidelines (mail requests should be addressed to the attention of IPF)
    Application Procedure: Submit application form, $3 for return shipping/handling, project description and budget, samples of work, support materials (can include resumé, biography, letters of support, reviews)
    Selection Process: Independent peer panel of artists
    Notification Process: 12 weeks after deadline
    Formal Report of Grant Required: Yes

Please read carefully!
Do not contact any listed organization unless you fulfill all eligibility requirements.

TECHNICAL ASSISTANCE PROGRAMS AND SERVICES
Programs of Special Interest: SWAMP coordinates Media Arts Touring and Media Residency activities which bring artists into the community (schools, universities, community settings). Media Education workshops train artists and educators to conduct residencies. SWAMP also acts as a fiscal sponsor for established film and video artists. The Independent Images Conference promotes independent media production, exhibition, and education in the Southwest and Mid-America region (fees involved).

SQUEAKY WHEEL/BUFFALO MEDIA RESOURCES

372 Connecticut Street
Buffalo, NY 14213
716-884-7172

EQUIPMENT ACCESS
Film: Production and post-production for 16mm, Super 8
Video: Production for Video 8, Hi-8, Beta; post-production for Hi-8 to 3/4"
Comments: Squeaky Wheel offers equipment access at low rates to its members.

TECHNICAL ASSISTANCE PROGRAMS AND SERVICES
Programs of Special Interest: Squeaky Wheel publishes a media directory for upstate New York, exhibits the work of local media artists, conducts technical and grantwriting workshops, and offers consultations on fundraising and distribution. "Axle Grease," a weekly public access cable show, features independent video and film from across the U.S. (no fees paid to artists); contact for details.

STATE ARTS COUNCIL OF OKLAHOMA

Jim Thorpe Building, Room 640
2101 North Lincoln Boulevard
Oklahoma City, OK 73105-4987
405-521-2931 (Voice/TDD)
FAX: 405-521-6418
CONTACT: COMMUNITY COORDINATORS

PROFILE OF FINANCIAL SUPPORT TO ARTISTS
Total Funding/Value of In-Kind Support: n/a

Please read carefully!
Do not contact any listed organization unless you fulfill all eligibility requirements.

Competition for Funding: n/a
Grant Range: n/a

DIRECT SUPPORT PROGRAMS
➤ **ORGANIZATIONAL SUPPORT BY PROJECTS**
Purpose: To support artist organizations, art projects and independent artists who are sponsored by nonprofit or tax-exempt organizations
Eligibility:
    Citizenship: Open
    Residency: Organization must be Oklahoma-based
    Special Requirements: Individual artist must apply through an Oklahoma-based nonprofit organization
    Art Forms: All disciplines
Type of Support: Matching grants on a project by project basis
Scope of Program: n/a
Application/Selection Process:
    Deadline: September (contact for specific date) for "$5,000 or More" category for period starting the following July; 60 days before the project in the "Less than $5,000 or Minority" categories
    Preferred Initial Contact: Call or write for application/guidelines
    Application Procedure: Organization submits application form and support material
    Selection Process: Peer panel and council review
    Notification Process: Letter
    Formal Report of Grant Required: Yes

TECHNICAL ASSISTANCE PROGRAMS AND SERVICES
Programs of Special Interest: The arts council administers Artists-in-Residence and Traditional Artists programs (some out-of-state artists eligible) and the Oklahoma Touring and Oklahoma Apprenticeship programs (Oklahoma artists only); maintains a resource library; and provides a showcase for Oklahoma visual artists through rotating exhibits at the State Capitol and through the permanent State Arts Collection in Oklahoma City. In addition, the arts council coordinates an annual showcase of roster artists, visual and performing, providing them with additional needed support.

SUNDANCE INSTITUTE

Columbia Pictures
10202 West Washington Boulevard
Culver City, CA 90232
310-204-2091
FAX: 310-204-3901

PROFILE OF FINANCIAL SUPPORT TO ARTISTS

Total Funding/Value of In-Kind Support: n/a

Competition for Funding: Total applications, 3,000 in 1992; total individuals funded/provided with in-kind support, 15

Grant Range: n/a

DIRECT SUPPORT PROGRAMS

➤ **FEATURE FILM PROGRAM**

Purpose: To support original, provocative, daring scripts that reflect the independent vision of the writer or writer/director

Eligibility:

Special Requirements: Sundance is particularly interested in supporting new talent, artists in transition (e.g., choreographers, actors, playwrights), and filmmakers who have already made a feature and are looking for a creative arena for the development of their next project; if supported projects are produced, Sundance asks writers/directors to contribute 1/2% to 1% of production budget to the institute

Art Forms: Film (directing, screenwriting)

Type of Support: The institute offers the following opportunities, all held in Sundance, Utah: 5-day Screenwriters Lab (January or June), including one-on-one problem-solving story sessions with professional screenwriters; a June Filmmaking Lab including hands-on directing experience in rehearsing, shooting and editing scenes on videotape; and a Producer's Conference in July for filmmakers supported in June; airline travel, accommodations, and food for 1 writer/filmmaker per project is provided by the institute (Sundance will consider paying for accommodations and food for additional partners)

Scope of Program: 10-15 projects per year

Application/Selection Process:

Deadline: July 1 (January Screenwriters Lab); December 1 (June Filmmakers Lab); no postmarks accepted

Preferred Initial Contact: Call or write for application/guidelines

Application Procedure: Submit application form for labs, $15 fee, synopsis of project/screenplay; finalists submit full screenplays

Selection Process: Staff, panel of artists

Please read carefully!
Do not contact any listed organization unless you fulfill all eligibility requirements.

Notification Process: Mid-December (January Lab), mid-April (June Lab)

TECHNICAL ASSISTANCE PROGRAMS AND SERVICES

Programs of Special Interest: The Sundance Film Festival showcases the talents of emerging filmmakers. To apply, send a request for festival information and a SASE to Sundance Institute. Applications are available in September. Deadlines are in the fall, annually; contact the organization for exact dates.

TENNESSEE ARTS COMMISSION (TAC)

320 Sixth Avenue, North
Suite 100
Nashville, TN 37243-0780
615-741-1701
TDD: 800-848-0298 (via Tennessee Relay Service)
FAX: 615-741-8559

TECHNICAL ASSISTANCE PROGRAMS AND SERVICES

Programs of Special Interest: Tennessee film and video artists may seek 2-week to year-long residencies in schools through the Arts in Education Program. TAC maintains a slide registry for Tennessee visual artists.

TEXAS COMMISSION ON THE ARTS (TCA)

920 Colorado Street, 5th Floor
P.O. Box 13406
Austin, TX 78711
512-463-5535 or 800-252-9415 (Texas only)
TDD: 800-735-2989 (via Texas Relay Service)
FAX: 512-475-2699
CONTACT: RITA STARPATTERN, PROGRAM ADMINISTRATOR, VISUAL AND COMMUNNICATION ARTS

PROFILE OF FINANCIAL SUPPORT TO ARTISTS

Total Funding/Value of In-Kind Support: n/a
Competition for Funding: n/a
Grant Range: n/a

Please read carefully!
Do not contact any listed organization unless you fulfill all eligibility requirements.

DIRECT SUPPORT PROGRAMS
➤ **ORGANIZATIONAL, PROJECT, AND TOURING SUPPORT—MEDIA ARTS**

Purpose: To support media organizations, media projects, and independents through funding and touring opportunities

Eligibility:
    Residency: Texas
    Special Requirements: Individual artists must apply through a Texas-based nonprofit organization
    Art Forms: Film, video, radio

Type of Support: Grants for organizational, project, and touring support

Scope of Program: n/a

Application/Selection Process:
    Deadline: December 1, annually
    Preferred Initial Contact: Call or write for application/guidelines
    Application Procedure: Submit application form
    Selection Process: Peer panel review
    Notification Process: Letter
    Formal Report of Grant Required: Yes

TECHNICAL ASSISTANCE PROGRAMS AND SERVICES
Programs of Special Interest: Individual artists may apply for residencies through the Arts in Education program.

TUCSON COMMUNITY CABLE CORPORATION (TCCC)

124 East Broadway
Tucson, AZ 85701
602-624-9833
FAX: 602-792-2565
CONTACT: MARK TAYLOR, DIRECTOR OF MANAGEMENT INFORMATION

EQUIPMENT ACCESS
Video: Production and post-production for VHS, S-VHS, 3/4", Hi-8
Comments: TCCC offers free public access to its equipment and facilities.

TECHNICAL ASSISTANCE PROGRAMS AND SERVICES
Programs of Special Interest: TCCC offers free technical assistance services (training and use of equipment) and offers small grants of up to $100 to Tucson producers for public access programming.

Please read carefully!
Do not contact any listed organization unless you fulfill all eligibility requirements.

TUCSON/PIMA ARTS COUNCIL (T/PAC)

166 West Alameda
Tucson, AZ 85701
602-624-0595
FAX: 602-624-3001
CONTACT: ALBERT SOTO, GRANTS OFFICER, OR DAVID HOYT JOHNSON, VISUAL
ARTS PROGRAM DIRECTOR

PROFILE OF FINANCIAL SUPPORT TO ARTISTS

Total Funding/Value of In-Kind Support: $15,000 for FY 1991-92
(fellowships only)
Competition for Funding: Total applications, 117; total individuals
funded/provided with in-kind support, 5
Grant Range: $3,000

DIRECT SUPPORT PROGRAMS

➤ **VISUAL ARTS FELLOWSHIPS**

Purpose: To support the development of Tucson and Pima County
artists by enabling them to set aside time to create new works, complete
works in progress, or pursue new avenues of artistic expression
Eligibility:
    Citizenship: Open
    Residency: Pima County, 1 year
    Age: 18 or older
    Special Requirements: No students enrolled in more than 3 credit
    hours at a college or university; previous recipients ineligible for 3
    years
    Art Forms: Visual arts (includes film/video, crafts, photography)
Type of Support: $3,000; recipients may be requested to make their
work available for a public exhibition
Scope of Program: 5 awards in 1992
Application/Selection Process:
    Deadline: Early December, annually; contact for exact date
    Application Procedure: Submit application form, resumé, slides
    of work
    Selection Process: Panel of arts professionals
    Notification Process: Letter to all applicants
    Formal Report of Grant Required: No

TECHNICAL ASSISTANCE PROGRAMS AND SERVICES

Programs of Special Interest: T/PAC administers additional grant
programs: Technical Assistance Grants are available to assist artists

Please read carefully!
Do not contact any listed organization unless you fulfill all eligibility requirements.

who wish to travel to attend workshops and conferences; Cultural Heritage grants are awarded for projects that reflect the cultural heritage or diversity of the Tucson community; application for both programs are considered on a quarterly basis. T/PAC also administers Arts-in-Education and Public Art programs for Tucson and Pima County. The council offers workshops, assistance with grant preparation for regional and national grants, the Rural Arts Traveling Exhibit, the Visual Artist Roster and Slide File, and the Art/Law Attorneys Roster.

UCROSS FOUNDATION

2836 U.S. Highway 14-16 East
Clearmont, WY 82835
307-737-2291
FAX: 307-737-2322
CONTACT: ELIZABETH GUHEEN, EXECUTIVE DIRECTOR

PROFILE OF FINANCIAL SUPPORT TO ARTISTS
Total Funding/Value of In-Kind Support: n/a
Competition for Funding: Total applications, 250; total individuals funded/provided with in-kind support, 65-70
Grant Range: n/a

DIRECT SUPPORT PROGRAMS
➤ RESIDENCY PROGRAM
Purpose: To provide individual workspace and living accommodations for selected artists and scholars so that they may concentrate, in an uninterrupted fashion, on their ideas, theories, and works
Eligibility:
    Age: 18 or older
    Special Requirements: Previous residents ineligible for 2 years
    Art Forms: All disciplines
Type of Support: 2-week to 2-month residencies with no charge for room, board, or studio space
Scope of Program: 65-70 residencies per year
Application/Selection Process:
    Deadline: October 1 and March 1, annually
    Preferred Initial Contact: Write for application/guidelines, include SASE
    Application Procedure: Submit application form, samples of work, references, resumé

Please read carefully!
Do not contact any listed organization unless you fulfill all eligibility requirements.

Selection Process: Peer panel of artists
Notification Process: Letter 8 weeks after deadline
Formal Report of Funding Required: No

UNITED ARTS COUNCIL OF GREENSBORO, INC.

Greensboro Cultural Center
P.O. Box 877
Greensboro, NC 27402
919-333-7440
FAX: 919-275-2787
CONTACT: JUDITH K. RAY, COMMUNITY DEVELOPMENT DIRECTOR

PROFILE OF FINANCIAL SUPPORT TO ARTISTS
Total Funding/Value of In-Kind Support: $6,000 for FY 1991 (Emerging Artists Program)
Competition for Funding: Total applications, 52; total individuals funded/provided with in-kind support, 27
Grant Range: $250-$1,000

DIRECT SUPPORT PROGRAMS
➤ **EMERGING ARTISTS PROGRAM**
Purpose: To encourage artists in their formative years by helping them cover the costs of professional development activities such as presenting their work for exhibits, training, travel, and production of new work
Eligibility:
  Citizenship: U.S.
  Residency: Guilford County only
  Special Requirements: No students
  Art Forms: All disciplines
Type of Support: $250-$1,000 for specific activity
Scope of Program: 24 awards in FY 1991
Application/Selection Process:
  Deadline: Deadline varies; contact for exact date
  Preferred Initial Contact: Call or write for application/guidelines
  Application Procedure: Submit application form, samples of work, resumé, financial statement, project budget
  Selection Process: Organization staff, board of directors, individuals outside of organization
  Notification Process: Letter within 8 weeks of deadline
  Formal Report of Grant Required: Yes

Please read carefully!
Do not contact any listed organization unless you fulfill all eligibility requirements.

TECHNICAL ASSISTANCE PROGRAMS AND SERVICES
Programs of Special Interest: The Sternberger Artists Center provides low-cost studio space to artists.

UTAH ARTS COUNCIL (UAC)

617 East South Temple
Salt Lake City, UT 84102
801-533-5895
TDD/FAX: 801-533-6196

PROFILE OF FINANCIAL SUPPORT TO ARTISTS
Total Funding/Value of In-Kind Support: $519,000 for FY 1993

Competition for Funding: Total applications, 1,362; total individuals funded/provided with in-kind support, 448 (includes each artist participating in Utah Performing Arts Tour)

Grant Range: Up to $5,000

DIRECT SUPPORT PROGRAMS
➤ **INDIVIDUAL ARTISTS' SERVICES PROGRAM**
CONTACT: TAY HAINES, PROGRAM COORDINATOR
Phone: 801-533-5895

Purpose: In addition to technical services for individual artists, artists may apply for an Artist Grant of up to $500 for unique professional development opportunities

Eligibility:
    Citizenship: n/a
    Residency: Utah, one year prior to application
    Age: 20 years or older
    Special Requirements: Degree-seeking students may apply only if the award is received after study is completed; artists who are normally part of a group may apply individually, provided all artistic documentation is easily identifiable as solely their own; artists can receive only one Artist Grant award per year
    Art Forms: All disciplines

Type of Support: Up to $500

Scope of Program: Approximately $18,000 available per year

Application/Selection Process:
    Deadline: FY 1993: February 1, 1994; FY 1994 deadlines available in April, 1994
    Preferred Initial Contact: Write or call for information

Please read carefully!
Do not contact any listed organization unless you fulfill all eligibility requirements.

Application Procedure: Submit application form, documentation, resumé
Selection Process: Peer and staff committee, board committee and Utah Arts Council board
Notification Process: By letter within four weeks of deadline
Formal Report of Grant Required: Yes

TECHNICAL ASSISTANCE PROGRAMS AND SERVICES
Programs of Special Interest: Artists selected for the council's Artist Bank are eligible for school and community residencies, workshops and performances. The council maintains a Utah Artists' Resource Slide File which includes slide documentation on approximately 1,400 Utah artists. Artists enrolled in the 1% for Art Slide Registry (open to residents and non-residents) pay a $10 registration fee and are eligible for the state's 1% for Art Commissions administered by the council; contact David Holz, Design Arts Coordinator, at 801-533-4039.

UTAH FILM & VIDEO CENTER (UFVC)

20 South West Temple
Salt Lake City, UT 84101
801-534-1158
CONTACT: MARY CRANNEY, DIRECTOR

PROFILE OF FINANCIAL SUPPORT TO ARTISTS
Total Funding/Value of In-Kind Support: $11,250 in FY 1992-93
Competition for Funding: Total applications, 12; total individuals funded/provided with in-kind support, 12
Grant Range: n/a

DIRECT SUPPORT PROGRAM
➤ C. LARRY ROBERTS MEMORIAL GRANT
Purpose: To support the ongoing efforts of film and video artists
Eligibility:
  Citizenship: n/a
  Residency: Utah
  Age: Open
  Special Requirements: Non-commerical media arts projects only; projects that are commissioned or for which the artist is employed or paid are not eligible; recipients must provide video copy of work for UFVC archive; students are eligible
  Art Forms: Film, video

Please read carefully!
Do not contact any listed organization unless you fulfill all eligibility requirements.

Type of Support: Up to $2,000 in FY 1992-93

Scope of Program: 3 awards totalling $2,000 in FY 1992-93

Application/Selection Process:
   Deadline: June 1, annually
   Preferred Initial Contact: Write or call for information
   Application Procedure: Submit letter with background and description of project, video sample of past work
   Selection Process: Review by panel, UFVC board
   Notification Process: Letter
   Formal Report of Grant Required: No

EQUIPMENT ACCESS

Film: Production and post-production for 16mm, Super 8

Video: Production and post-production for 1/2" and S-VHS; exhibition opportunities for 3/4"

Comments: UFVC provides equipment access at discounted rates to members ($25 annual fee) and to students. UFVC's Associate Directors are film/videomakers who offer assistance as needed. Equipment orientation and instruction are offered to all users. Equipment access can be granted to individuals who apply for it; $4,300 of equipment access was granted for 7 projects in FY 1992-93.

TECHNICAL ASSISTANCE PROGRAMS AND SERVICES

Programs of Special Interest: UFVC has a reference library, offers screening opportunities and will serve as a fiscal sponsor for media artists. Other cash grants may be available to Utah media artists throughout the year, depending on contributions to the center; award amounts and deadlines vary accordingly.

THE VERMONT COMMUNITY FOUNDATION

P.O. Box 30
Middlebury, VT 05753
802-462-3355
FAX: 802-462-3357

PROFILE OF FINANCIAL SUPPORT TO ARTISTS

Total Funding/Value of In-Kind Support: $50,000 in FY 1992 (includes organizations and individuals)

Competition for Funding: Total applications, n/a; total individuals funded/provided with in-kind support, 12

Grant Range: $300-$4,000

Please read carefully!
Do not contact any listed organization unless you fulfill all eligibility requirements.

DIRECT SUPPORT PROGRAM

➤ **VERMONT ARTS ENDOWMENT FUND**

Purpose: To support the development, completion or presentation of new work by Vermont artists; to enhance the career development of artists and administrators

Eligibility:
    Citizenship: n/a
    Residency: Vermont
    Special Requirements: Artists may apply directly and, if funded, must find a fiscal agent with tax-exempt status; matching funds may be required, especially for grants of over $1,000
    Art Forms: All disciplines
    Type of Support: $300-$4,000
    Scope of Program: $20,000 to 12 individuals in 1992

Application/Selection Process:
    Deadline: November 1, annually
    Preferred Initial Contact: Call or write for application/guidelines
    Application Procedure: Submit Proposal Summary Form, project description (including purpose, amount requested and other sources of funding), work samples, budget, resumé
    Selection Process: Arts committee, VCF board of trustees
    Notification Process: Letter in December
    Formal Report of Grant Required: Yes

VERMONT COUNCIL ON THE ARTS (VCA)

136 State Street, Drawer 33
Montpelier, VT 05633-6001
802-828-3291 (Voice/TDD)
CONTACT: CORNELIA CAREY, GRANTS OFFICER

PROFILE OF FINANCIAL SUPPORT TO ARTISTS

Total Funding/Value of In-Kind Support: $45,990 for FY 1993 (for Fellowships, Artists' Project Grants and Artists' Development Grants)

Competition for Funding: Total applications, 320; total individuals funded/provided with in-kind support, 36

Grant Range: $100-$3,500

DIRECT SUPPORT PROGRAMS

➤ **FELLOWSHIPS**

Purpose: To support the creative development of Vermont artists

Please read carefully!
Do not contact any listed organization unless you fulfill all eligibility requirements.

Eligibility:
   Residency: Vermont
   Age: 18 or older
   Special Requirements: Students ineligible
   Art Forms: Disciplines rotate on a 3-year cycle: media arts, music, painting/works on paper, theater arts in 1994; design arts, sculpture, dance, fiction/nonfiction in 1995; crafts, interdisciplinary, photography, poetry in 1996
Type of Support: $3,500 fellowships
Scope of Program: 10 fellowships, 6 finalist awards in 1992 (finalist awards discontinued in 1993)
Application/Selection Process:
   Deadline: Spring, annually; contact for exact date
   Application Procedure: Submit application form, resumé, samples of work
   Selection Process: Advisory panels with approval of VCA board of trustees
   Notification Process: Letter by late summer
   Formal Report of Grant Required: Yes

➤ **ARTISTS' PROJECT GRANTS**

Purpose: To fund specific arts projects by Vermont artists
Eligibility:
   Residency: Vermont (for collaborative projects, at least 50% of participants must be Vermont residents)
   Special Requirements: Artists must apply through a nonprofit organization; no full-time students; project must include plans for a public presentation in Vermont
   Art Forms: All disciplines
Type of Support: $500-$3,500 grants
Scope of Program: $4,000 granted for 3 projects in 1992
Application/Selection Process:
   Deadline: Spring, annually; contact for exact date
   Preferred Initial Contact: Discuss project ideas and application procedure with Grants Officer
   Application Process: Submit application form, work samples, resumé
   Selection Process: Advisory panel with approval of VCA board of trustees
   Notification Process: Letter by late summer
   Formal Report of Grant Required: Yes

➤ **ARTISTS' DEVELOPMENT GRANTS**

Purpose: To assist the professional development of Vermont artists by supporting such areas as research and development for a new project, attending workshops, colonies or conferences, and documenting work

Please read carefully!
Do not contact any listed organization unless you fulfill all eligibility requirements.

Eligibility:
    Residency: Vermont
    Age: 18 or older
    Special Requirements: Full-time students ineligible; previous recipients of fellowships and development grants ineligible for 1 year
    Art Forms: All disciplines
Type of Support: $100-$400 for individuals; up to $800 for collaborative submissions
Scope of Program: $8,000 granted for 32 projects in 1992
Application/Selection Process:
    Deadline: Rolling deadline; 60 days before event
    Preferred Initial Contact: Call to discuss proposal with Grants Officer
    Application Procedure: Submit application form, resumé
    Selection Process: Council staff
    Notification Process: 30 days after receipt of application
    Formal Report of Grant Required: Yes

TECHNICAL ASSISTANCE PROGRAMS AND SERVICES

Programs of Special Interest: Artists may apply to participate in the Arts in Education program; information about successful applicants appears in the *Artists Register*, which is provided to potential sponsors. The VCA maintains a slide registry used as a resource for selection of artists for the Art in State Buildings program and other projects. The council maintains a job bank and lists of other opportunities for artists, as well as the Resource Center, a noncirculating library of information about the arts. The council holds informative workshops, including Grant Seekers Workshops for artists and organizations seeking VCA funding.

VIDEO DATA BANK

112 South Michigan Avenue
Third Floor
Chicago, IL 60603
312-345-3550
FAX: 312-541-8072

TECHNICAL ASSISTANCE PROGRAMS AND SERVICES

Programs of Special Interest: The Video Data Bank is the largest national distributor of tapes by and about contemporary artists; its collection features experimental and independently produced videos. Artists accepted into distribution are paid royalties for the rentals and sales of their work. Submissions are accepted throughout the year; contact for guidelines. Video Data Bank houses three

Please read carefully!
Do not contact any listed organization unless you fulfill all eligibility requirements.

primary collections: Independent Video, including over 1,000 recent titles by independent producers, collectives and artists; Early Video History, including seminal works from video's formative period; and On Art and Artists, a collection of some 300 interviews with contemporary artists, critics and performers, also including documentaries on artists as well as performance and video art. Video Data Bank has produced several video library series in an effort to make independent video available to a diverse group of people. Video Drive In presents videos internationally to large public audiences.

VIDEO FOUNDATION TO ASSIST CANADIAN TALENT (VIDEOFACT) †

151 John Street
Suite 301
Toronto, Ontario
Canada M5V 2T2
416-596-8696
CONTACT: JULIE THORBURN, PROGRAM DIRECTOR

PROFILE OF FINANCIAL SUPPORT TO ARTISTS
Total Funding/Value of In-Kind Support: n/a
Competition for Funding: n/a
Grant Range: n/a

DIRECT SUPPORT PROGRAMS
Purpose: To support the number and quality of music videos produced in Canada through providing financial assistance toward the production of music videos
Eligibility:
　　Citizenship: Canada (landed immigrants also eligible)
　　Special Requirements: Producers, managers, artists, record labels, record or video production companies are eligible; video director or production company, or video production facilities must be located in Canada; 2 of the following must be located in Canada: composer, lyricist, principal performer, performance/production
　　Art Forms: Music video
Type of Support: Up to 50% of project cost to a maximum of $12,500
Scope of Program: $950,000 available in 1990-91
Application/Selection Process:
　　Deadline: 5 per year

Preferred Initial Contact: Call or write for application/guidelines
Application Procedure: Submit application form, samples of work, resumé, project budget
Selection Process: Board of directors
Notification Process: Phone call or letter 4 weeks after deadline
Formal Report of Grant Required: Yes

VIRGIN ISLANDS COUNCIL ON THE ARTS (VICA)

41-42 Norre Gade
St. Thomas, VI 00802
809-774-5984
FAX: 809-774-6206

PROFILE OF FINANCIAL SUPPORT TO ARTISTS

Total Funding/Value of In-Kind Support: $171,000 in FY 1992

Competition for Funding: Total applications, 71; total individuals funded/provided with in-kind support, 56 (figures include organizations and individuals)

Grant Range: $500-$10,000

DIRECT SUPPORT PROGRAMS

➤ **SPECIAL PROJECTS**

Purpose: To financially assist individual and arts organization projects, including partial support for research, participation in professional development workshops or seminars, and materials for specific projects

Eligibility:
    Residency: U.S. Virgin Islands
    Special Requirements: Must have matching funds
    Art Forms: All disciplines

Type of Support: Up to $10,000 to cover up to 50% of project cost

Scope of Program: In FY 1992, 19 individuals applied and 15 received grants

Application/Selection Process:
    Application Procedure: Submit application form, project narrative, supplemental materials
    Selection Process: VICA board members, panelists and VICA staff
    Notification Process: Letter within 2 weeks of board meeting
    Formal Report of Grant Required: Yes

Please read carefully!
Do not contact any listed organization unless you fulfill all eligibility requirements.

TECHNICAL ASSISTANCE PROGRAMS AND SERVICES
Programs of Special Interest: VICA staff assists individual artists, arts organizations and community organizations seeking funding from other sources. The council is now offering an Artist Registry, a list of artists working in all disciplines in St. Thomas, St. John and St. Croix.

VIRGINIA CENTER FOR THE CREATIVE ARTS (VCCA)

Mt. San Angelo
P.O. Box VCCA
Sweet Briar, VA 24595
804-946-7236
CONTACT: WILLIAM SMART, EXECUTIVE DIRECTOR

PROFILE OF FINANCIAL SUPPORT TO ARTISTS
Total Funding/Value of In-Kind Support: n/a

Competition for Funding: Total applications, 3,000; total individuals funded/provided with in-kind support, 310

Grant Range: n/a

DIRECT SUPPORT PROGRAMS
Purpose: To provide a retreat where writers, visual artists, and composers may pursue their work, free from the distractions and responsibilities of day-to-day life

Eligibility:
    Age: Usually 20 or older
    Art Forms: Music composition (chamber, choral, new, orchestral), opera, theater (general and experimental), visual arts (no crafts), architecture, photography, film, literature (no scholarly theses), interdisciplinary, multidisciplinary

Type of Support: 1- to 3-month residencies including room, board, and studio; artists asked to pay $30 per diem fee if possible

Scope of Program: 310 residencies in 1992

Application/Selection Process:
    Deadline: January 25, May 25, September 25, annually
    Preferred Initial Contact: Call or write for application/guidelines
    Application Procedure: Submit application form, $15 application fee, samples of work, references, resumé
    Selection Process: Peer panel of artists
    Notification Process: Letter or phone call 2 months after deadline
    Formal Report of Grant Required: No

VIRGINIA COMMISSION FOR THE ARTS

Lewis House, 2nd Floor
223 Governor Street
Richmond, VA 23219-2010
804-225-3132 (voice/TDD)
FAX: 804-225-4327

TECHNICAL ASSISTANCE PROGRAMS AND SERVICES

Programs of Special Interest: The commission administers an Artists-in-Education Residency program. Contact directly for further details.

VIRGINIA FOUNDATION
FOR THE HUMANITIES AND PUBLIC POLICY (VFH)

145 Ednam Drive
Charlottesville, VA 22901-4629
804-924-3296
FAX: 804-296-4714

PROFILE OF FINANCIAL SUPPORT TO ARTISTS

Total Funding/Value of In-Kind Support: Approximately $200,000 annually (figures reflect Grant Program only)
Competition for Funding: n/a
Grant Range: Up to $15,000

DIRECT SUPPORT PROGRAM

➤ **VFH GRANT PROGRAM**

Purpose: To support the development of public educational programs of benefit to Virginians, including media projects with a humanities basis

Eligibility:
   Citizenship: Open
   Residency: Virginia, or projects relating to Virginia
   Special Requirements: Projects must involve the humanities; individuals must be sponsored by a nonprofit organization which will serve as fiscal agent; organization must be a public or private nonprofit organization or educational institution that is Virginia-based or has a significant Virginia audience
   Art Forms: All disciplines

Please read carefully!
Do not contact any listed organization unless you fulfill all eligibility requirements.

Type of Support: Grants up to $15,000; average grants $5,000-$10,000

Scope of Program: Total of $50,000 available annually

Application/Selection Process:
  Deadline: February 1, May 1, October 1, annually
  Preferred Initial Contact: Write or call for information
  Application Procedure: Request special guidelines for media projects; submit material as requested by guidelines
  Selection Process: Review by staff and board
  Notification Process: Phone call and/or letter within 6 weeks of deadline
  Formal Report of Grant Required: Yes

➤ **FELLOWSHIP PROGRAM**

Purpose: To support research in the Humanities; for media projects, this includes script development and use of Virginia Center for Media and Culture facilities for post-production

Eligibility:
  Citizenship: Open
  Residency: Virginia, or projects relating to Virginia
  Special Requirements: Fellowship recipients must be in residence at the center during their fellowship
  Art Forms: All disciplines

Type of Support: Fellowships include a stipend of up to $3,000 per month (depending on length of tenure or other financial support) and, for media projects, may include equipment access

Scope of Program: 15 fellowships annually; media applicants compete with all other proposals

Application/Selection Process:
  Deadline: Summer and Fall residencies: November 1, annually; January and Spring residencies: April 1, annually
  Preferred Initial Contact: Write or call for information
  Application Procedure: Submit material as requested by guidelines
  Selection Process: Review by staff, external panel and board
  Notification Process: Phone call and/or letter within 2 months of deadline
  Formal Report of Grant Required: Yes

EQUIPMENT ACCESS

CONTACT: STAFF, VFH CENTER FOR MEDIA AND CULTURE

Film: Post-production for 16mm

Video: Post-production for 3/4", Hi-8

Comments: Equipment access is available at low-cost to independent media artists and to nonprofit cultural organizations; applications

Please read carefully!
Do not contact any listed organization unless you fulfill all eligibility requirements.

accepted throughout the year; priority given to Virginia-based artists and organizations, and to those doing media projects in the humanities—especially those pertaining to the history and culture of Virginia.

TECHNICAL ASSISTANCE PROGRAMS AND SERVICES

Programs of Special Interest: The Virginia Foundation for the Humanities offers programs and services for media artists and professionals through its Center for Media and Culture. The center offers an annual conference for media professionals, humanities scholars and cultural agencies, publishes a newsletter, and is developing an on-line database of producers, writers, scholars and funders. The Filmmakers' Bureau allows artists to travel around Virginia to present and discuss their films; filmmakers must be residents of Virginia or their work must pertain to Virginia. The center also offers special programs including seminars, technical workshops and screenings.

VISUAL COMMUNICATIONS/ SOUTHERN CALIFORNIA ASIAN AMERICAN STUDIES CENTRAL, INC.

263 South Los Angeles, Suite 307
Los Angeles, CA 90012
213-680-4462
CONTACT: LINDA MABALOT, EXECUTIVE DIRECTOR

EQUIPMENT ACCESS

CONTACT: AMY KATO, OPERATIONS MANAGER
Film: Production for Super 8
Video: Post-production (off-line/cuts only) for S-VHS
Comments: Visual Communications provides equipment access at discounted rates to members.

TECHNICAL ASSISTANCE PROGRAMS AND SERVICES

Programs of Special Interest: Visual Communications serves as a fiscal sponsor for a limited number of member media artists. Artists must submit a treatment, tape and budget, and projects must focus on Asian Pacific subjects or themes. The organization also selects independent works to be screened at the Los Angeles Asian Pacific American International Film and Video Festival, Los Angeles Free-waves, Pioneering Visions Exhibition Series, and Ethnovisions Series. These works are programmed to be screened in the community and in the school systems. Consultation services are

Please read carefully!
Do not contact any listed organization unless you fulfill all eligibility requirements.

available for artists seeking funding from Los Angeles city programs and other sources. Membership fees vary.

VISUAL STUDIES WORKSHOP (VSW)

31 Prince Street
Rochester, NY 14607
716-442-8676

PROFILE OF FINANCIAL SUPPORT TO ARTISTS

Total Funding/Value of In-Kind Support: n/a
Competition for Funding: n/a
Grant Range: Up to $500

DIRECT SUPPORT PROGRAMS

➤ **UPSTATE MEDIA REGRANT PROGRAM**

CONTACT: PIA CSERI-BRIONES, EQUIPMENT ACCESS MANAGER

Purpose: To assist emerging media artists and independent producers to advance their work

Eligibility:
  Residency: Upstate New York
  Special Requirements: No students
  Art Forms: Video, audio, time-based computer art

Type of Support: $500 grants

Scope of Program: 6 awards per year

Application/Selection Process:
  Deadline: Spring, annually; contact for exact date
  Preferred Initial Contact: Write or call for guidelines
  Application Procedure: Submit resumé, samples of work, artist's statement
  Selection Process: Panel of artists and arts professionals
  Notification Process: After panel meeting, 6-8 weeks after deadline
  Formal Report of Grant Required: No

➤ **NO TV & MOVIES CABLE TELEVISION SERIES**

CONTACT: MEDIA CENTER COORDINATOR

Purpose: To exhibit independent video and film in VSW's Viewing/Listening Room and on cable television

Eligibility:
  Special Requirements: Applicants must have sole control over every phase of production
  Art Forms: Video, film dubbed to video (maximum length, 28 minutes)

Please read carefully!
Do not contact any listed organization unless you fulfill all eligibility requirements.

Type of Support: Work exhibited in Viewing/Listening Room and on Rochester Community TV, possibly in other locations throughout New York State; artists are paid $16.50 per minute

Scope of Program: n/a

Application/Selection Process:
  Deadline: Summer or fall, annually; contact for exact date
  Preferred Initial Contact: Call or write for guidelines
  Application Procedure: Submit work on high quality 3/4" tape, artist's statement, resumé, SASE for return of material
  Selection Process: Staff
  Notification Process: Letter or phone call 6 weeks after deadline
  Formal Report of Grant Required: No

➤ **ARTIST-IN-RESIDENCE PROGRAM**

Purpose: To allow artists the facilities and time to pursue their work

Eligibility:
  Residency: U.S.
  Special Requirements: No students
  Art Forms: Media arts

Type of Support: 1-month residency including access to facilities, living space, $1,000 honorarium; film and video artists are expected to hold a screening at the Media Center and, as a visiting artist, attend up to 3 evening classes

Scope of Program: Varies; the program may not be offered every year

Application/Selection Process:
  Deadline: Varies; see Preferred Initial Contact
  Preferred Initial Contact: Write or call to be placed on mailing list; notification will be sent when program is offered
  Application Procedure: Submit samples of work, artist's statement, project proposal, list of equipment needs, resumé
  Selection Process: Peer panel of artists, staff
  Notification Process: 3 weeks after deadline
  Formal Report of Grant Required: No

EQUIPMENT ACCESS

CONTACT: PIA CSERI-BRIONES, EQUIPMENT ACCESS MANAGER

Film: Production and post-production for 16mm, Super 8

Video: Production for Hi-8 and post-production for 3/4", Hi-8

Comments: Also available are an Amiga graphics station and a MIDI sound studio. Low-cost access is available to artists and independent producers working on noncommercial projects. Further rate reductions are available through Media Artist Subsidy Grant Programs; call for application forms. Special hours and possible low-cost housing for out-of-town users.

Please read carefully!
Do not contact any listed organization unless you fulfill all eligibility requirements.

TECHNICAL ASSISTANCE PROGRAMS AND SERVICES

Programs of Special Interest: VSW presents individual and group exhibitions in the Viewing/Listening Room 4-5 times per year, and periodically presents media installations, screenings and workshops. Each year, students curate an Annual National Student Media Arts Exhibition. The Media Center houses a collection of over 2,000 video titles, some of which are available for viewing on site. VSW is affiliated with the State University of New York at Brockport for an MFA Program, evening classes in film and video, and a Summer Institute. The Center sponsors area artists for grant applications to agencies such as the New York State Council on the Arts.

V TAPE

183 Bathurst Street
Toronto, Ontario
Canada M5T-2R7
416-863-9897
FAX: 416-360-0781

TECHNICAL ASSISTANCE PROGRAMS AND SERVICES

Programs of Special Interest: V Tape is a non-exclusive, nonprofit distribution and information center for artists and independent producers. Services include video rentals and sales to institutions, an in-house library of over 1,000 titles currently available for distribution, files on video producers and a print library including magazines, catalogues and reviews. Consultation services are available for educators, curators and video programmers.

WASHINGTON PROJECT FOR THE ARTS (WPA)

400 Seventh Street, NW
Washington, DC 20004
202-347-4813
FAX: 202-347-8393
CONTACT: LINDA LEWETT, VIDEO COORDINATOR

EQUIPMENT ACCESS

Video: Post-production for 3/4", Hi-8; Amiga Interface

Please read carefully!
Do not contact any listed organization unless you fulfill all eligibility requirements.

Comments: Access at minimal rates is available for independent producers working on nonprofit projects. A few artists are given free access to facilities and an exhibition opportunity at WPA's discretion.

TECHNICAL ASSISTANCE PROGRAMS AND SERVICES
Programs of Special Interest: WPA conducts workshops in editing and production.

WASHINGTON STATE ARTS COMMISSION (WSAC)

P.O. Box 42675
Olympia, WA 98504-2675
206-753-3860
TDD: 206-587-5500 (via Washington State Relay Service-Seattle)
    800-833-6388 (Outside Seattle)
FAX: 206-586-5351

PROFILE OF FINANCIAL SUPPORT TO ARTISTS
Total Funding/Value of In-Kind Support: $50,000

Competition for Funding: Total applications, 300; total individuals funded/provided with in-kind support, 10

Grant Range: $5,000

DIRECT SUPPORT PROGRAMS
➤ ARTIST FELLOWSHIP AWARDS

Purpose: To provide artists with funds to create new work, improve skills, or pursue artistic development

Eligibility:
    Residency: Washington State
    Special Requirements: Must demonstrate at least 5 years professional achievement; no students enrolled in degree programs; preference to artists who have not won WSAC fellowship in past 5 years
    Art Forms: Media arts awarded each year; other disciplines rotate on a 2-year cycle

Type of Support: $5,000 awards

Scope of Program: 10 awards per year

Application/Selection Process:
    Deadline: Fall, annually; contact for specific date
    Application Procedure: Submit application form, samples of work, resumé

Please read carefully!
Do not contact any listed organization unless you fulfill all eligibility requirements.

Selection Process: Peer panel of artists, commission
Notification Process: Letter in spring
Formal Report of Grant Required: Yes

TECHNICAL ASSISTANCE PROGRAMS AND SERVICES
Programs of Special Interest: The Washington State Arts Commission operates an Artist in Residence program which sends artists into the community for two-week residencies in schools, hospitals, prisons, etc. Contact Arts in Education at (206) 753-3861; Art in Public Places facilitates purchasing and commissioning of artwork for state agencies, institutions of higher learning, and public schools. It also sponsors several art exhibitions which tour the public school system. Open competitions announced through direct mail from WSAC mailing list. Preference to Washington artists or artists from the western states region. Contact Art in Public Places at (206) 753-5894.

WEST VIRGINIA DIVISION OF CULTURE AND HISTORY

Cultural Center, 1900 Kanawha Boulevard
Charleston, WV 25305-0300
304-558-0220 (Voice/TDD)
FAX: 304-558-2779
CONTACT: LAKIN COOK, EXECUTIVE DIRECTOR, ARTS & HUMANITIES SECTION

PROFILE OF FINANCIAL SUPPORT TO ARTISTS
Total Funding/Value of In-Kind Support: $23,000 in 1992 (figures reflect media arts program only)
Competition for Funding: Total applications, 20; total individuals funded/provided with in-kind support, 4
Grant Range: $5,000-$8,000

DIRECT SUPPORT PROGRAMS
➤ MEDIA ARTS PROGRAM
Purpose: To support media arts projects in the areas of artists' fees, production and post-production costs, and presentation costs
Eligibility:
  Citizenship: U.S.
  Residency: West Virginia
  Special Requirements: Individual artists must illustrate additional sources of financial support in their budget and project description and illustrate project's relationship to West Virginia
  Art Forms: Film, video, audio

Please read carefully!
Do not contact any listed organization unless you fulfill all eligibility requirements.

Type of Support: Up to $10,000 in matching funds to organizations that serve as conduit agencies for individual artists

Scope of Program: $23,000 awarded to individuals in 1992

Application/Selection Process:
    Deadline: April 1, annually
    Preferred Initial Contact: Call or write for information
    Application Procedure: Submit application form, sample of work or extensive treatment
    Selection Process: Peer panel of media artists and administrators review applications and make recommendations; commission makes final decisions
    Notification Process: Letter by August 1
    Formal Report of Grant Required: Yes

➤ **TRAVEL FUND**

Purpose: To provide artists and arts administrators with financial assistance to attend out-of-state seminars, workshops, conferences, and showcases important to their field of expertise (in-state events of national scope may be funded in some cases)

Eligibility:
    Citizenship: U.S.
    Residency: West Virginia
    Age: Open
    Special Requirements: Professional artists and arts administrators only; previous recipients ineligible for 1 year
    Art Forms: All disciplines

Type of Support: 50%, up to $200, of travel costs; funds available on a first-come, first-served basis

Scope of Program: $5,000 given to 25-30 recipients annually

Application/Selection Process:
    Deadline: At least 6 weeks before event (early application encouraged)
    Preferred Initial Contact: Call or write for guidelines/application
    Application Procedure: Submit application form, financial statement
    Selection Process: Staff review according to commission guidelines
    Notification Process: Within 3 weeks of application
    Formal Report of Grant Required: Yes

TECHNICAL ASSISTANCE PROGRAMS AND SERVICES

Programs of Special Interest: West Virginia Division of Culture and History provides support for the West Virginia International Film Festival. The Artist/Arts Administrator Opportunities File holds information on workshops, calls for proposals, and job opportunities. The selective West Virginia Artists List and Register contains background information on individual artists. Artists interested in the

Arts in the Community program should develop a proposal with a sponsor who will apply for funding; eligible projects include workshops and presentations of media artists' works.

WISCONSIN ARTS BOARD (WAB)

101 East Wilson Street, 1st Floor
Madison, WI 53703
608-266-0190
TDD: 608-267-9629
FAX: 608-267-0380
CONTACT: ELIZABETH MALNER,
PERCENT FOR ART & INDIVIDUAL ARTISTS COORDINATOR

Profile of Financial Support to Artists
Total Funding/Value of In-Kind Support: $156,634 for FY 1993

Competition for Funding: Total applications, 470; total individuals funded/provided with in-kind support, 60

Grant Range: $1,000-$5,000

Direct Support Programs
➤ **INDIVIDUAL ARTIST PROGRAM—MEDIA ARTS**

Purpose: To assist artists in advancing their careers, in pursuing a specific project, or in developing their skills as a professional

Eligibility:
  Citizenship: U.S.
  Residency: Wisconsin, 1 year
  Special Requirements: No students pursuing degrees in the fine arts; recipients of New Work Awards and Development Grants must match grants in cash or in-kind support
  Art Forms: Film, radio, video apply in even-numbered years

Type of Support: Fellowships ($5,000 unrestricted grants), New Work Awards ($3,500 matching grant for pursuit of a project-oriented activity), Development Grants ($1,000 matching grant for professional development activity)

Scope of Program: 2 Fellowships, 2 New Work Awards, 3 Development Grants awarded in 1993 (for FY 1994)

Application/Selection Process:
  Deadline: September 15, annually
  Preferred Initial Contact: Call or write for application/guidelines
  Application Procedure: Submit application form, video/audio cassette, resumé, artist's statement; artists chosen for New Work

---

Please read carefully!
Do not contact any listed organization unless you fulfill all eligibility requirements.

Awards and Development Grants must submit project description before receiving grant
Selection Process: Peer panel of artists, board of directors
Notification Process: Letter in January
Formal Report of Grant Required: Yes

TECHNICAL ASSISTANCE PROGRAMS AND SERVICES
Programs of Special Interest: The WAB sponsors workshops in such areas as grantwriting, audience development, and marketing. Artists selected for inclusion in the *Arts-in-Education Artists Directory* are eligible for school and community residencies.

WOMEN IN FILM FOUNDATION (WIFF)

6464 Sunset Boulevard
Suite 530
Los Angeles, CA 90028
213-463-6040
CONTACT: SUSIE SPECK MAYOR, FOUNDATION ADMINISTRATOR

PROFILE OF FINANCIAL SUPPORT TO ARTISTS
Total Funding/Value of In-Kind Support: n/a
Competition for Funding: n/a
Grant Range: $2,000-$25,000

DIRECT SUPPORT PROGRAMS
➤ **FILM FINISHING FUND—GENERAL AWARDS**
Purpose: To support filmmakers and videomakers who have demonstrated advanced and innovative skills, and whose work relates to WIFF's goals of increasing employment and promoting equal opportunities for women, enhancing the media image of women, and influencing prevailing attitudes and practices regarding and on behalf of women
Eligibility:
　Citizenship: n/a
　Residency: Open nationally
　Special Requirements: Independent producers and nonprofit corporations are eligible; projects in development or pre-production will not be considered; a substantial number of the creative personnel involved with the project must be women; film or video must be accessible to English-speaking audiences (must at least have English subtitles); all recipients must supply a videotape copy of their completed work for the foundation's archives
　Art Forms: Film, video

Type of Support: Up to $5,000 grant for completion of films or videotapes

Scope of Program: 4-5 annually

Application/Selection Process:

    Deadline: Varies annually; contact for exact date

    Preferred Initial Contact: Write for guidelines in January (include SASE)

    Application Procedure: Submit $20 application fee, project description and budget, distribution and exhibition plans, biographies of key personnel, sample of work-in-progress; SASE for return of work

    Selection Process: Committee

    Notification Process: Letter within 4 months

    Formal Report of Grant Required: No

TECHNICAL ASSISTANCE PROGRAMS AND SERVICES

Programs of Special Interest: Women in Film Foundation also offers 7 specific completion grants (same deadline, application/selection process as General Awards): Loreen Arbus "Focus on Disability" Grant, an annual award of up to $5,000 for a film or video dealing with issues of disability or providing opportunities for disabled performers; Loreen Arbus "Focus on Discrimination" Grant, an annual award of up to $10,000 for a film or video depicting the subject of discrimination in any form; Max Goldenson and Karen Hansen "Women and Children in War" Grant, a grant of up to $10,000 for a film or video program that depicts women and children in war; The Norman G. Brooks and Fern Field Brooks Award, a grant of up to $5,000 for an independent film or video produced by a woman which explores and offers solutions to local and/or global environmental issues; The Weddington Production Film Sound Grant, an in-kind completion grant to a woman based in Los Angeles for post-production services; Hollywood Film and Video Grant, which provides post-production services to a woman based in Los Angeles to complete her independent film; The Tichi Wilkerson/ Arthur Kassel Grant, which provides up to $25,000 in post-production services at the Beverly Hills Video Group.

WOMEN MAKE MOVIES (WMM)

462 Broadway
Suite 500
New York, NY 10013
212-925-0606
CONTACT: DOROTHY THIGPEN,
DIRECTOR OF PRODUCTION SERVICES & MEMBERSHIP

PROFILE OF FINANCIAL SUPPORT TO ARTISTS
Total Funding/Value of In-Kind Support: n/a
Competition for Funding: n/a
Grant Range: n/a

DIRECT SUPPORT PROGRAMS
➤ **VIDEO PRODUCTION WORKSHOPS FOR WOMEN**

Purpose: To provide video training and equipment access, free of charge, to women for community-based productions, with special outreach to women of color

Eligibility:
  Citizenship: n/a
  Residency: Borough of Manhattan
  Age: Over 18 years of age
  Special Requirements: Must be female and have an interest in media and community issues; no students
  Art Forms: Video

Type of Support: "Hands-on" video production training and access to Hi-8 video equipment and editing over a four-month period, with direct consultation and support from an instructor to completion of video project

Scope of Program: 9-12 women chosen for each four-month workshop series; two series (summer, winter) per year

Application/Selection Process:
  Deadline: Revolving deadline; contact for details
  Preferred Initial Contact: Write or call for information
  Application Procedure: Submit application form, project proposal, personal statement and one letter of reference from community representative
  Selection Process: Peer panel of artists and community representatives
  Notification Process: Recipients by phone, non-recipients by mail

Please read carefully!
Do not contact any listed organization unless you fulfill all eligibility requirements.

TECHNICAL ASSISTANCE PROGRAMS AND SERVICES

Programs of Special Interest: WMM offers fiscal sponsorship for selected media projects that are in accordance with the organization's goals and whose key personnel are WMM members ($30 membership fee). Sponsorship allows a film or video project to receive tax-deductible and tax-exempt contributions from individuals, foundations, and government agencies. Low-cost workshops are offered to the public annually in Spring and Fall. Topics such as fundraising, screenwriting, film/video production management and distribution are addressed by established media artists. Each workshop series ends with a networking event for participants and WMM members.

WYOMING ARTS COUNCIL

2320 Capitol Avenue
Cheyenne, WY 82002
307-777-7742
TDD/FAX: 307-777-5499
CONTACT: LILIANE FRANCUZ, VISUAL ARTS PROGRAM MANAGER

PROFILE OF FINANCIAL SUPPORT TO ARTISTS

Total Funding/Value of In-Kind Support: $42,500 for FY 1992 (not including AIE residencies)
Competition for Funding: Total applications, 175; total individuals funded/provided with in-kind support, 21
Grant Range: $250-$2,500

DIRECT SUPPORT PROGRAMS

➤ **FELLOWSHIPS**
Purpose: Fellowships are designed to assist emerging Wyoming artists at crucial times in their careers
Eligibility:
   Citizenship: U.S.
   Residency: Wyoming
   Age: 18 or older
   Special Requirements: No students; previous fellowship winners ineligible for 4 years; maximum of 2 fellowships per individual
   Art Forms: All disciplines, including film and video
Type of Support: $2,500 awards; $3,000 to organizations to exhibit work of fellowship recipients also available

Please read carefully!
Do not contact any listed organization unless you fulfill all eligibility requirements.

Scope of Program: 12 Fellowships; $30,000 total for program

Application/Selection Process:

> **Deadline:** Contact the council for deadline information
> **Preferred Initial Contact:** Call or write for application/guidelines
> **Application Procedure:** Submit application form, samples of work, references, artist's statement
> **Selection Process:** Peer panel of artists and board of directors
> **Notification Process:** Letter in October/November
> **Formal Report of Grant Required:** Yes

➤ **INDIVIDUAL ARTIST GRANTS**

Purpose: To support specific projects that promote, preserve, encourage, and stimulate culture in the state

Eligibility:

> **Citizenship:** U.S.
> **Residency:** Wyoming
> **Age:** 18 or older
> **Special Requirements:** No students
> **Art Forms:** All disciplines, including film and video
> **Type of Support:** Up to $1,000 matching grant for specific project
> **Scope of Program:** 7 awarded in 1992 totalling $7,000
> **Application/Selection Process:**
> **Deadline:** March 1, annually
> **Preferred Initial Contact:** Write or call for application/guidelines
> **Application Procedure:** Submit application form, samples of work, references, resumé, project budget and description
> **Selection Process:** Peer panel of artists and board of directors
> **Notification Process:** Letter
> **Formal Report of Grant Required:** Yes

TECHNICAL ASSISTANCE PROGRAMS AND SERVICES

Programs of Special Interest: The council maintains an Artist Registry/ Slide Bank to promote the work of Wyoming artists and sponsors Artspeak, an annual gathering of artists that includes workshops. Artists selected for inclusion in the Arts in Education Program Artist Roster are eligible for school and community residencies.

Please read carefully!
Do not contact any listed organization unless you fulfill all eligibility requirements.

YADDO

P.O. Box 395
Saratoga Springs, NY 12866
518-584-0746
CONTACT: ADMISSIONS COMMITTEE

PROFILE OF FINANCIAL SUPPORT TO ARTISTS
Total Funding/Value of In-Kind Support: n/a
Competition for Funding: Total applicants, 900; total individuals funded/provided with in-kind support, 200 (figures approximate for 1992)
Grant Range: n/a

DIRECT SUPPORT PROGRAMS
➤ RESIDENCIES
Purpose: To provide a working community for artists
Eligibility:
   Special Requirements: Artists working at the professional level only
   Art Forms: Visual arts, literature, music composition, choreography, film/video, performance art; collaborative projects are encouraged for up to 3 artists
Type of Support: 2- to 8-week residencies, including room, board, and working space; residents encouraged to make a voluntary payment (suggested rate of $20/day), but qualified applicants accepted regardless of ability to pay
Scope of Program: 211 residencies in 1991
Application/Selection Process:
   Deadline: January 15 and August 1, annually
   Preferred Initial Contact: Write for applications; a SASE is appreciated but not required
   Application Procedure: Submit application form, $20 application fee, samples of work, names of sponsors, professional and biographical information
   Selection Process: Peer panel of artists
   Notification Process: Letter several months after deadline

Please read carefully!
Do not contact any listed organization unless you fulfill all eligibility requirements.

ZELLERBACH FAMILY FUND

120 Montgomery
Room 2125
San Francisco, CA 94104
415-421-2629
CONTACT: LINDA HOWE, ART ADMINISTRATOR

PROFILE OF FINANCIAL SUPPORT TO ARTISTS
Total Funding/Value of In-Kind Support: n/a
Competition for Funding: n/a
Grant Range: $1,000 - $5,000

DIRECT SUPPORT PROGRAMS
➤ **COMMUNITY ARTS DISTRIBUTION COMMITTEE**

Purpose: To encourage artists at a beginning stage of their development and to enrich the community through the sharing of their work

Eligibility:
    Residency: San Francisco Bay Area
    Special Requirements: Must be sponsored by a nonprofit organization; subject must be local art or artists; guidelines stipulate that the final work of art needs to go back to the community in some form; to qualify, project must involve some work of art accessible to the general public; multi-ethnic subjects encouraged
    Art Forms: All disciplines, including media and visual arts

Type of Support: Average grant $1,000–$5,000 for exhibition/ presentation of work

Scope of Program: In 1991, 7 grants to film/videomakers, 8 grants to visual artists (painters, sculptors, photographers, etc.)

Application/Selection Process:
    Deadline: Deadlines vary; contact for details
    Preferred Initial Contact: Call or write for application/guidelines
    Selection Process: Panel review
    Notification Process: Letter
    Formal Report of Grant Required: Yes

Appendix: ORGANIZATIONS OFFERING AWARDS BY NOMINATION ONLY

Some organizations choose to make awards to artists through a process of nomination rather than application. Listed below are three such organizations. They ask that individuals not contact them seeking grants; please respect their choice of process.

Lyndhurst Foundation
Rockefeller Foundation (Intercultural Film/Video Program)
Southeastern Center for Contemporary Art

APPENDIX: STATE HUMANITIES COUNCILS

The following is a list of state humanities councils. If you are a filmmaker or video maker working on a documentary project, you may be eligible for grant support from your state humanities council or from the council of the documentary subject's state. The primary recipients of humanities council funding are organizations. Individuals who wish to apply are required to have a fiscal sponsor. Before going through the application process, artists may wish to discuss a project idea with council staff to determine whether it is suitable for funding. As with any source of funding, please be sure to check guidelines carefully and respect all eligibility requirements.

Alabama Humanities Foundation
2217 Tenth Court South
Birmingham, AL 35205
205-930-0540
FAX: 205-930-0986

Alaska Humanities Forum
430 West 7th Avenue
Suite 1
Anchorage, AK 99501
907-272-5341
FAX: 907-272-3979

Arizona Humanities Council
Ellis-Shackelford House
1242 North Central Avenue
Phoenix, AZ 85004
602-257-0335
FAX: 602-257-0392

Arkansas Humanities Council
10816 Executive Center Drive
Suite 310
Little Rock, AR 72211
501-221-0091
FAX: 501-221-0093

California Council for the Humanities
312 Sutter
Suite 601
San Francisco, CA 94108
415-391-1474
FAX: 415-391-1312

315 West 9th Street
Suite 702
Los Angeles, CA 90015
213-623-5993

614 Fifth Street
Suite C
San Diego, CA 92101
619-235-2307

Colorado Endowment for the Humanities
1623 Blake Street
Suite 200
Denver, CO 80202
303-573-7733
FAX: 303-573-7722

Commonwealth of the Northern Mariana Islands Council for the Humanities
Caller Box AAA-3394
Saipan, MP 96950
670-235-4785
FAX: 670-235-4786

Connecticut Humanities Council
41 Lawn Avenue
Wesleyan Station
Middletown, CT 06457
203-347-6888 or 347-3788
FAX: 203-347-0783

Delaware Humanities Forum
1812 Newport Gap Pike
Wilmington, DE 19808-6179
302-633-2400
FAX: 302-633-1888

D.C. Community Humanities Council
1331 H Street, NW
Suite 902
Washington, DC 20005
202-347-1732
FAX: 202-347-3350

Florida Humanities Council
1514 1/2 East Eighth Avenue
Tampa, FL 33605-3708
813-272-3473
FAX: 813-272-3479

Georgia Humanities Council
50 Hurt Plaza, SE
Suite 440
Atlanta, GA 30303-2936
404-523-6220
FAX: 404-523-5702

Guam Humanities Council
123 Archbishop Flores Street
Suite C
Agana, Guam 96910
671-472-4507
FAX: 671-472-4524

Hawaii Committee for the Humanities
First Hawaiian Bank Building
3599 Wai'alae Avenue
Room 23
Honolulu, HI 96816
Tel/FAX: 808-732-5402

Idaho Humanities Council
217 West State Street
Boise, ID 83702
208-345-5346
FAX: 208-345-5347

Illinois Humanities Council
618 South Michigan Avenue
7th Floor
Chicago, IL 60605
312-939-5212
FAX: 312-939-1265

Indiana Humanities Council
1500 North Delaware Street
Indianapolis, IN 46202
317-638-1500
FAX: 317-634-9503

Iowa Humanities Board
Oakdale Campus
University of Iowa
Iowa City, IA 52242
319-335-4153
FAX: 319-335-4077

Kansas Humanities Council
112 West Sixth Street
Suite 210
Topeka, KS 66603
913-357-0359
FAX: 913-357-1723

Kentucky Humanities Council
417 Clifton Avenue
University of Kentucky
Lexington, KY 40508-3406
606-257-5932
FAX: 606-257-5472

Louisiana Endowment for the Humanities
The Ten-O-One Building
1001 Howard Avenue
Suite 3110
New Orleans, LA 70113
504-523-4352
FAX: 504-529-2358

Maine Humanities Council
P.O. Box 7202
Portland, ME 04112
207-773-5051
FAX: 207-773-2416

Maryland Humanities Council
601 North Howard Street
Baltimore, MD 21201-4585
410-625-4830
FAX: 410-625-4834

Massachusetts Foundation for the Humanities
One Woodbridge Street
South Hadley, MA 01075
413-536-1385
FAX: 413-534-6918

80 Boylston Street
Suite 1000
Boston, MA 02116

Michigan Humanities Council
119 Pere Marquette Drive
Suite 3B
Lansing, MI 48912-1231
517-372-7770
FAX: 517-372-0027

5201 Woodward Avenue
4th Floor
Detroit, MI 48202-4093
313-993-7770
FAX: 313-993-8045

Minnesota Humanities Commission
26 East Exchange Street
St. Paul, MN 55101
612-224-5739
FAX: 612-224-0419

Mississippi Humanities Council
3825 Ridgewood Road
Room 311
Jackson, MS 39211-6453
601-982-6752
FAX: 601-982-6610

Missouri Humanities Council
911 Washington Avenue
Suite 215
St. Louis, MO 63101-1208
314-621-7705
FAX: 314-621-5850

Montana Committee for the Humanities
P.O. Box 8036
Hellgate Station
Missoula, MT 59807
406-243-6022
FAX: 406-243-4836

Nebraska Humanities Council
Lincoln Center Building, Suite 225
215 Centennial Mall South
Lincoln, NE 68508
402-474-2131
FAX: 402-474-4852

Nevada Humanities Committee
1034 North Sierra Street
Reno, NV 89503
702-784-6587
FAX: 702-784-6527

New Hampshire Humanities Council
19 Pillsbury Street
P.O. Box 2228
Concord, NH 03302-2228
603-224-4071
FAX: 603-224-4072

New Jersey Committee for the Humanities
390 George Street
Suite 602
New Brunswick, NJ 08901-2019
908-932-7726
FAX: 908-932-1179

New Mexico Endowment for the Humanities
209 Onate Hall
Corner of Campus & Girard NE
Albuquerque, NM 87131
505-277-3705
FAX: 505-277-7991

New York Council for the Humanities
198 Broadway
10th Floor
New York, NY 10038
212-233-1131
FAX: 212-233-4607

North Carolina Humanities Council
425 Spring Garden Street
Greensboro, NC 27401
919-334-5325
FAX: 919-334-3014

North Dakota Humanities Council
P.O. Box 2191
Bismarck, ND 58502
701-255-3360
FAX: 701-223-8724

Ohio Humanities Council
695 Bryden Road
P.O. Box 06354
Columbus, OH 43206-0354
614-461-7802
FAX: 614-461-4651

Oklahoma Foundation for the Humanities
Festival Plaza
428 West California
Suite 270
Oklahoma City, OK 73102
405-235-0280
FAX: 405-235-0289

Oregon Council for the Humanities
812 SW Washington
Suite 225
Portland, OR 97205
503-241-0543
FAX: 503-241-0024

Pennsylvania Humanities Council
320 Walnut Street, #305
Philadelphia, PA 19106
215-925-1005
FAX: 215-925-3054

**Fundacion Puertorriquena de las
Humanidades**
Apartado Postal S-4307
San Juan de Puerto Rico 00904
809-721-2087
FAX: 809-721-2684

Bacon House Mews
606 18th Street, NW
2nd Floor
Washington, D.C. 20006
202-371-8111

**Rhode Island Committee for the
Humanities**
60 Ship Street
Providence, RI 02903
401-273-2250
FAX: 401-454-4872

South Carolina Humanities Council
1610 Oak Street
Columbia, SC 29204
803-771-8864
FAX: 803-771-8874

South Dakota Humanities Council
P.O. Box 7050, University Station
Brookings, SD 57007
605-688-6113
FAX: 605-688-4032

Tennessee Humanities Council
P.O. Box 24767
Nashville, TN 37202
615-320-7001
FAX: 615-321-4586

Texas Committee for the Humanities
3809 South Second Street
Austin, TX 78704
512-440-1991
FAX: 512-440-0115

Utah Humanities Council
350 South 400 East
Suite 110
Salt Lake City, UT 84111-2946
801-359-9670
FAX: 801-531-7869

Vermont Council on the Humanities
145 Ednam Drive
Charlottesville, VA 22903
804-924-3296
FAX: 804-296-4714

Virgin Islands Humanities Council
P.O. Box 1829
St. Thomas, VI 00803
809-776-4044
FAX: 809-779-8294

**Washington Commission for the
Humanities**
615 Second Avenue
Suite 300
Seattle, WA 98104
206-682-1770
FAX: 206-682-4158

West Virginia Humanities Council
723 Kanawha Boulevard
Suite 800
Charleston, WV 25301
304-346-8500
FAX: 304-346-8504

Wisconsin Humanities Committee
716 Langdon Street
Madison, WI 53706
608-262-0706
FAX: 608-263-2595

Wyoming Council for the Humanities
P.O. Box 3643, University Station
Laramie, WY 82071-3643
307-766-6496
FAX: 307-766-6810

ALPHABETICAL INDEX OF ORGANIZATIONS

INDEX OF ORGANIZATIONS BY GEOGRAPHIC AREA SERVED

INDEX OF ORGANIZATIONS BY MEDIUM AND FORMAT

INDEX OF ORGANIZATIONS BY TYPES OF SUPPORT

CAREER DEVELOPMENT/ WORKSHOPS/TRAINING

REGISTRIES

SCREENINGS/EXHIBITIONS

SCREENWRITING

STUDENTS

STUDY GRANTS

TRAVEL GRANTS

See International Opportunities and/or
Professional Development

SELECTED READING

The following publications are available from the American Council for the Arts. To order, call ACA Books toll-free at 800-321-4510.

The Artist's Tax Guide and Financial Planner by Carla Messman. Practical advice on preparing a tax return that takes advantage of every legitimate deduction. Published by Lyons & Burford. 288 pp. Paper, 1992. ISBN: 1-55821-130-6 $16.95

Business and Legal Forms for Fine Artists by Tad Crawford. This success kit includes forms and sample contracts for the fine artist's every need. 128 pp. Paper, 1990. ISBN: 0-927629-01-1 $12.95

Caring for Your Art by Jill Snyder. The best methods to store, handle, mount and frame, display and secure art. A co-publication with Allworth Press. 176 pp. 32 illus. Paper, 1991. ISBN: 0-9607118-1-3 $14.95

Creating Space by Cheryl Kartes. This guide will help you solve the unique problems associated with developing real estate for artists. 320 pp. 100 illust. Paper, 1993. ISBN: 0-915400-92-8 $19.95

Health Insurance by Lenore Janacek. The various types of health insurance plans and how self-employed people can find the right one. Includes a guide to organizations offering health insurance to artists. A co-publication with Allworth Press. 232 pp. Paper, 1993. ISBN 0-879903-11-3 $15.95

How to Survive and Prosper as an Artist by Caroll Michels. A new edition of this complete program, covering law, insurance, accounting, resumes, presentations and public relations. Published by Henry Holt and Company. 265 pp. Paper, 1992. ISBN: 0-8050-0604-4 $8.95

Legal Guide for the Visual Artist by Tad Crawford. Revised and expanded, this guide tells you how to deal with censorship, sales, contracts and grants. 224 pp. Paper, 1989. ISBN: 0-927629-00-3 $18.95

Licensing Art and Design by Caryn R. Leland. How to succeed in the financially rewarding licensing market. Published by Allworth Press. 112 pp. Paper, 1990. ISBN: 0-92769-04-6 $12.95

Money for Visual Artists, 2nd edition researched by Douglas Oxenhorn. Updated and expanded guide to opportunities for visual artists. Includes more than 40 new entries. Co-published with Allworth Press. 236 pp. Paper, 1993. ISBN 1-879903-05-9 $14.95

Money for International Exchange in the Arts by Jane Gullong. A guide to support for all kinds of international opportunities, including grants, fellowships, awards, residencies and exchanges. Co-published with Allworth Press. 150 pp. Paper, 1992. ISBN 1-879903-01-6 $14.95

Money for Performing Artists edited by Suzanne Niemeyer. The essential resource guide for composers, musicians, choreographers, dancers, actors, playwrights and other performing artists. Co-published with Allworth Press. 240 pp. Paper, 1991. ISBN 0-915400-96-0 $14.95

ABOUT THE AMERICAN COUNCIL FOR THE ARTS

Founded in 1960, the American Council for the Arts (ACA) is a national organization whose purpose is to define issues and promote public policies that advance the contributions of the arts and the artist to American life. To accomplish its mission, ACA conducts research, sponsors conferences and public forums, publishes books, reports, and periodicals, advocates before Congress for legislation that benefits the arts, and maintains a 15,000-volume specialized library. ACA is one of the nation's primary sources of legislative news affecting all of the arts and serves as a leading advisor to arts administrators, individual artists, educators, elected officials, arts patrons and the general public.

BOARD OF DIRECTORS

THE VISUAL ARTIST INFORMATION HOTLINE

The Marie Walsh Sharpe Art Foundation in cooperation with the American Council for the Arts (ACA) on October 1, 1990 launched a nationwide, toll-free information hotline serving visual artists. Since that date, the Hotline has responded to over 10,000 calls from artists living in all 50 states, the District of Columbia, Puerto Rico and the Virgin Islands.

Individual fine artists in any of the visual arts—painting, sculpture, drawing, crafts, photography, mixed media, film, video—may call the Hotline at (800) 232-2789 and speak directly with the staff of ACA's Information Services Program, located in New York City, which operates the Hotline as one of ACA's services to artists. Hours of operation are Monday through Friday, 2-5 PM Eastern Time. When the line is busy or calls are made outside regular hours, a message can be left which will be answered by mail.

Primarily a referral service, the Hotline directs artists to a variety of programs and services that are offered by organizations at the national, regional, state and local level. The Hotline is not set up to assist nonprofit groups.

Artists call most frequently about the following: funding—including grants, fellowships and emergency funds; insurance—organizations which offer group health and fine art insurance to their members; artist communities; public art programs; international opportunities; studio space; legal information—the Hotline identifies organizations which assist artists with legal questions or problems.

The Hotline is one of the programs for visual artists initiated by the Sharpe Foundation's Artists Advisory Committee. Marie Walsh Sharpe, a Colorado Springs philanthropist, created the foundation before her death in 1985 to benefit visual artists. In spring 1993, the Hotline became a project of a consortium of private foundations, including the Sharpe Art Foundation, which provide support and advise ACA in the operation of the Hotline.